NetObjects Fusion® 11

David N. Plotkin

New York Chicago San Francisco Lisbon
London Madrid Mexico City Milan New Delhi
San Juan Seoul Singapore Sydney Toronto

The *McGraw-Hill* Companies

Library of Congress Cataloging-in-Publication Data

Plotkin, David.
  How to do everything NetObjects Fusion 11/David N. Plotkin.
    p. cm.
  ISBN 978-0-07-149849-4 (alk. paper)
  1. NetObjects Fusion. 2. Web sites—Design. I. Title.
  TK5105.8885.N48P56 2009
  006.7—dc22

                                    2008049422

How to Do Everything: NetObjects Fusion® 11

1234567890   FGR FGR   019

ISBN   978-0-07-149849-4
MHID   0-07-149849-4

Sponsoring Editor
Megg Morin

Editorial Supervisor
Janet Walden

Project Manager
Vastavikta Sharma,
International Typesetting
and Composition

Acquisitions Coordinator
Carly Stapleton

Technical Editor
Oana Ilyes

Copy Editor
Bob Campbell

Proofreader
Madhu Prasher

Indexer
Claire Splan

Production Supervisor
James Kussow

Composition
International Typesetting
and Composition

Illustration
International Typesetting
and Composition

Art Director, Cover
Jeff Weeks

This book is dedicated to my wife Marisa. Life is a partnership, and she is the best partner ever. And that is after 32 years of marriage. Amazing, isn't it?

About the Author

David Plotkin is the Data Quality Manager for AAA of Northern California, Nevada, and Utah. He has written multiple books on computer software, including digital photography software and web site building software. He is an accomplished photographer and avid cyclist. He lives in Walnut Creek, California, with his wife Marisa, a writer of children's books (www.marisamontes.com).

About the Technical Editor

Oana Ilyes graduated from the West University of Timisoara, Faculty of Letters, History and Teologie with a Bachelor's degree in Romanian/English language and literature and has an M.A. degree in British and American Studies: Traductology. Since graduating, she has been a technical writer, reviewer, and editor in the software industry, producing innovative and effective documentation.

Contents at a Glance

Contents

Acknowledgments

If you've ever looked at the list of names that scrolls by at the end of a movie, you know that it "takes a village" to create a work of art. Books are not that much different, and it would be impossible for me to acknowledge the contributions of everyone who has helped make this a manuscript that I am proud to put my name on. In no particular order, they are

- Megg Morin, my acquisitions editor. If you are ever lucky enough to write a computer book, you can't do any better than Megg, who is patient and knowledgeable and protects her authors. I have written many other books for Megg, and working with her is always an enjoyable experience.
- Carly Stapleton, my acquisitions coordinator. After I get done writing and shooting screens and pulling my hair out (what there is left), its time to turn my documents into a book. Carly keeps track of everything and makes sure everything gets turned in properly.
- Janet Walden and her department, who took all the stuff I sent them and turned it into this book. They were fun to work with, which has not always been the case with other books.
- Oana Ilyes, my technical editor. Fusion is not a well-known product (though that is a shame), so finding someone who was intimately familiar with it and could make sure I got everything correct from a technical standpoint was hard. We really lucked out in finding Oana, who lives in Romania, yet speaks English (or writes it, anyway) very well. She made sure that things were correct, and made constructive suggestions on phrasing, content, and structure that improved the book.
- Chris Dolan, who ran the Fusion beta program and always made sure I had the latest version—and answered my questions before I found Oana.
- John White, at NetObjects technical support. Some of the more complex ins and outs were more than I could handle, and John was my "go to" guy for the really tough questions. And when work needed to be done to get the site up and running, John was able to take care of that as well. The supplemental material on the web site (www.htde-netobjectsfusion.com) would not have been possible without John's help.

- Micah Klesick, who runs his own web site on Fusion, and who encouraged me to learn the software and write the book. His excellent web site can be found at www.learnNOF.com.
- Finally, my wife Marisa, who had to live through my working on two books at once, and had to get used to my answering every request to do something around the house with "I'm working on my book." She is a writer herself (of children's books), though she shakes her head at the idea of working so hard on a book for a product that is continually evolving.

Introduction

In the beginning, there was Notepad. Believe it or not, people used to code their web sites using HTML and a text editor. This was horribly inefficient and required a good understanding of HTML coding and a programmer's mindset. This never appealed to me.

As the years have progressed, applications have appeared that make it possible for you to build a web site pretty much the way you create a word processing document. That is, you can build the web pages and link them together without writing much (or any) HTML code, and the applications give you a pretty good idea of what the finished pages will look like on the Web. These applications have evolved into two categories. The first is a free or very low cost simple web builder, often hosted remotely by your web presence provider. These applications tend to have limited functionality but are fine for quickly creating web sites that are largely composed of text and some images. The second type of application tends to be quite expensive ($500 or more) and provides powerful toolsets for full web functionality—with an associated long learning curve that requires a considerable investment in time and effort to learn to use well.

But what about the middle ground—the applications that allow quite a bit of power but are relatively easy to use and learn? And don't cost a fortune? This category is surprisingly sparsely populated. Microsoft's discontinued FrontPage addressed this need, but its replacement requires an infrastructure that only an IT department could be proud of. Fortunately, those of us who would like to have a product in this category are not out of luck. NetObjects Fusion has been around for many years, and it improves by leaps and bounds with each new version. Version 11 adds a lot of functionality and streamlines some things that could have been easier in earlier versions. And, unlike some other products, it doesn't require a special configuration on the web server—it generates all the code it needs to run without any help.

How to Do Everything: NetObjects Fusion 11 is designed to help you understand what Fusion can do, and become productive quickly. The book is solution driven—if you need to do something (such as add an image and create hyperlinks for it), you can find a section that will tell you how to do that. You *can* read the book from cover to cover, but you don't have to.

Who Should Read This Book

The book, like the software itself, is directed at people who are serious about building and maintaining web sites. This is because if you only need to do simple things, then you could make do with the freebies that are out there. You don't have to be vastly experienced at building web sites, because the book addresses the simple things (building pages, adding text and images, and so on) first, and enables you to grow as you gain more experience and need to add functionality. As you work on your web site, you are going to discover things you need to do. Fusion will make that possible, and this book will describe how to get the work done. For example, there are some pretty involved features, such as collecting data that is input by a site visitor into a form and storing it in a database. The book provides a detailed walk-through of how to use the software to accomplish this as well—when you're ready.

How This Book Is Organized

How to Do Everything: NetObjects Fusion 11 is organized in logical blocks. The very first thing you'll learn is how to navigate through the software, use the various views, configure the toolbars and panels, and create web sites and pages. These are covered in Chapters 1, 2, and 3.

Once you know how to navigate and create pages, it's time to place information on those pages. The next section teaches you the ins and outs of placing text on a page, positioning that text, and formatting it to your liking. Graphics (including vector objects) and sound add interest to your pages, and you can arrange almost anything in grids by using tables. These topics are covered in Chapters 4, 5, 6 and 7.

If you've ever seen a web site that is impossible to navigate but has an overwhelming number of fonts, colors, and such, you'll know how important it is to design and structure your site correctly. You can establish a common look to your web site (and customize that look) and set up links and buttons to navigate through your site using the information in Chapters 8 and 9.

Chapters 10–15 show you how to add some pretty advanced functionality to your web site. This includes two kinds of photo gallery, Java and ActiveX controls, a search facility, a site map, and forms (with the necessary database to hold the information). You can even add FAQs (Frequently Asked Questions), a Guestbook, and security, which requires a user to sign up and use a userid and password to access the web site. Finally, you can publish the contents of a database or spreadsheet onto a web page.

Of course, at some point you'll need to publish your web site to your web presence provider. This is covered in Chapter 16. You may want to skip ahead and look at that chapter when you are ready to publish your site.

About This Book's Companion Web Site

When you're writing about web-building software, there are just some things that are pretty hard to describe—and that work much better if you can actually try them.

To that end, I set up a web site, which you can find at **www.htde-netobjectsfusion .com**. There you can try things like a Guestbook, check out Frequently Asked Questions, navigate using navigation bars and image maps, view data published from a database, and get explanations of various components. I didn't try to make the site especially "pretty," but you can certainly leave me feedback (using the form specifically for that purpose) on what you'd find useful for me to add to the site.

PART I

Build Web Sites and Pages

1

Navigate in NetObjects Fusion

HOW TO...

- Understand the different views
- Change what you see in each view
- Show, hide, and relocate the toolbars and panels
- Get Help from NetObjects Fusion

NetObjects Fusion provides two main views of a web site: Site view and Page view. By switching back and forth between these two views, you can quickly build up a site structure as well as customize the individual web pages in the site.

Understand the Site View

The Structure tab of Site view (see Figure 1-1) provides a view that shows the structure of the web site, much like an organization chart. Not everyone thinks of their web site in terms of a structure, but various tools included with NetObjects Fusion (such as the Navigation Bars that help you navigate through the site) leverage this structure to perform useful tasks automatically. For more information on site navigation, see Chapter 9.

 Note To switch to Site view from any other view, click the Site button in the Views Bar toolbar.

Zoom In and Out

You can change how much of the structure you see in Site view, zooming in to enlarge the structure or zooming out to see more of the structure (especially helpful for large web sites). To change the zoom level, click the magnifying glass tool in the Standard

Click and drag
a toolbar here

View Bar
toolbar

Standard
Tools toolbar

Common
Actions toolbar

Property
Inspector panel

Click this "pin" to
collapse the panel
without closing it

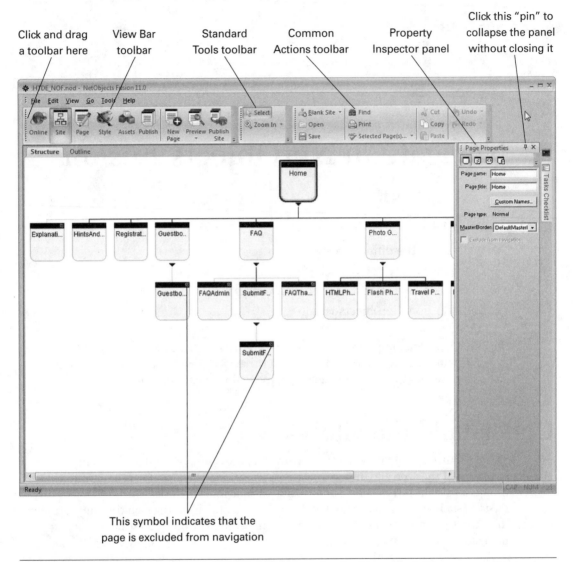

This symbol indicates that the
page is excluded from navigation

FIGURE 1-1   The structure of a web site is a hierarchy, looking much like an org chart.

Tools toolbar to choose the Zoom tool (either zoom in or zoom out), or
click the tiny down arrow alongside the tool to pick the tool you want
from the drop-down menu.

 Use the ALT key to switch tools temporarily. For example, if you currently have the
Zoom Out tool selected, pressing the ALT key switches to the Zoom In tool as long
as you have the ALT key pressed.

If you don't like the default vertical orientation (seen previously in Figure 1-1), you can switch to a horizontal orientation by choosing View | Orientation | Horizontal. Use View | Orientation | Vertical to switch back.

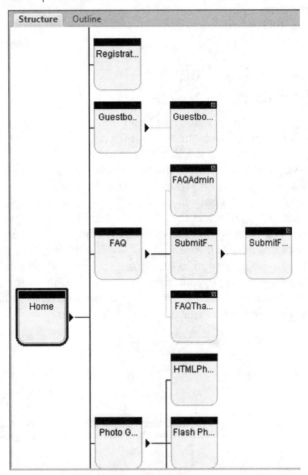

Understand the Relationship Between Pages

Each of the rounded squares in Site view represents a page in the web site. For example, the Home page is at the top of the stack and is the starting point for navigating the site. Each page on a given level is a "sibling" of the pages on that level, and the automatic Navigation Bars (see Chapter 9) provide a way to navigate along the lines either to siblings or to the child pages of a page (the pages at the next level down). The dark lines represent the navigation paths through the site. However, if you exclude a page from navigation, it won't show up in the Navigation Bars, and the connecting line is drawn in gray. The page also displays a red "not" symbol in the upper-right corner.

You can collapse the structure (for viewing only) by clicking the down arrow that appears below any page that has child pages. If you do so, the down arrow turns into a plus sign—clicking the plus sign re-expands the site structure.

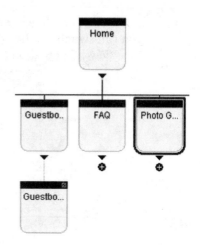

Rearrange the Pages in Site View

As you'll see in Chapter 3, you can build the structure for an entire web site without leaving Site view, and in fact, this is a handy way to lay out your web site quickly. As it turns out, however, sometimes you'll need to rearrange the structure of the web site, and this is easy to do in Site view as well.

The first step is to select the page you want to move. The selected page (FAQ, in the following illustration) shows a blue border, unless the page has been excluded from navigation, in which case it shows a red border. Either way, the next step is to click and drag the page (and its children, if it has any) on top of a different page in the web site and watch for the red arrow to appear (visible in the image as a downward-pointing wedge at the bottom of the page thumbnail) that indicates where the page will be dropped when you release the mouse button.

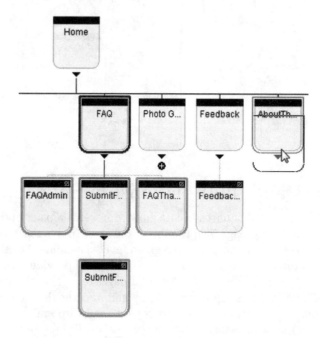

Here is what the various arrows mean:

- **Right or left arrow**   Indicates that the page (and its children) will be dropped as a sibling on the indicated side of the target web page.
- **Up arrow**   Indicates that the dragged page will become the parent of the target page.
- **Down arrow**   Indicates that the dragged page will become the child of the target page. If the target page already has child pages, the dragged page becomes the new parent of the existing child pages.

Work with the Outline View

A variation on Site view is available if you click the Outline tab (see Figure 1-2). The site itself is displayed like an outline in the left pane, and a view-only set of page properties are shown in columns in the right pane.

Clicking a page in the left pane that has child pages displays the properties for the child pages (including the "Child Name") in the right pane. If the selected page in the left pane has no child pages, the Child Name column will display "None" in the right pane.

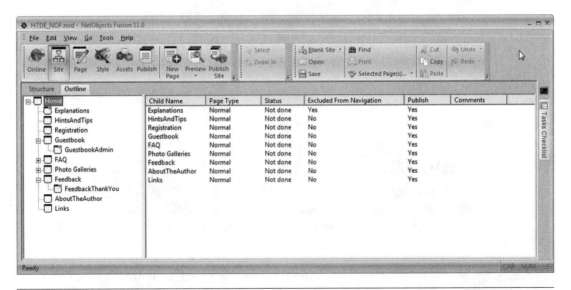

FIGURE 1-2   View the properties of the children of the selected page in the Outline tab of Site view.

Toggle the Panels with the View Menu

A limited variety of "panels" are available in Site view, such as the Property Inspector panel visible at the right edge of the screen in Figure 1-1, seen previously. You can turn a particular panel on or off by using the entries in the View menu. Each entry is a toggle: select the item to turn the panel on; reselect it to hide the panel. The entries for panels in the View menu include

- **Standard Tools**   This is actually the toolbar that includes the Select tool and the Zoom tool.
- **Property Inspector**   Displays a variety of properties for the selected item. In Site view, these are pretty much limited to the properties of the selected page, but in Page view (discussed later in this chapter), the Property Inspector can display page properties as well as properties for other items you select (such as tables, images, and hyperlinks) on a page.
- **Tasks Checklist**   A prebuilt list of tasks associated with the task category chosen from the drop-down list at the top of the Tasks Checklist.
- **Output**   This panel is a list of tasks you have done as you create and edit the site or pages within the site. When the Tasks Checklist and the Output panel are both open, they share a panel—pick the one you want to see from the tabs at the bottom of the panel.

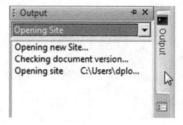

Understand the Page View

Page view (see Figure 1-3) is where you create web pages and add text, images, hyperlinks, tables, multimedia objects, and much more. Once you have the basic structure of your web site laid out, you'll spend the vast bulk of your time in Page view.

To switch to Page view from any other view, click the Page button in the Views Bar toolbar. From Site view, you can also double-click one of the pages in the site structure.

Ruler   Margin marker   Guide

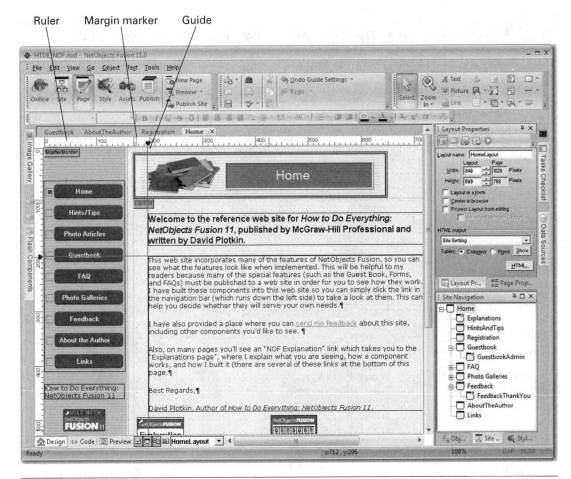

FIGURE 1-3   Use Page view to edit your web pages

As with Site view, you have toolbars, panels, and layout tools. You can also configure what items you see on each page, and whether the Page labels are visible or not (these can be helpful in identifying page areas and borders when you first start using the software).

Zoom In and Out

In addition to the Zoom tool in the Standard Tools toolbar, you can pick a zoom level from the fly-out menu that appears when you choose View | Zoom. Values

How to... # Configure the Tasks Checklist for Your Own Use

The Tasks Checklist by default contains a set of tasks for building an overall web site. As you complete these tasks, you can check them off in the list.

But what if you want to add your own tasks or task groupings to help you make sure you've done everything you need to? You can do exactly that, using the tools that appear in the toolbar at the top of the Tasks Checklist panel. If you can't see the tools, it is because Tasks Checklist isn't being displayed wide enough. To remedy this situation, click and drag the right edge to expand the view.

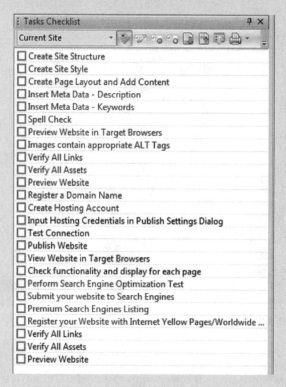

The first step is to establish your own categories for groups of tasks. For example, you might want a category for creating individual pages. To create a category, either click the Manage Categories icon (second from the right end) or choose Manage Tasks Checklist from the drop-down list near the top-left corner of the Tasks Checklist panel. Either way, a list of current categories appears—initially, just the Current Site category. Choose the Add Category button (the left-most button in the new toolbar), fill in the name of the category in the Task Category dialog box, and click OK. Note that you can also select a category name and choose Remove Category (center icon) or Edit Category (right icon) to perform those tasks on the selected category.

The next step is to add tasks to the category. To do that, pick the category from the drop-down list (if you just built a category, it now appears in that list). This makes the complete set of icons available for adding, deleting, and editing task names, as well as rearranging the order of the tasks using the Move Up and Move Down icons.

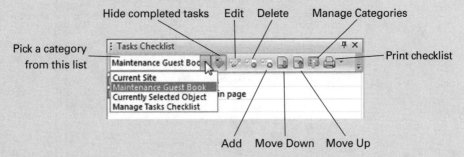

To add a task, click the Add button in the toolbar to display the Edit Task dialog box. The Task field is empty because this is a new task.

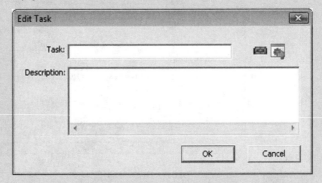

Fill in the task (and a description if you wish), and click OK to add the task to the list.

range from 25% to 200%. To quickly return to a 100% view, you can use the CTRL-0 keyboard shortcut.

Turn on Rulers, Guides, and Grids

To help you lay out your page, NetObjects Fusion provides rulers and guides (CTRL-U), and a grid (CTRL-D). These can be turned off or on from the View menu. To configure the units on the ruler, choose Tools | Options | Application to open the Application

Options dialog box. Click the Program tab, and choose the Measurement Units from the drop-down list near the bottom of the dialog box.

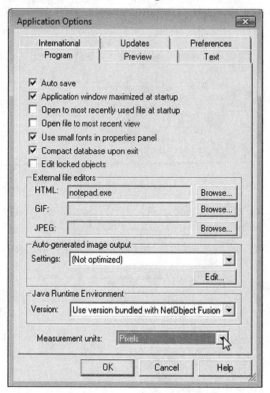

You can add a guide (seen previously in Figure 1-3) to the ruler by clicking in the ruler. The guide (which looks like a blue triangle with a line) helps you align page items by dragging them to line up an edge with the guide line. If the guide is in the wrong place, simply click and drag it to a new location in the ruler. To discard the guide entirely, click and drag it up (left ruler) or left (top ruler) off the ruler.

To help you align objects on the page even more, you can turn on "snapping," which snaps the item you are dragging to either the guides (View | Snap To Guides or CTRL-SHIFT-U) or the grid (View | Snap To Grid or CTRL-SHIFT-D). You can even have various objects snap to each other's edges by turning on snap to object outlines (View | Snap To Object Outlines).

As you'll discover in future chapters, the web page is made up of two main component parts: the Layout and the MasterBorder. You can see the MasterBorder on the left side and the top (including the Banner) of the page in Figure 1-3. You can adjust the split between the MasterBorder and the central portion of the page (the Layout) by clicking and dragging the margin markers, which look like thin gray rectangles in the ruler.

Choose a Workspace

Although you can pick a workspace in Site view, this feature is much more useful in Page view. A *workspace* is a snapshot of your working area, including which panels you have open (and/or minimized), the panel locations, the toolbar layouts, and which layout tools (such as the ruler) you are using. To choose the workspace to use, select View | Workspace and pick the workspace from the submenu. By default, Fusion provides two workspaces: Basic and Advanced. Once you have modified one of the default workspaces and exit the software, the Last Used workspace becomes available in the View | Workspace menu.

Probably the most useful aspect of workspaces is the ability to create and save different workspaces when working on different types of web sites. If you are working on a single site, you may either use the Last Used workspace or save your own workspace.

Just lay out everything the way you want it, and then use the following steps:

1. Choose View | Workspace | Save Workspace As.
2. Fill in the name of the Workspace and make sure that the workspace is saved to the Layout folder.
3. Click Save. From then on, the workspace will appear in the View | Workspace submenu.

Tip   The best way to hide everything on the screen and provide a big working area is to choose View | Full Screen (CTRL-SPACE). When you do that, a "Full Screen" toolbar appears (with a single button) near the top of the screen. Click this button to return to working with the last-defined workspace.

How to... ## Remove Custom Workspaces

NetObjects Fusion does not provide an easy way to remove a custom Workspace once you create it. The only way to discard a workspace you create is to delete the workspace file (which ends in .xml) from the Layout folder. To delete a custom workspace, use the following steps:

1. Choose View | Workspace | Save Workspace As to open the Save As dialog box.
2. Select the custom workspace file you want to delete and press the DELETE key. Click Yes to confirm the file deletion.
3. Once the file has been deleted, click Cancel to cancel out of the save operation.

The custom workspace still appears in the View | Workspace menu, but if you choose it, you'll get an error. To remove the workspace from the menu, close and reopen NetObjects Fusion.

Turn Page Components On and Off

The fourth section of the View menu (counting down from the top) displays a list of page components, which you can turn on and off by making a selection from the menu. The items are visible on the page (see Figure 1-4). Most of these items (especially the MasterBorder) are helpful in laying out the page, but if you find specific items too busy, you can "adjust to taste."

Turn Panels On and Off

There are a few panels available in Site view (such as Property Inspector, Task List, and Output panel), but Page view has a vast number of additional panels that include the multitude of tools you need to build a web page. In addition to the panels directly

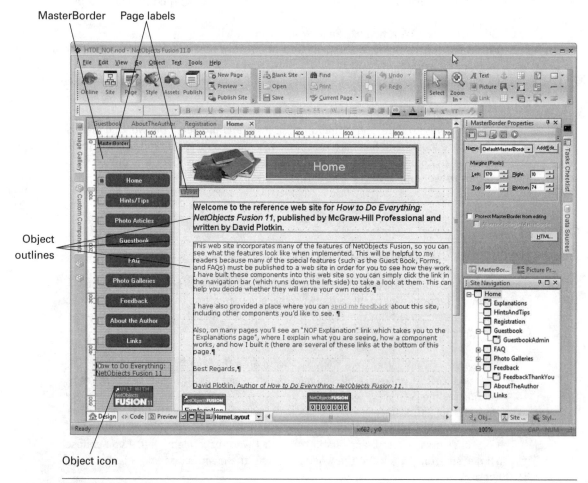

FIGURE 1-4 You can use the View menu to turn specific items on and off in Page view.

visible in the View menu, you can select from many additional panels by selecting them from the View | More Panels submenu.

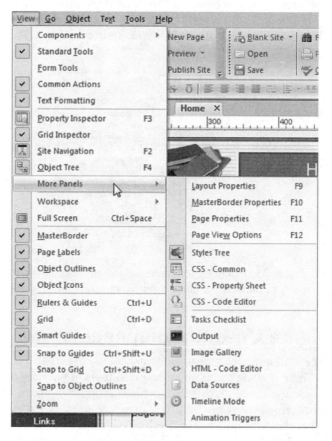

Some of the panels (such as the first four in the View | More Panels submenu) swap (change content) automatically when you select an item on the page. These are known as "property inspector" panels. For example, if you click the page MasterBorder, the MasterBorder Properties panel appears (by default at the top of the stack of panels on the right side). However, if you then click in the Layout section of the page, the MasterBorder Properties panel is replaced by the Layout Properties panel. In addition, you can view the Page view Options "panel" (the fourth one in the View | More Panels submenu) by clicking the second icon from the right in the Page Properties panel.

Some of the panels are "compound" panels: selecting one of the options in the View | More Panels submenu opens a whole set of panels, nested together with tabs at the bottom so that you can switch to one of the other panels in the set. A good example of one of these compound panels is the Site Navigation panel, which is opened as part of the set with Object Tree and Style Tree.

 Of course, you can use the techniques for moving panels (discussed later in this chapter) to unhook the compound panels and make the panels individually visible.

Configure Custom Components

One of the wonderful aspects of NetObjects Fusion is that it includes a vast array of tools. These include database tools, Flash tools, prebuilt code for FAQ, forms, a guestbook, news reader, RSS feed, Google search, ad banners, animated buttons, and much more. However, it can be pretty overwhelming to navigate through all these tools to find the one you want to use. To help with this, NetObjects Fusion bundles related tools into component groups. For example, this image shows the tools you'll need to build the FAQ page for your web site.

To turn each component group on or off, make a selection from the View | Components submenu.

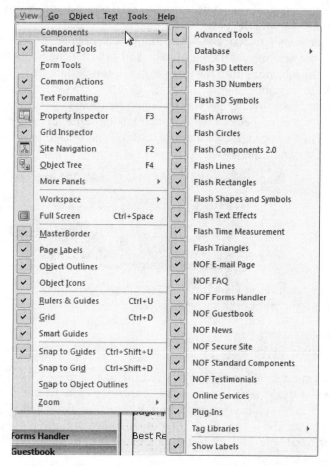

NetObjects Fusion places the component group into its appropriate panel. For example, if you choose to view the NOF Guestbook component group, it is placed in the Custom Components panel. All of the Flash tools (Flash 3D Numbers, Flash 3D Letters, Flash Lines, etc.) are placed in the Flash Components panel. If you have closed the Flash Components panel, choose View | Components and select the Flash components you need. The Flash Components panel then displays the selected Flash components.

Understand Page Design Mode

Page Design mode is the more or less WYSIWYG (what you see is what you get) environment where you lay out the page. You can place tables, frames, text blocks, images, hyperlinks, buttons, and more into the page, as described later in this book. In addition, there are elements (like the labels and object borders) that you can turn on and off. These do not show up in the final version you see in a browser but are helpful in designing the page.

Fusion keeps track of the pages that you have opened in a site. These pages are added to the tabs in Page Design mode. You can then switch between these pages by clicking the tab containing the page name in the design area. To close a page, click the small "x" in the tab.

It may occur to you that you can open multiple pages in Page view/Design mode. Maybe it is best to specify how it works: Fusion remembers the pages that have been open in Page view, and adds them in tabs in Page Design mode, offering the possibility to switch between them.

If you are in Page view but don't see Page Design mode, click the Design button in the lower-left corner of the working area.

Preview the Page

You can get an even better idea of what the page will look like by clicking the Preview button near the lower-left corner of the working area. In this mode, the "extras" (such as the labels and object outlines) are removed. You can't edit the page in this mode, but it appears "live"—any flash components play, and the mouse cursor turns into the pointing hand when you pass it over a hyperlink (though you can't click the link to navigate to the page).

Another way to preview the page is to open it in a browser by selecting Go | Preview (or choosing Preview from the Views Bar toolbar), selecting the browser you want to use from the submenu, and then picking the resolution from the browser submenu.

Did You Know?

You Can Move Items with Great Control

Clicking and dragging items certainly works for moving them, but you may have trouble getting the degree of control you want. To move items with a finer touch, you can select the item and move it a pixel at a time using the arrow keys. To move it ten pixels at a time, hold down the SHIFT key while pressing an arrow key.

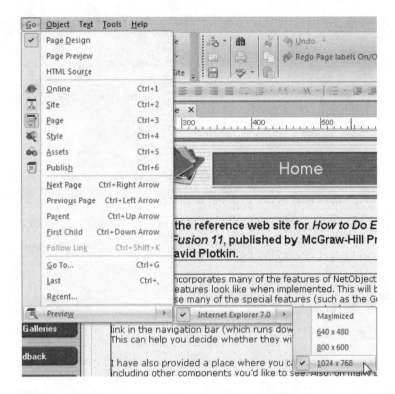

To configure the browser(s) to use for preview, see "Set Important Options," later in this chapter.

Of course, not all the features will work—many require that the site be published to an actual web site that supports the various scripts and components you can build into the site. But for a basic "look" at the pages, and to experiment with navigation, Preview is really handy.

View the HTML Source

Although you don't have to know HTML to work in NetObjects Fusion, it can be helpful to view the HTML "source code" (see Figure 1-5) that the tool generates to render the page. To do this, click the Code button near the lower-left corner of the working area. The HTML source code is not editable in this view, but if you know your way around HTML, studying the code may help you figure out why something is not behaving the way you expect.

Navigate Your Site in Page View

Although the easiest way to navigate through your web site is to switch to Site view and double-click the page you want to view or work on next (or double-click the page you want in the Site Navigation panel), you can actually navigate your site from within Page view using the Go menu.

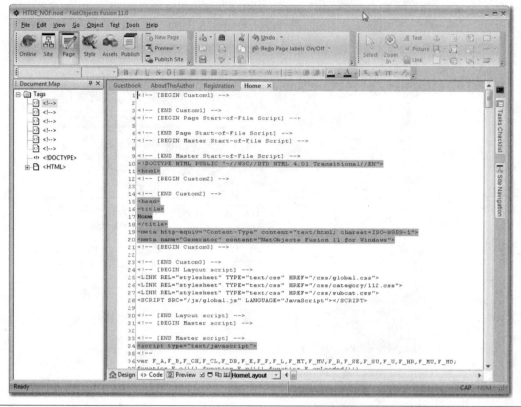

FIGURE 1-5 The HTML that renders the web page is visible in Code mode.

The options include

- **Next Page** (CTRL-RIGHT ARROW) Navigates to the page to the right of the current page at the same level.
- **Previous Page** (CTRL-LEFT ARROW) Navigates to the page to the left of the current one at the same level.
- **Parent** (CTRL-UP ARROW) Navigates to the parent page of the current page.
- **First Child** (CTRL-DOWN ARROW) Navigates to the left-most child page of the current page.
- **Follow Link** (CTRL-SHIFT-K) After selecting any text, image, or other object that has a hyperlink, choose Follow Link to open that link in a browser. Note that this does not work for the buttons or text links in Navigation Bars.

Configure the Toolbars and Panels

NetObjects Fusion provides a variety of menus, toolbars, and panels to create and edit your web site. You have considerable power in configuring what you want to see and how you want to arrange these tools.

Move and Configure the Toolbars

As with many Windows applications, the toolbars and their associated tools are located across the top of the screen, just below the menu bar. The available tools change as you switch to different views to create and edit your web site. The toolbars are quite flexible—you can click and drag a toolbar to a different position in the toolbar area, or even into the working area, where it becomes a floating window.

 To relocate a toolbar, click and drag the dotted line at the left end of the toolbar. To drag a toolbar around the working area, or from the working area (where it has become a window) back into the toolbar area, click and drag the title bar. You can even relocate the menus, though I am not sure why you'd want to.

Each toolbar has two different display modes: Standard and Smart Layout. The Standard display mode, which is also the default one, shows all the tools as tiny icons, and as you move your mouse over an icon, this Standard mode displays a tooltip with the name of the tool.

The second mode (Smart Layout) is much more useful. The toolbar uses all the available space to show as much information as possible. As you grow the toolbar, you'll see larger icons and text, as shown here.

 To increase or decrease the space available for a toolbar, you can either drag an adjacent toolbar out of the way (giving you more room) or click and drag the dotted line at the left end of an adjacent toolbar to lengthen or shorten it—thereby affecting the space available for surrounding toolbars.

As the space for the toolbar shrinks, the icons and text shrink as well, until you are left with tiny icons that pack things in tightly.

If there isn't enough room to show all the icons in the toolbar, a tiny double-headed arrow appears in the upper-right corner of the toolbar. Clicking this button displays the "missing" icons in a drop-down menu.

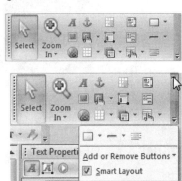

To enable Smart Layout, click the tiny down arrow at the right edge of the toolbar and select the Smart Layout check box in the drop-down list.

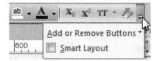

Dock, Move, and Resize Panels

You can position a panel almost anywhere in the workspace by clicking and dragging the panel title bar. As you begin to drag the panel, you'll see a set of arrow buttons (see Figure 1-6). If you simply ignore those buttons and click and drag the panel,

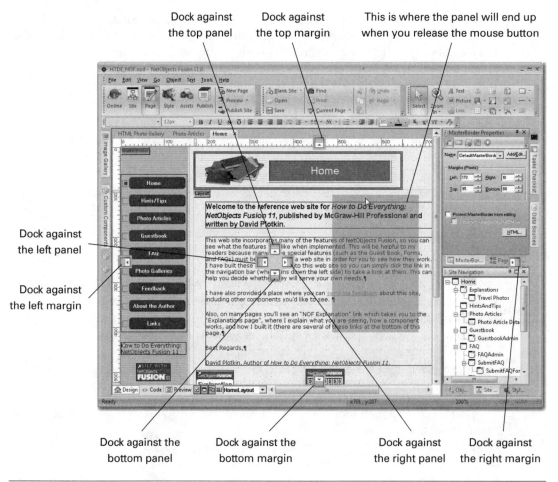

FIGURE 1-6   Drag a panel on top of an arrow button to position it against a margin.

it turns into a free-floating panel. However, if you drag the panel on top of one of the arrows, it will be docked against the appropriate margin. A blue rectangle shows where the panel will be docked when you release the left mouse button.

 When you "dock against a panel," this means that the panel you are dragging docks against the edge of any panel that is already docked against the side of the working area. For example, in Figure 1-6, if you drag a panel to dock against the right panel, it will dock to the left of the existing MasterBorder Properties and Site Navigation panels, shrinking the available working area. If there is no panel already docked against the side of the working area (such as on the left side), the dragged panel docks against that side—just as if you had chosen to dock against the left margin. If there *is* a panel already docked against that side, the existing panel is pushed out into the working area to make room for the new panel being docked against the side of the working area.

If you drag a panel on top of another panel, you'll see a slightly different set of buttons, which indicate where the panel will end up (in relation to the existing panel).

Dragging the panel on top of one of the arrow buttons places the panel on that side of the existing panel, as you would expect. For example, dragging the panel on top of the down-pointing arrow stacks the two panels, one above the other (especially helpful in Page view, discussed later in this chapter). However, if you drag the panel on top of the center button, the dragged panel and the existing panel are combined into one panel; you pick the one you want to work with from the tabs at the bottom of the combined panel.

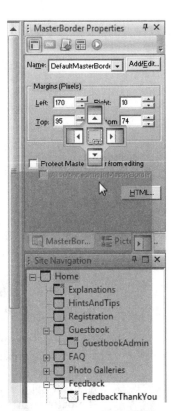

You can resize free-floating panels by clicking and dragging any margin. If the panel is docked, you can only change the width (if docked to the left or right side) or the height (if docked to the top or bottom) when the panels are docked. However, if multiple panels are docked to a side and stacked (as shown in Figure 1-7), you can change the split between the panels by clicking and dragging the margin between the panels.

Collapse Panels to Move Them Out of the Way

There are a variety of other controls for manipulating panels as well. First of all, you can close the panel by clicking the small "x" in the upper-right corner. Just to the left of the "x" is a small pin icon. Clicking this pin collapses the panel and places it out of the way. If the panel is docked against a side of the

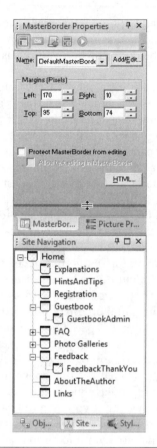

FIGURE 1-7   Click and drag the split between panels to change the amount of room each panel has.

workspace, the collapsed panel shows up as a narrow slide against that side, as shown here (against the right margin).

If, instead, the panel is a free-floating workspace window, nothing seems to happen until you click somewhere not on the panel, at which point the panel "rolls up" to show just the title bar for the panel.

 To redisplay an unpinned panel, click the title bar either in the workspace (free-floating panel) or in the margin (docked panel). To redisplay the panel normally, click the pin again in the displayed panel.

Set Important Options

As with most programs, NetObjects Fusion has a large number of options you can set to configure how the program works. Some of the more important ones include

- **Set the new page size** From the General tab of the Current Site Options dialog box (choose Tools | Options | Current Site), fill in the Height and Width for the new page in the New Page Size section.

- **Set the Site Generation scripts** There are two main "languages" (PHP and ASP) for generating scripts that run functionality like FAQs on your web site. Which one you use will depend on information provided by your web site provider. To select one of these options, pick it from the Scripts drop-down list in the Site Generation section of the Current Site Options dialog box. If the web site provider can use AJAX technology (which provides powerful interactive functionality), you can select the Enable AJAX Technology check box.

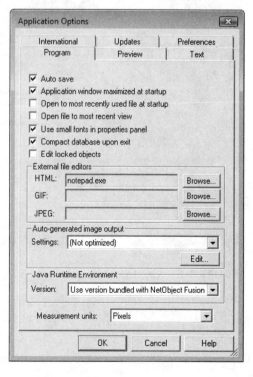

- **Configure the Program items** A variety of check boxes appear in the Program tab of the Application Options dialog box. These check boxes enable you to configure how the program opens and saves files. They include the four options, described next.

  - **Auto Save** Select this check box to have NetObjects Fusion save the file (ending in .nod) periodically. I generally leave this check box unselected. Although auto save ensures you don't lose your work, it also means that you can't easily change your mind about recent changes by simply closing and reopening the site.

  - **Application window maximized at startup** Select this check box to open a full-size application window when you start the program, saving you the trouble of dragging the window border to or maximizing the window to give yourself more working room.

  - **Open to most recently used file at startup** If you're like me, you normally work on a specific web site, rather than maintaining a whole bunch of different sites. If that suits your working style, select this check box in the Program tab of the Application Options dialog box so that NetObjects Fusion opens and automatically loads the last file (web site) you used. If you *don't* select this check box, NetObjects Fusion opens to the "Online View" (see Figure 1-8) where you can pick from recently used files.

- **Open file to most recent view** If you really want to pick up where you left off, select this check box as well, which then opens in the same view (such as Site view, Page view, etc.) as when you closed the NetObjects Fusion the last time you used it.

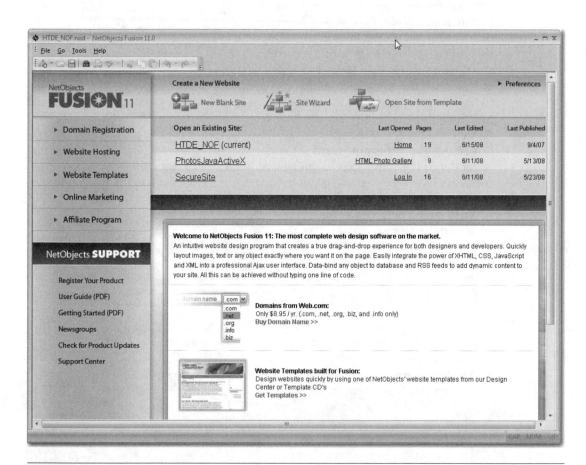

FIGURE 1-8 Use the Online view to pick from a list of web sites to open.

- **Set up external tools**   It can be very handy to open an application automatically to edit HTML, GIF, or JPEG image files. To specify such applications, use the Program tab of the Application Options dialog box (choose Tools | Options | Application). In the External File Editors section, click the Browse button next to each file line and specify the executable file (like notepad.exe) from the Open dialog box. Once you've set this up, simply right-click HTML text or a picture file, and pick Open File In External Editor from the shortcut menu.
- **Configure the Browser Preview**   Use the Preview tab of the Application Options dialog box to configure which browser(s) will be available in the Go | Preview menu. To add a browser to the list, click Add to bring up the New Browser dialog box. Fill in the name of the browser (such as Internet Explorer 7.0) and click Browse to pick the executable file from the Open dialog box. To choose what to preview, pick either Current Page or Entire Site from the Preview scope section. If you pick Entire Site, you can actually navigate through the site during the preview, but it takes much longer to prepare the preview. To pick a Window size, choose one of the options from the Window Size section.

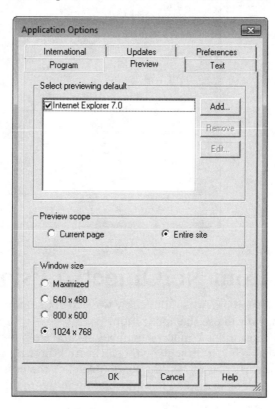

- **Set the default text sizes**   Use the Text tab of the Application Options dialog box to set the default font to use for Proportional fonts and for Fixed Width fonts. Choose the font you want to use from each drop-down list, and the matching size from the adjacent drop-down list. Each font drop-down list shows only the appropriate list of fonts. For example, the Fixed Width list shows only fixed-width fonts (such as Courier New).

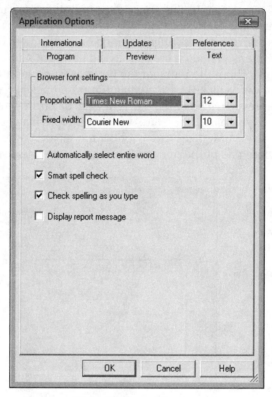

Get Help from NetObjects Fusion

NetObjects Fusion provides quite a few ways to get help in understanding its features and learning how to use the application.

As with most other Windows applications, the Help menu (Help | Help Topics) provides a dialog box from which you can search through the contents, use an index, or search for particular terms. Simply double-click the entry in the left-side panel of the Help dialog box to display the information in the right-side panel.

If multiple topics in the Index tab match the item you double-clicked, a smaller Topics Found dialog box appears with the topics. Simply click one and then click Display.

Another way to get help is to right-click an object and select What's This? from the shortcut menu. This action pops up a textual description about the item.

This trick also works with certain fields in the Properties panels, except that with the panels, all you need to do is right-click the field to display the Help description. Such fields include most drop-down lists, check boxes, and controls (like the Paint Can button for picking a color).

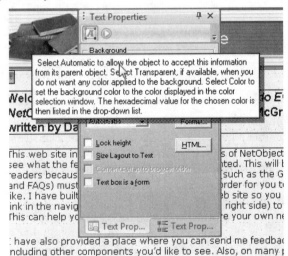

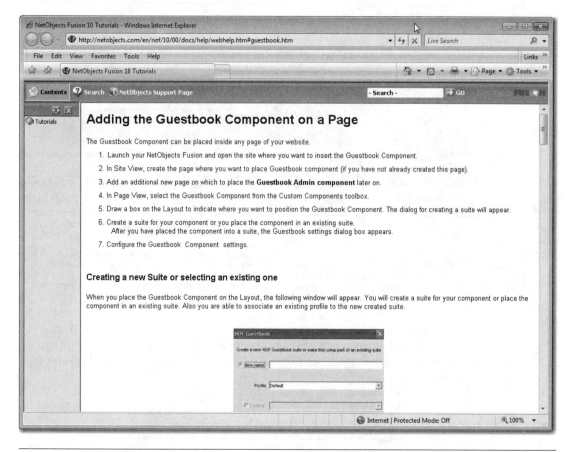

FIGURE 1-9 Online tutorials provide step-by-step instructions on how to use certain complex components.

With some components (such as FAQ TOC), the Help pop-up (available when right-clicking a component) also includes a link to an online tutorial.

The Online Tutorial offers surprising amounts of detail as it walks you through how to build some complex components, as shown in Figure 1-9.

Another special case of panel-based help is shown in the Flash Components. Right-clicking a Flash item (such as the Grow and Pulse effect in the Flash Rectangles section) shows a preview of the effect so that you don't have guess at what you're getting. Pretty slick!

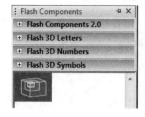

2

Build an Initial Web Site

HOW TO...

- Build a web site using a wizard
- Start building a web site from a blank site
- Save your work
- Open a web site to work on it
- Buy or create a web site template
- Publish your web site locally

There are a variety of ways for you to start building a web site. You can start from scratch with a blank site or use a site wizard to help you define your content. You can also design a web site using an existing template or web site as a starting point. It all depends on whether you have a good idea of what you want, or you wish to start from a template designed for a certain purpose.

Build a Site from the Site Wizard

The Site Wizard walks you through building a brand-new site. To use it, make sure you are in the Online view and either click the Site Wizard button or click the tiny arrow to the right of the Blank Site tool (the left-most tool in the toolbar), and then pick Using Site Wizard from the drop-down menu. You can also select File | New Site | Using Site Wizard. However you do it, the Site Wizard dialog box opens.

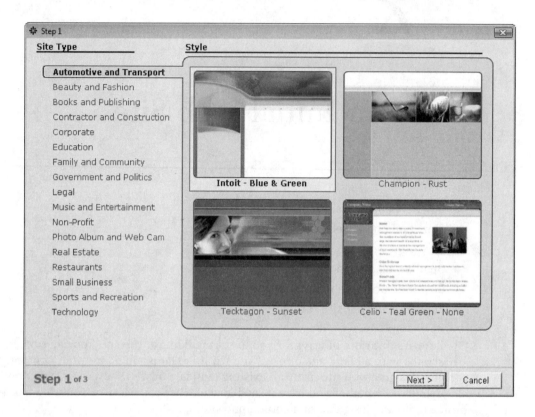

The first step is to pick a Site Type. The types are listed in the left panel of the dialog box by business type (Automotive And Transport, Legal, Music And Entertainment, and more). For each type, there are several styles available. Pick the Site Type by clicking it, and then pick the Style by clicking one of the thumbnails. When you're done with this step, click Next to move to Step 2. This is where you pick the pages you want added to the site, as well as the basic layout.

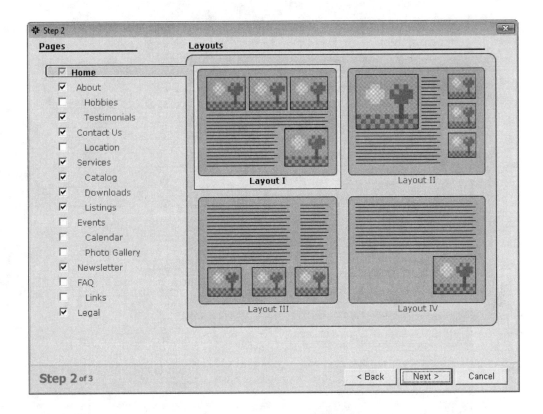

You have considerable flexibility in picking the layouts. The first step is to select the page from the Pages list; then you pick one of the four layouts from the Layouts thumbnails. You can pick a different layout for each page. This works well, as the layouts available for (say) the calendar page differ considerably from the layouts for the Photo Gallery or Newsletter. Once you have picked the pages and layouts, click Next to move to Step 3. This is where you put in optional information about yourself or your business. The nice thing about this is that NetObjects

Fusion automatically fills in such information on web pages where it is used while generating the site.

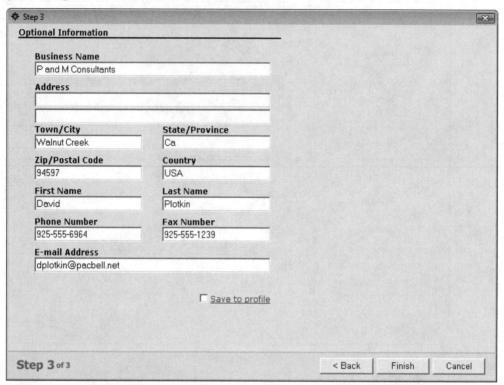

 If you don't have a profile, NetObjects Fusion gives you the opportunity to create one so that you don't have to build it from scratch in the future. You do, however, have the opportunity to adjust any of the information in Step 3 before clicking Finish to generate and open the web site. After the web site is generated, it is automatically added to the Online view.

Create a Web Site with the Blank Site Tool

You can create a new web site using the "blank site" template (which actually contains a single home page but nothing else) by clicking the New Blank Site button, choosing File | New Site | Blank Site, or choosing Blank Site from the Blank Site tool drop-down list. This action opens the New Blank Site dialog box.

Fill in the name of the site (which is also used as the name of the folder that contains the web site files) in the File name field, and then click Save to create the site.

How to... Add a Web Site to the Online View

You can configure which web sites you want to appear (and their order) in the Open An Existing Site list of the Online view.

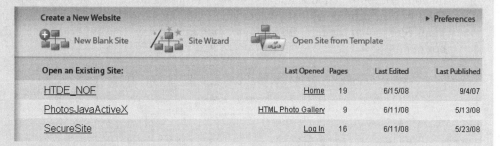

The list normally includes any site that you have opened using NetObjects Fusion, up to the limit about to be described.

To open a web site that does not appear in the list (and thus get it into the list), choose File | Open Site and navigate to the .nod file in the Open dialog box. Then click Open.

To remove a web site from the list, click the Preferences button in the upper-right corner of the Online view to open the Edit Site Project Preferences dialog box.

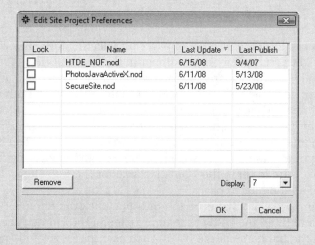

Select the name of the web site you want to remove from the list, and then click Remove.

You can specify up to 12 web sites (the default is 7) to appear in the Online view by choosing the number from the Display drop-down list in the lower-right corner of the dialog box. You can also specify which column to sort on (the default is the Last Update date) by clicking the column header in the Edit Site Project Preferences dialog box. The tiny arrow (which is displayed in the Last Update column in the illustration) appears in the sort column, pointing in the sort direction (ascending or descending). To switch the sort order of a column, simply click the column heading to reverse the arrow direction.

Create a New Web Site from an Existing Site

You can create a new web site by patterning it after an existing site—either one that is stored locally on your computer or an Internet site. To import a site that already exists on your computer, choose File | New Site | From Existing Site, or pick From Existing Site from the drop-down list you get when you click the tiny arrow to the right of the Blank Site tool at the left end of the toolbar. Either way, the Import Web Site dialog box opens.

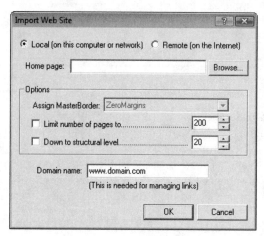

You can limit the number of pages by selecting the Limit Number Of Pages To check box and specifying a number in the adjacent field. You can also limit the structural level (how many levels down from the home page are imported) by selecting the Down To Structural Level check box and specifying a limit in the adjacent field.

To import a site that already exists on your computer, select the Local (On This Computer Or Network) radio button. In the Home Page field, specify the location of the home page for the web site (an .htm or .html file). You can also specify the location of the home page by clicking Browse and navigating to the home page .html file. Make sure to fill in the Domain Name for the web site so that NetObjects Fusion can find all the related pages.

To import a site that is on the Internet, click the Remote (On The Internet) radio button and fill in the URL of the home page in the Home Page field. Don't forget to include the full name of the page—such as http://www.htde-netobjectsfusion.com/index.htm. Importing a large web site this way can take a while, as it has to download everything—including images.

Create a Web Site from a Template

Another way to create a new web site is to create it from a template. To do that, click the Open Site From Template button in the Online view. You can also click File | New Site | From Template, or click the Blank Site tool and choose From Template in the drop-down list. Doing so opens the Select A Template File dialog box, from which you can navigate to a template file (either a .zip or a .nft file), click the file, and then choose Open to create the new web site from the template.

One thing you'll notice right off is that NetObjects Fusion doesn't come with many templates. You have two ways to remedy this—buy templates from the publisher or create your own and save them. To buy templates, click the Website Templates link at the left side of the Online view.

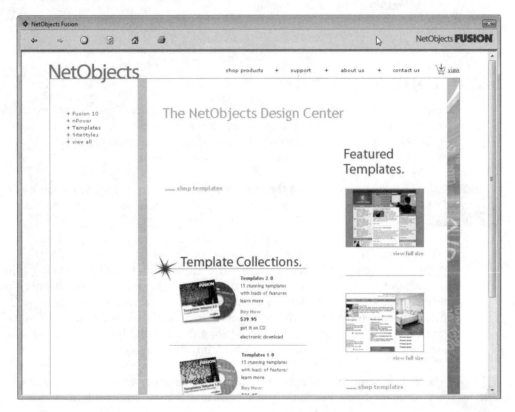

This opens the Design Center, from which you can select and purchase templates to download and use.

To create your own templates, use the following steps:

1. Create the web site you want to use as a template, using the tools provided by NetObjects Fusion.
2. Make sure you're in Site view (where you can see the structure of the web site).
3. If you only want to export certain pages, select those pages in the Site view. To select multiple pages, click the first page, then hold down the CTRL key and select the additional pages.
4. Choose File | Export As Template, and then choose either Entire Site or Selected Pages from the submenu. This opens the Save Template dialog box.
5. Fill in the name of the template and click Save to save the template for future use.

You Can Move a Web Site from One Computer to Another

To do so, save the web site as a template on one computer, and then copy the template to the target computer and create a new web site from the template. Do *not* just copy the .nod file from one computer to another—it won't open properly on the target computer.

Save Your Web Site

Unlike some other web site–building packages, NetObjects Fusion saves your work in a file, which it opens when you want to work on the site. As with just about any Windows application, you can save the site (and your current work) by selecting File | Save or File | Save As to save the file under a new name.

If you just want to close the site without closing the application, choose File | Close Site. This returns you to the Online view, where you can pick another site to work with.

If you are concerned about forgetting to save your site, you can configure NetObjects Fusion to do it for you. From the Application Options dialog box (choose Tools | Options | Application), select the Auto Save check box. With this check box selected, each time you make a change, NetObjects Fusion saves the change. Of course, this also means that you can't revert to an earlier saved version (if you don't like the changes you made) by simply closing the site and reopening it. For this reason, I usually leave the Auto Save check box unselected.

Even though you can't revert to an earlier version of a site if you use Auto Save, the Undo functionality (Edit | Undo or CTRL-Z) is quite robust. Fusion keeps a significant history of changes, so you can undo quite a few changes. Unfortunately, if you typed text, each undo removes only a single character.

Open a Web Site

There are a number of ways you can open a web site in NetObjects Fusion. First of all, if the web site appears in the Open An Existing Site list in the Online view, you can simply click the name of the site to open it and view it in Site view. Another way to open the site from either the Online view or the Site view is to choose File | Open Site, and then pick the file (.nod) for the site you want from the Open dialog box (and click Open). Note that you can only have a single web site open at any time—if you already have a web site open and you open another one, the first one closes.

Publish Your Web Site Locally

Much like the Preview function discussed in Chapter 1, you can publish your web site locally on your hard drive so that you can preview what it looks like in your browser. And, as with the Preview function, specialized components on the pages won't work when you publish locally. To publish locally, click the Publish Site button in the Views Bar toolbar to open the Publish Site dialog box.

 Click the Publish Site button, *not* the Publish button. The Publish button takes you to another view of your web site (as described in Chapter 16), where you can compare your local copy with what has been published to the Internet.

Make sure to choose Local Publish in the Publish Files To drop-down list, and pick what you want to publish from the Pages To Publish drop-down list. If you choose Select Page(s), another dialog box opens to enable you to select the check boxes for the pages you want to publish.

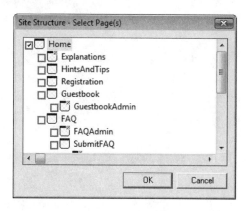

If you've only changed a few items, you can select the Publish Changed Assets Only check box. Of course, at some point you need to have published your entire web site for this to make any sense.

Once you've got everything set up, click Publish to render the HTML pages to your hard drive. Once that is complete, the home page opens in your default browser.

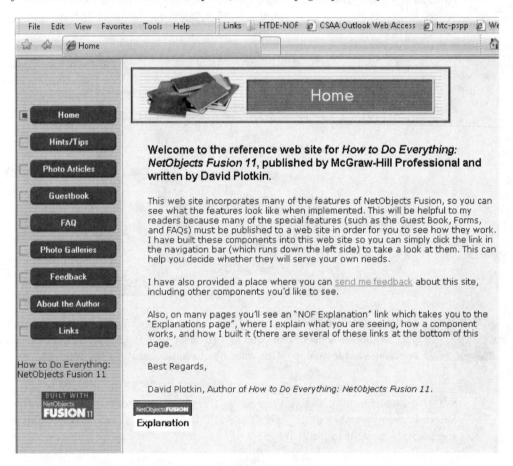

3

Build a New Web Page

HOW TO...

- Create new pages for your web site
- Specify the properties of the pages
- Create and configure MasterBorders
- Create and configure Layouts
- Customize Layouts with Layout Regions

Once you've opened your new web site, the next step is to add web pages to the structure of the site in Site view. By adding pages this way, you can visualize the structure and how to navigate your web site. Once you've added and done the basic configuration of the pages in your site, you can start laying out the pages themselves, adding various components to each page.

Create New Pages in Site View

The Structure tab of Site view (see Figure 3-1) is ideally set up to do the initial structural design of your web site, especially if you ensure that the Property Inspector panel is available (choose View | Property Inspector or press F3 to display the panel).

To add a new page in Site view, click the page that will be the parent of the new page and then use one of the following tools to create the new page:

- Right-click the parent page and pick New Page from the shortcut menu.
- Click the New Page button in the Views Bar toolbar.
- Choose Edit | New Page (CTRL-N).

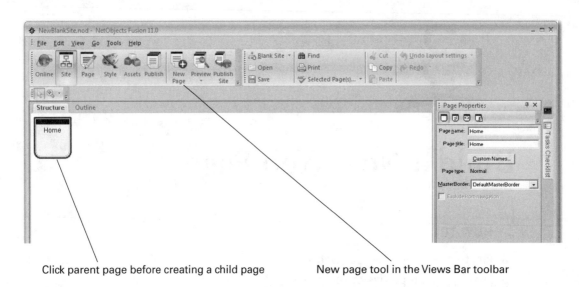

Click parent page before creating a child page   New page tool in the Views Bar toolbar

FIGURE 3-1 A basic web site starts with a Home page—but you can add on from there.

The new page is created as a child of the selected page with a page name and a page title of "untitled" followed by a number.

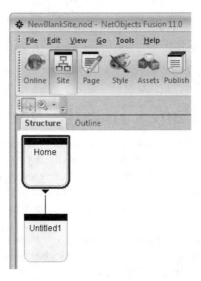

Insert a Template into a Web Site

Of course, if you already have a web site or a template built, it is highly inefficient to rebuild it one page at a time in Site view. Fortunately, you don't have to. To add an entire template as the child of an existing page, select the page, and choose Insert

Template from the shortcut menu (or select File | Insert Template). From there you simply pick a template to use (.zip or .nft file) and proceed as described in Chapter 2 for building a new site.

The major difference between creating a site from a template and adding a template into an existing site is that when creating a site from a template, the imported template includes the home page. This works well if you want to use the structure of the template, along with the style, MasterBorders, and so forth. Add a template when you want to add specific functionality (such as secured pages) or components (such as a Guestbook or Forms) that you've already created in another site.

Another difference between creating a site from a template and adding a template into an existing site is that various components (such as MasterBorders) have default names, and if these names collide (that is, both the existing site and the template have components with the same name), you'll have to choose how to resolve the collision. For example, if the MasterBorders have the same name, you'll get the dialog box shown.

Once you've resolved any collisions, the new site is created, with the entire template inserted as a child of the originally selected page (see Figure 3-2).

Another issue you may have to deal with is that the inserted template may have pages with the same name (such as Home) as pages in the original web site. This can be confusing, as the page name is used in Navigation Bars (see Chapter 9). The page name is also used in generating the HTML page when you publish your site, but NetObjects Fusion is smart enough to create a unique name (such as Home1.html) when creating the pages. Still, it is best to make sure that each page has a unique name, as described later in this chapter.

Import a Document as a Page

If you already have a document built (in Word or a Rich Text Format), you can add that document as a page in your web site. To do that, select the parent page in the Site view and choose File | Import | Document. This opens the Import Document dialog box.

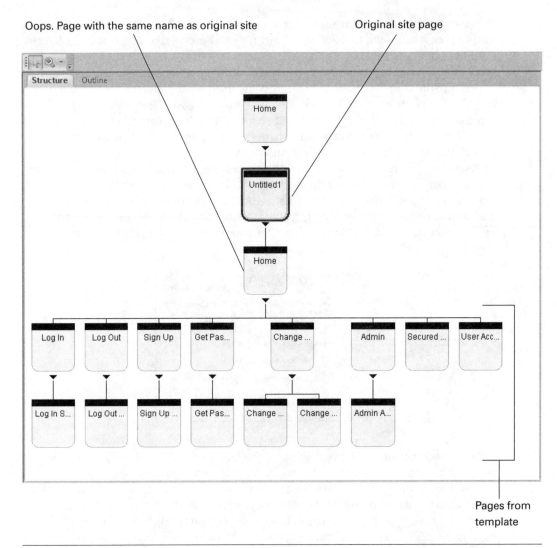

FIGURE 3-2 A new site, with a template inserted as the child of a site page

Navigate to the file location and select the file you want to include. Choose the type of MasterBorder you want from the Assign MasterBorder drop-down list, and click Open to create the page.

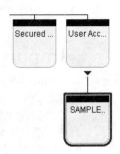

 Don't try to load too large a document (more than about two pages long) into the new web page. If you do, the page will refuse to open in Fusion, though you will be able to see it when you publish the web site and view it in a browser.

Fill in the Page Properties

Click the left-most tab in the Page Properties panel (the tooltip reads "Page") to set the name, title, and other properties of the page.

The items you can set from this panel are

- **Page name**   This is the name of the page, as it appears in the Navigation Bar(s) and (by default) in the banner for those page styles that use a banner. By default, it is also the Page title. The Page name should be short enough to fit in the buttons, banner, and text of the web page.
- **Page title**   This is the title of the page, which appears in the title bar or tab of the browser. Thus, the page title should be fairly descriptive.
- **Custom Names**   Click Custom Names to open the Custom Names dialog box. Here you can specify the text to place on the Navigation button (when using Navigation Bars, see Chapter 9), the banner that appears at the top of the page, and what file extension to use for the page. It's usually best not to change the file extension, as the page may not work correctly if you specify the wrong extension—and NetObjects Fusion does a good job of specifying the correct file extension.

- **MasterBorder**   A MasterBorder is the area that specifies the framed areas at the top, left, right, and bottom areas of the page. As you will see later in this chapter, you can set up the size of the MasterBorder, add text and graphics to the MasterBorder, and specify Navigation Bars. You can then save the MasterBorder with its own name. The default MasterBorder (called DefaultMasterBorder) and any MasterBorders you create appear in the MasterBorder drop-down list, and you can pick one for each page. The other item that appears is called ZeroMargins—which means not having a MasterBorder. That is, the frame areas are missing from the page— along with anything that normally appears in those areas, such as the page banner, Navigation Bars, and graphics.

- **Exclude from navigation** As I have mentioned several times already, the pages that appear in the web site structure normally also appear in the various navigation aids, such as the Navigation Bar (see Chapter 9). However, sometimes you don't want site users to know that a page exists. Good examples of this are pages where you administer FAQs, the Guest Book, and so on. As the site administrator, you can navigate to those pages by entering their URL in the browser, but site visitors should not have a button or link to navigate to those pages, which they should not be using. To exclude a page from navigation, select the Exclude From Navigation check box in the Page Properties.

You cannot exclude the Home page from navigation.

Set the Page Management Properties

Clicking the Management tab (the second one from the left) in the Page Properties panel provides another set of controls.

The controls here enable you to do the following:

- **Adjust the Page status to Done** You can adjust the page status to indicate that it is done by selecting the Done check box. This doesn't actually change anything except to give a visual cue in the Site view (a small green check mark), but it does allow you to scan the site structure and see quickly which pages still need work.

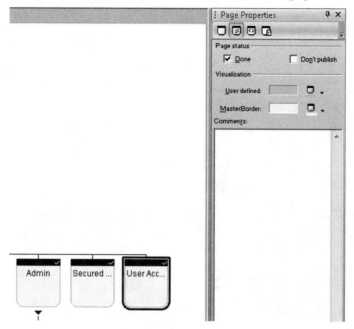

- **Adjust the Page status to Don't Publish**   If you're still working on a page and don't want to publish it, select the Don't Publish check box. This actually does prevent the page from being published, and it also puts a visual cue (a small red "x") in the Site view. Just remember that if you don't publish a parent page, the child pages attached to it are not going to be accessible.

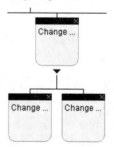

- **Set the color (visualization) of a page**   If you want a page to stand out in the web site structure, you can change the page color. To do so, select the page, click the Color drop-down list, and pick a color from the grid. The page turns to the selected color.
- **Set the color of a page by its MasterBorder**   The other way to change the color of a page is to select the page and pick a color from the MasterBorder color drop-down. The page color changes to the selected color, as does the color

of every other page with the same MasterBorder. This is a good visual way to segregate web pages with the same MasterBorder by color.

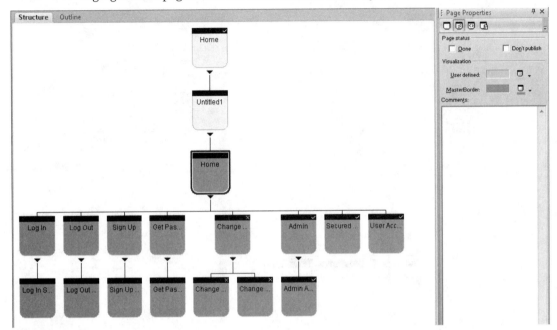

 Note   To actually *see* the pages displayed in the colors described in the last two bullets, you must select which visualization you want. To do so, choose View | Page Color Coding, and then select either User Defined or MasterBorder.

- **Comments**   You can add a description to the page if you wish by typing it into the Comments box. This comment doesn't appear anywhere in the web page itself, but it can be helpful to remind you what you wanted to use the web page for.

Set the Web Page Meta Tags

Clicking on the third tab from the left in the Page Properties panel enables you to add "Meta tags" to a web page. Meta tags are essentially words that web search engines use to find and categorize your web site, as well as information (such as your name and address) that can be embedded in the HTML code of your web pages that helps to identify the pages and the web site. Keep in mind that the Meta tags are not visible to people looking at the page; you can see the Meta tags only if you view the source code of the page.

To add Meta tags to a page, click the Meta Tag drop-down list to pick a category of information you want to add.

The next step is to add the Meta tags (words) themselves in the text area below the Meta Tag drop-down list. You can add multiple Meta tags by separating them with commas, as I've done here with keywords.

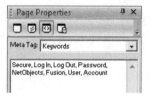

If you wish, you can use the check boxes at the bottom of the panel to "push down" the Meta tags to other pages in the web site. If you have the Home page selected, you can select the Apply Meta Tags To All Pages check box, which (as you would expect) applies the Meta tags to all the pages in the web site. If you have any other page selected, the check box changes slightly to enable you to Inherit Meta Tags From Parent. This option enables you to control how far down the hierarchy you want the Meta tags inherited. If you leave this check box unselected, you can add Meta tags starting from scratch. However, if you select this check box, the page will inherit the Meta tags from the parent page, and you can add more Meta tags or adjust the Meta tags for the page by starting from the Meta tags present on the parent page.

Once you have the Meta tags set, you can preview the page code (see Figure 3-3) to see what they'll look like in the page. As you can see, the Meta tags each appear on a line designated by the category you chose.

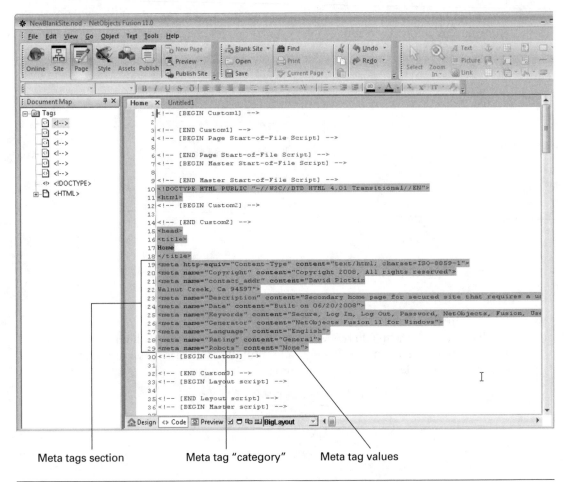

Meta tags section   Meta tag "category"   Meta tag values

FIGURE 3-3 Preview the page code by selecting the Code button from Page view.

Set the Page Protection Properties

Clicking the right-most tab in the Page Properties panel displays the Protect options.

The check boxes in the Protect Page section "protect" the selected pages from various changes, such as deletion, copying (to create another page), moving the page to another place in the site structure, and adding a child page. Actually, they don't really protect anything because you can always simply deselect the check box to allow the action. Instead, these check boxes provide more of a warning to

remind you that you didn't want to allow these actions to take place. The warning appears as an alert box in the Site view, as shown here.

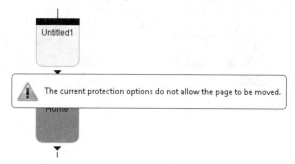

 To set the protection options for a parent page and all the child pages of that parent, just make sure that the child pages have the Inherit Protection Options From Parent check box selected.

The check boxes in the Protect Page Content section provide protection/reminders for the content you change in Page view. You can protect the Layout from editing, or just allow editing of the text (by selecting the Allow Text Editing In Layout check box). You can also protect the MasterBorder from editing (including changing the size) or just allow text editing in the MasterBorder. Unlike the alert box you see in Site view, the content editing protection simply disallows editing by changing the mouse cursor into a "not" symbol when you have chosen an editing tool (like the Text tool) and the mouse is over a protected area (such as a MasterBorder). The labels for the protected area (like MasterBorder or Layout) also show a "lock" symbol. The Properties panel also shows a lock as the left-most icon.

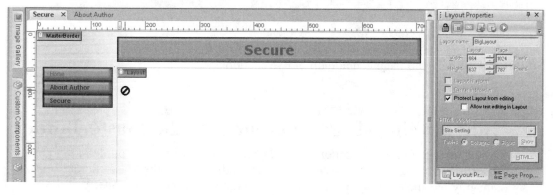

Understand the Parts of a Page

Each page in your web site is composed of two parts—the MasterBorder and the Layout (see Figure 3-4). Each section serves its own purpose, and adding items to the appropriate section of the page can make the job of creating a web page much easier.

MasterBorder

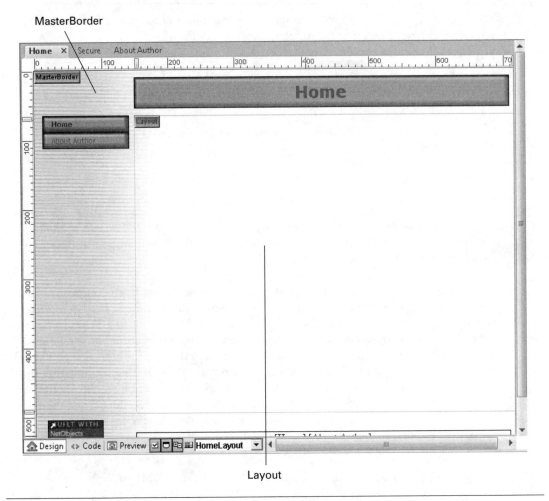

Layout

FIGURE 3-4 Each web page is made up of two sections.

Add Multiple-Page Content with the MasterBorder

The MasterBorder is the section of the page that contains all four borders. If you have the rulers turned on, you can see the margin indicators for the MasterBorder—they are gray rectangles, as shown in Figure 3-5. The most important property of the MasterBorder is that any object you place in a MasterBorder appears at that same exact location on every other page that uses the same MasterBorder. For example, in Figure 3-5, the page banner that appears in the top margin of the MasterBorder will appear in the top margin of all other pages that use that same MasterBorder. Further, if you click and drag an object to change its location on one page, it will appear in that

Top margin of MasterBorder

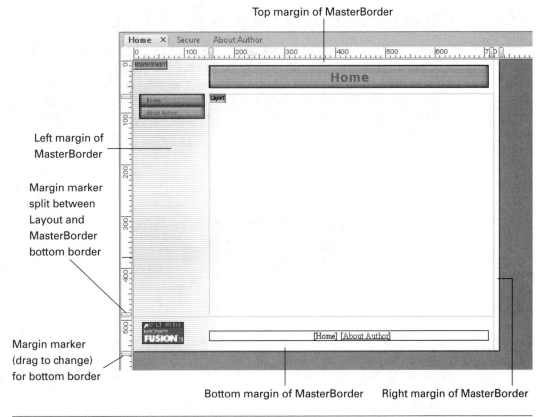

Left margin of
MasterBorder

Margin marker
split between
Layout and
MasterBorder
bottom border

Margin marker
(drag to change)
for bottom border

Bottom margin of MasterBorder   Right margin of MasterBorder

FIGURE 3-5   Objects in the MasterBorder appear in the same place on every page.

same (adjusted) location on every other page that uses the same MasterBorder. The same is true for object size, the font used in text objects, and all other properties of items that appear in the MasterBorder.

As you have probably guessed by now, you can have multiple MasterBorders available in a web site, and you can apply a particular MasterBorder to a page, thus customizing the page. This is especially useful for "subsites" (web sites that live within another site), as you can have consistency within each subsite without them all having to look the same.

To choose a different MasterBorder, simply select it from the Name drop-down list in the MasterBorder Properties panel.

Some Items Vary from Page to Page

For example, the page banner displays the name of the page on which it appears. Nevertheless, despite this variation, the location of the page banner is the same on every page that uses the same MasterBorder. The same is true of the Navigation Bar (which appears in the left margin in Figure 3-5). It displays the pages you can navigate to from that page—but the bar is in the same place on every page.

To create a new MasterBorder, use the following steps:

1. Click Add/Edit to open the Edit MasterBorder List dialog box.

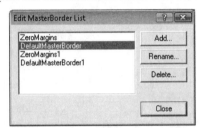

2. Click Add to open the New MasterBorder dialog box.
3. Enter the name of the MasterBorder, and pick the MasterBorder to base the initial design on from the Base On drop-down list.
4. Click OK to create the new MasterBorder, which initially looks like the MasterBorder you chose in the Base On drop-down list. The new MasterBorder appears in the list of MasterBorders in the Edit MasterBorder List dialog box.
5. Click Close to close the Edit MasterBorder List dialog box. Once you've created the MasterBorder this way, you can change the margins (as described later in this chapter), add objects, and so on to customize it.

You can also rename an existing MasterBorder by clicking Rename, filling in the new name in the Rename MasterBorder dialog box, and clicking OK. Any page that formerly used the MasterBorder will now show (and use) the new name in the MasterBorder Properties panel.

Add Single-Page Content in the Layout

The "Layout" area of the page is where you place content that you want to appear on only a single page—that is, the content that is unique to that page. The details, options, and size of the Layout section are controlled by the Layout Properties panel, which replaces the MasterBorder Properties panel when you click an empty area of the Layout section.

If you think you are going to need different versions of the Layout area for a single page, you create alternate Layout areas and then switch between them as needed. For example, you might have a "seasonal" page on your web site where you highlight various holidays as they come up (Easter, Valentine's Day, Mother's Day, etc.). You could create a Layout for each occasion, and then switch Layouts and republish the page as appropriate.

To create a new Layout for a page, click the Layout name pop-up list and click Add.

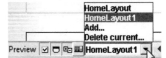

This automatically creates a new, blank Layout, named the same as last-used Layout except with a number to make it unique. All you have to do now is go ahead and customize this Layout for the page.

 If you change your mind about a new Layout, you can delete a Layout by making it the current Layout (pick it from the Layout drop-down list) and then choosing Delete Current from the Layout drop-down list. The option to delete the current Layout appears only if you have more than one Layout for a page.

In addition to the name and the size (discussed later in this chapter), the Layout Properties dialog box enables you to set some properties of the Layout that control how it works. These options are

- **Layout is a form**   A form is a special area of a web page in which you can place fields to collect data, and then specify where that data is stored (see Chapter 13). Selecting this check box turns the entire Layout area into a form, so that you don't have to add a Form Area to the Layout, and thus you can place any of the Form objects available on the Form tools toolbar directly on the Layout.
- **Center in browser**   Selecting this check box sets the published web page to display in the center of the web browser if the web page is smaller than the browser window.

Did You
Know?

You Can Rename a Layout

The default name for a Layout is pretty useless as far as identifying anything about the Layout—it is essentially just the original page name (which is something like "Untitled4") followed by "Layout" and a number. But renaming a Layout is really easy. Simply select the name in the Layout Name field of the Layout Properties panel, and type in a new name. This works for any Layout associated with the page—simply select the Layout from the Layout drop-down list at the bottom of the screen and then change the name in the Layout Name field.

- **Protect Layout from editing**   Prevents you from editing the Layout area until you uncheck this check box. If you want to allow text objects in the Layout but not other types of objects (such as pictures), select the Allow Text Editing In Layout check box. This check box has exactly the same effect as the Protect Layout From Editing check box that appears in the Page Properties panel (under the Protection tab) in the Site view (discussed earlier in this chapter).

Note   The complexities of picking an approach for HTML output and how to render tables (which appear in the Layout Properties and Layout Region Properties) are discussed in Chapter 16.

Make Your New Layout Look Like Your Old Layout

If you want your new Layout to look similar to your old Layout, use the following steps:

1. Go back to your old Layout and click in a blank area of the Layout.
2. Copy everything in the old Layout to the clipboard by choosing Edit | Select All (or press CTRL-A) followed by Edit | Copy (CTRL-C).
3. Switch to the new Layout and choose Edit | Paste (CTRL-V) to paste everything into the new Layout.

One thing you do need to watch out for: when you paste the objects into the new Layout, the Layout may automatically resize to hold the objects. You have two options to deal with this. The first is to make a note of the Width and Height of the Layout (visible in the Layout Properties panel) and, after clicking and dragging the objects to the location where you want them, type in the Layout Width and Height to reset the Layout size.

Another option is to choose Object | Size Layout To Objects (CTRL-SHIFT-L). This option (which is also available for the MasterBorder), resizes the Layout to be just big enough to hold the objects it contains.

Make Adjustments to the Layout and MasterBorder

As we've discussed previously, you can create additional Layouts and MasterBorders, and rename existing ones. But you can make many more adjustments to these two crucial components of a web page, including the size, the split between the Layout and MasterBorders, the background, frames, and many more properties.

 Note   The "Actions" that you can create for a page (and for other objects) will be discussed in Chapter 12. Actions are created by clicking the Actions tab (the right-most icon) in the Properties panel.

Adjust the Layout and MasterBorder Margin Sizes

You can adjust the size of the Page, the Layout, and the MasterBorder (remember, there are four margins for the MasterBorder). The various sizes interact with each other. For example, if you increase the height of the Layout or the height of the MasterBorder top or bottom margin, the height of the page changes as well.

Change the Layout Size

To adjust the size of Layout, you have two options. The first is to adjust the values in the Width and Height fields in the Layout column of the Layout Properties panel.

The second option is to click and drag the outermost gray ruler markers (see Figure 3-6).

 Tip   To make sure that each new page has the dimensions you want for your web site, remember that you can adjust the new page size in the General tab of the Current Site Options dialog box (Tools | Options | Current Site).

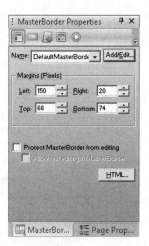

Change the MasterBorder Size

To change the MasterBorder margin sizes, click in the MasterBorder to display the MasterBorder Properties panel.

To change the size of each margin, enter the new value in the Left, Right, Top, or Bottom fields. Alternatively, you can click and drag the gray ruler markers as indicated in Figure 3-7 to adjust the margin size.

 Note   You cannot directly change the Width or Height in the Page column of the Layout Properties panel, so don't even try.

Change the Layout width   Change the page width

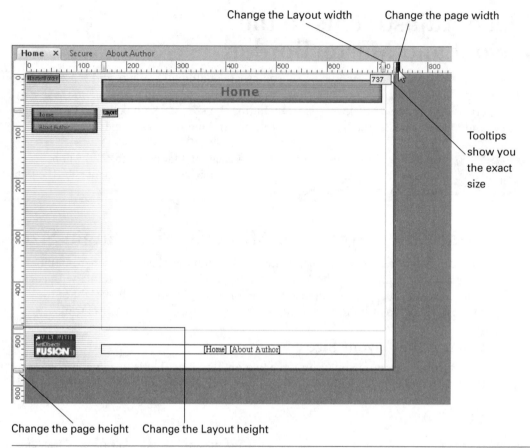

Tooltips
show you
the exact
size

Change the page height   Change the Layout height

FIGURE 3-6 Click and drag the outermost ruler markers to change the page size.

Adjust the Layout Background

When you pick a SiteStyle (which sets the colors and styles used for the web site—see Chapter 8), it establishes a lot of the properties of the web site, including the background properties of a Layout. However, you can override the background properties by clicking the Background tab (the second one from the right) in the Layout Properties panel.

Oddly enough, although the background color and image are located in the Layout Properties dialog box, any color or image you choose actually applies to the entire page, including the MasterBorder.

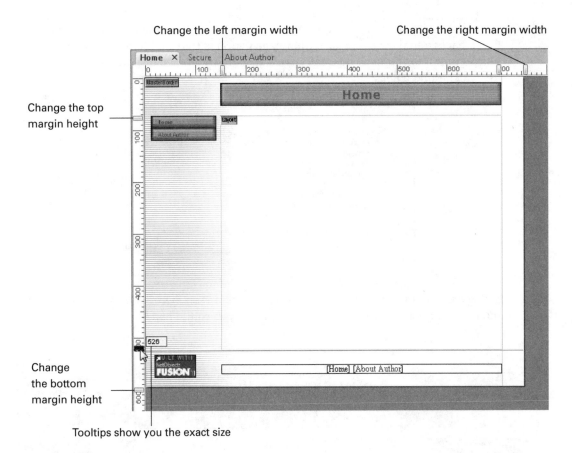

Change the left margin width

Change the right margin width

Change the top margin height

Change the bottom margin height

Tooltips show you the exact size

FIGURE 3-7 Adjust the size of each MasterBorder margin by clicking and dragging the appropriate ruler marker.

Choose a Background Color

To pick a background color, you can choose it from the Color drop-down list or click the Paint Can icon to pick a color from the ColorPicker. The Color drop-down list only provides three choices: Automatic (which uses the option specified by the SiteStyle), Transparent (no color), and the hexadecimal number (such as #FFFFFF) that represents the currently selected background color. You have considerably more flexibility if you click on the Paint can icon, as shown here.

You can pick one of the displayed colors, or click More Colors to open the full ColorPicker dialog box, described in the upcoming How To box.

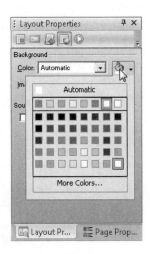

If the SiteStyle uses a background image, you won't see the change you made to the background color, because the image overlays it. If that happens, NetObjects Fusion prompts you to change the page's background image to None, so you can see the background color.

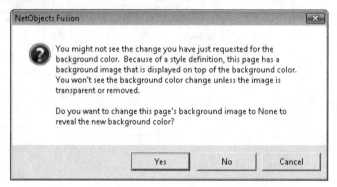

If you do choose to set the Background image to None (by clicking Yes in the dialog box), you will see the new background color (see Figure 3-8) you chose—and the Image drop-down list will display None, as you would expect.

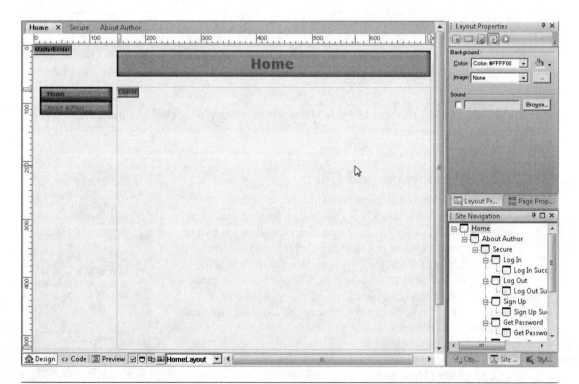

FIGURE 3-8   Turning off the background image lets you see the new background color.

How to... # Pick a Color from the ColorPicker Dialog Box

The ColorPicker dialog box enables you to pick any color your computer can produce for uses such as the page background color. To pick a color from the dialog box, use the following steps:

1. Click the color column (just to the left of the HSB and RGB fields) to pick the basic color you want to use, such as Blue or Red. The square to the left of the color column shows all the variations (shades) of that color.
2. Pick the color you want from the large square. The small rectangle to the right of the color column shows two colors. The top color is the currently selected color; the bottom color is the new color you will get if you click OK.
3. Once you click the color in the large square, a small color "web safe" color box will appear just to the right of the color rectangle. If you want to ensure that a visitor's browser will display the color you picked, click the Web Safe color square to pick that color.

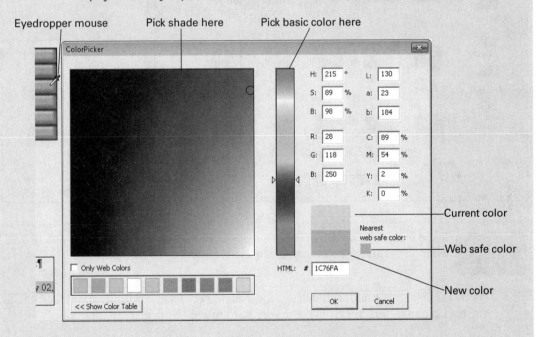

Eyedropper mouse   Pick shade here   Pick basic color here

Current color
Nearest web safe color:
Web safe color
New color

4. Click OK to choose the color you selected.

There are a number of other ways to pick a color when the ColorPicker dialog box is open. First of all, you can move the mouse pointer over any part of the workspace (or even a panel!). As you do, the pointer turns into an eyedropper, and you can pick any color by simply clicking it. Also, if you happen to know the values that correspond to the color you want to use, you can type the values into the text fields in the ColorPicker dialog box. The field groupings are HSB, RGB, Lab, and CMYK. You can also type the Hexadecimal value into the HTML field near the bottom of the dialog box.

Choose a Background Image

You can specify your own background image for a page if you wish, although most SiteStyles actually supply a background image as part of the style. The Image drop-down list provides three options: Automatic (the image supplied by the SiteStyle), None, and Browse. If you choose Browse (or click the Browse button alongside the Image drop-down list), you can pick the image you want to use from the Picture File Open dialog box.

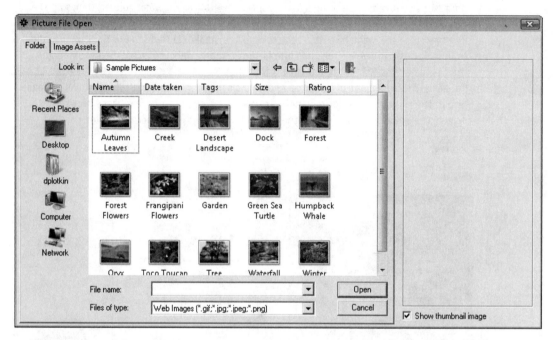

  If the image you want to use has already been used on the site, you should find it listed in the Image Assets tab of the Picture File Open dialog box.

If the image is smaller than the page, NetObjects Fusion will tile the image to fill the background—which can make it very hard to see the page contents.

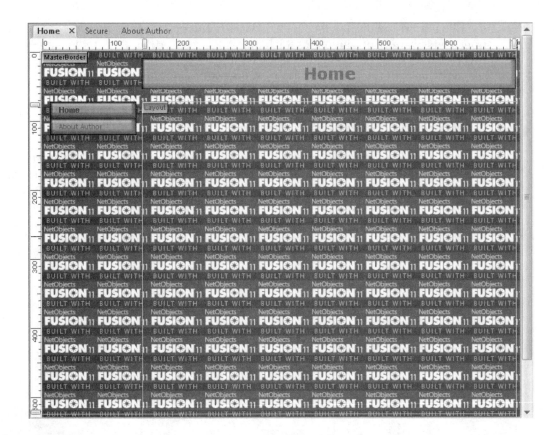

 Note The problem with most background images is that they make it hard to see other images and text objects on the page. That is, they are too "busy" and detract from the content you want your visitors to see. So use background images with extreme care!

Add a Background Sound

One of the most annoying things that can happen when you are surfing the web is for a web page to start playing music or making noises. But, if you insist on having your web pages do that, you can specify a Sound in the Layout Properties panel. To do so, click the Sound check box to open the Background Sound dialog box.

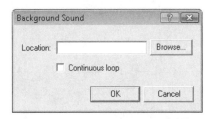

Click Browse to display the Open dialog box and pick a sound file. You can choose from a wide variety of sound files, including MP3, AIFF, MIDI, Real Audio, and others. If you want to be really annoying, select the Continuous Loop check box, so that the sound file will continue to play as long as the web page is displayed.

Work with Layout Regions

As we've already seen, you can set a variety of properties—such as background color and image—for the entire Layout. But what if you want to use a different background color for just a section of the Layout, or designate just a portion of the Layout as a form? Or even specify groupings of Actions (see Chapter 12) for just a portion of the Layout? You can do all that—and much more—by using *Layout Regions*.

A Layout Region is a designated section of a Layout or MasterBorder that you create using the Layout Region tool from the Standard Tools toolbar.

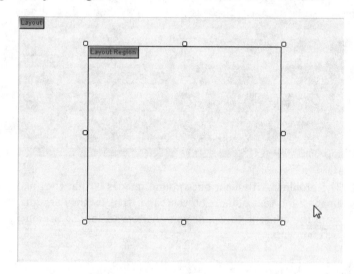

To create a Layout Region, select the tool and click and drag the Layout Region on the web page. Once you have done so, you can adjust the size by clicking and dragging the sizing handles of the Layout Region. You can also click and drag inside a Layout Region to relocate it on the page. You can even embed one Layout Region inside another, as I've done here.

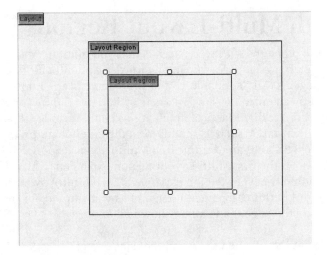

To configure the Layout Region, you can do the following from the Layout Region Properties panel.

- **Set the Grid Guides** If you'd like to see a grid in the Layout Region, select the Grid check box and then set the distance between the grid lines by specifying a quantity in the Width and Height fields.
- **Specify the Layout Region as a Form** To set up the Layout Region as a Form (so that you can add form fields and capture data), select the Form check box.
- **Choose a background color and image** Switch to the Background tab in the Layout Region Properties panel to set the color and image just as previously described for a Layout.

Work with Multi-Layout Regions

One of the problems with web pages is that you often need to pack a lot of information onto the page, making it crowded and difficult to understand. Multi-Layout Regions (MLRs) enable you to show some of the information on a page, and provide a mechanism for site visitors to switch to a different batch of information when they are ready. Practical applications could include step-by-step instructions about complex tasks, such as modifying a digital photograph to make it look better.

Figure 3-9 shows an example of a Multi-Layout Region using the TogglePane. The left side shows the first Multi-Layout Region expanded, while the right side shows a different Multi-Layout Region expanded. Each Multi-Layout Region has different information (in this case, a text box), and as you can see, far more information is available on the page than can be shown all at once.

 To get the situation shown on the right side of Figure 3-9, I clicked the top section header (closing that section) and then clicked the second section header, opening it.

In addition, you can even embed one Multi-Layout Region in another. So, for example, a TabTop region has been embedded in the third TogglePane (see the left side of Figure 3-10), while a TabBottom has been embedded in the fourth TogglePane (right side of Figure 3-10).

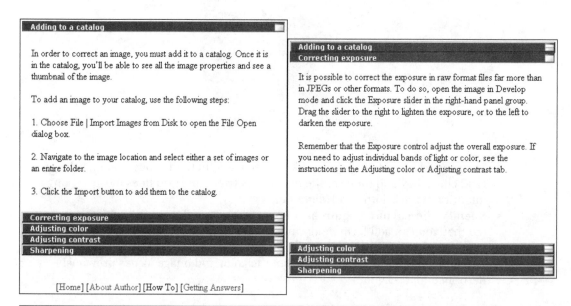

FIGURE 3-9 The first batch of information is visible (on the left); the second region contains different information (on the right).

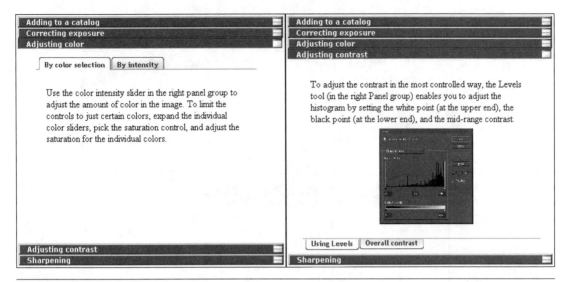

FIGURE 3-10 Embed one Multi-Layout Region in another to add even more information.

Understand the Types of Multi-Layout Regions

There are five types of MLRs: TabTop, TabBottom, Accordion, Wizard, and TogglePane. The overall purpose of these regions is the same, but the navigation tabs are different. For example, the TabTop region provides tabs at the top of the region to navigate to different content. On the other hand, any regions in an Accordion MLR open and collapse (like an accordion) to show different content. Figure 3-11 displays a preview of all five different MLRs.

The default MLR is visible at the bottom of the drop-down list in the Standard Tools toolbar. This MLR is fully customizable using "actions" (see Chapter 12)—the site designer can decide what navigation elements (such as buttons) to use and how to navigate through the various Layout Regions. For example, you can place three images on the page, along with three Layout Regions in the MLR. You can then set an action for each picture to display a different Layout Region.

MLRs Are Much More Efficient at Presenting Content

MLRs are more efficient at presenting information than regular web pages. This is because when you switch Layout Regions to view alternate content, only the portion of the web page included in the MLR must be refreshed from the web server. On a normal page (even one that looks as if it has tabs or other navigation objects), the entire page—including the MasterBorder—must be reloaded. By the way, this technology is known as "AJAX."

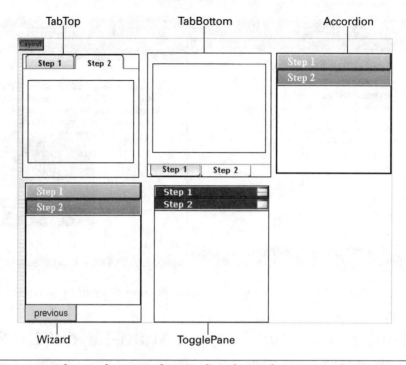

FIGURE 3-11   Choose the type of MLR that shows the content the way you want.

Create and Edit Multi-Layout Regions

To build a Multi-Layout Region, use the following steps:

1. Click the tiny down arrow alongside the tool to display the selection of available regions.

2. Click and drag in the Layout or the MasterBorder to create the MLR on the page. The MLR is represented on the page as a rectangle with a sample of the control for that MLR.

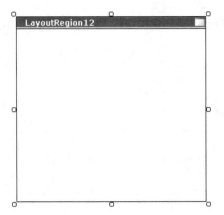

 You can resize the MLR by clicking and dragging the sizing handles. You can also move the MLR by clicking inside the MLR and dragging it to a new location. However, you cannot resize the MLR to be smaller than the content it contains.

3. In the Multi-Layout Region Properties panel, create the Layout Regions by clicking the plus (+) symbol. Each time you do, another Layout Region (which can contain content) is created in the panel.

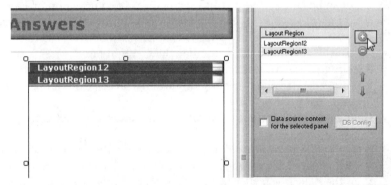

4. Rename each Layout Region to give it a descriptive name by double-clicking the Layout Region in the list, changing the name in the Edit dialog box, and clicking OK.

 To discard a Layout Region, select it in the list and click the minus (–) symbol.

5. To rearrange the order of the Layout Regions, select a region and click the up arrow or down arrow buttons. The order is important—the regions appear (either from left to right or from top to bottom) in the same order as the list.

Add Contents to the Multi-Layout Regions

To add content (such as text or graphics, as described later in the book) to the MLRs, you must first select the Layout Region from the list of Layout Regions in the Multi-Layout Region Properties panel. This is because only a single Layout Region (contained within an MLR) is visible at a time in Design mode. After picking each Layout Region, use the tools in the Standard toolbar and panel to add the content. For example, if you want to add a text box, click the Text tool and move the mouse cursor over the inside rectangle of the MLR. The rectangle turns blue to indicate that you are adding content to the Layout Region, and then you can click and drag to define the text box.

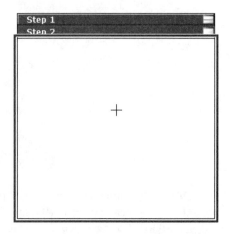

Configure the Multi-Layout Regions

An MLR can be configured just like a "regular" Layout Region or Layout. After selecting the MLR, you can use the Multi-Layout Region Properties panel to

- Adjust the grid and grid size under the General tab.
- Specify that the MLR is a form by selecting the Form check box (under the General tab). If you do specify the MLR as a Form, the embedded Layout Regions are also forms.
- Change the Background color and image under the Background tab.

Note The Multi-Layout Region Properties panel and the ability to drag and resize the MLR are available only if you click the control area (such as a tab or a header) of the MLR. If you click in the blank content area, you'll see instead the Layout Region Properties panel with the General and Background tabs.

Handle the Frame Aspects of MasterBorders

If you have some experience designing web pages, you may have already begun to suspect that MasterBorders are actually an implementation of a web concept called "frames." Frames separate the content area of each page from the borders, with the border content appearing on every page. And yes, that is exactly how I described MasterBorders earlier in the book.

Understand Frames in Fusion

In other web-building applications, you can specify frames and set properties of those frames—such as where a link located in the frame will open. With MasterBorders, the default behavior is normally what you want—clicking a link in a MasterBorder (such as a Navigation Bar) opens the resulting page in the Layout area. However, if you want to change that behavior, or to set some other properties frame by frame, you can use the AutoFrames icon in the MasterBorder Properties panel. For example, if you place a link in the top margin of the MasterBorder and want the new page to open in the left margin, you'll need to use the frame properties to do that (as explained in Chapter 9). To create frames in a MasterBorder, select the Frames tab in the MasterBorder Properties panel.

To add one of the four frames, click the button for that frame. For example, click the Left button to add a Left frame to the page, as shown in Figure 3-12.

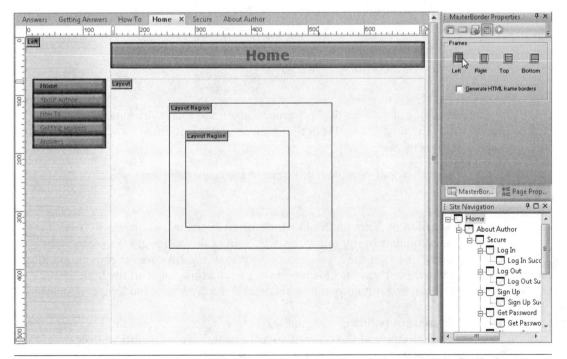

FIGURE 3-12 Frames are denoted by a grid background and name tag ("Left" in this example).

The order in which you add frames has an impact on the frame size. For example, if you select the Left frame first, it stretches all the way up the left side. If you then add a Top frame, it extends only to the edge of the Left frame. However, if you add the Top frame *first,* it extends all the way across the top, and if you then add the Left border, it extends only up to the bottom border of the Top frame.

Configure the Frames

Once you've added a frame, you can set the frame properties by clicking in the frame and choosing Frame Properties from the shortcut menu. This opens the Frame Properties panel.

Besides being able to set the background color and image (by clicking the Background tab in the Frame Properties panel), you can set the following properties under the General tab:

 Although you can view the Frame name in the Frame Name field, you can't change it.

- **User scrollable**   This set of radio buttons enables the user to specify whether to provide scroll bars in the frame (or not). Setting this to Yes always places scroll bars, whether or not they are needed. Setting this to No does *not* provide scroll bars, even if the content is too long to view (and thus spills off the bottom of the frame). Selecting Auto provides scroll bars if the content is too long to be viewed all at once.
- **Enable margin padding**   Normally, there is a two-pixel "padding" between the edge of the frame and the content area. To turn this padding off and get rid of that margin, deselect the Enable Margin Padding check box.
- **User-resizable frame**   Enables the site visitor to click and drag on the frame border to change the size. However, this check box only becomes available if you select the Generate HTML Frame Borders check box on the AutoFrames tab of the MasterBorder Properties panel.

Handle "No Frames" Support

Some older browsers don't support frames. To prevent site visitors using these browsers from being greeted with a blank page or an error message when they access your site, add alternate content for them using the HTML < noframes > tag.

You add the < noframes > tag and your alternate content to the frameset file is generated when you publish. Your content can include text, pictures, and links, using standard HTML tags. To modify the Frames to enable No Frames support, use the following steps:

1. In Page view, right-click the MasterBorder or a frame and choose Master HTML. The Object HTML dialog box appears.

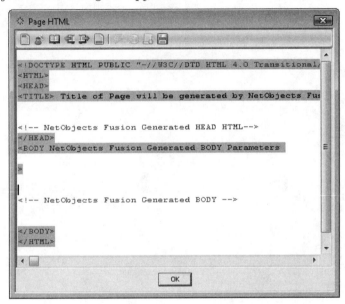

2. Click in the space between the < body > tags and enter

```
<noframes>
<h1>Thanks for visiting our site!</h1>
We're sorry you haven't had a chance to upgrade your browser yet and
can't see our framed site. We think the frames make it easier to find
what you want.
<p>If you want to obtain a more current browser, check out Microsoft's
<a href="http://www.microsoft.com">  Internet Explorer</a>!
</noframes>
```

3. Click OK to close the dialog box.

4

Create and Format Text

HOW TO...

- Create a text box and add text to a page
- Configure the text box
- Format the text, paragraph, and borders
- Use bulleted and numbered lists
- Embed objects in a text box
- Create and use variables in text

Despite all the fancy things you can do with a web page, there is still a need to impart information using text. Step-by-step directions, the "About" page, and just about every other page in your web site will need text. Thus, it is fortunate that Fusion makes it easy to add text and format it to your heart's content.

Add Text to a Web Page

To add text to a web page in a text box (as opposed to a table, which is covered in Chapter 6), all you have to do is select the Text tool from the Standard Tools toolbar, move the mouse pointer over the area where you want the text box to be located, and click and drag to create the text box.

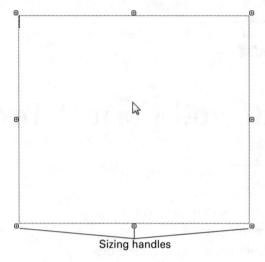

Sizing handles

 You can add a text box to a MasterBorder, a Layout, a Layout Region, a Multi-Layout Region, Table cells, and more.

To place text in the text box, type the text. You can edit the text using standard word processing techniques. For example, to select a portion of text, you can click and drag the text with the mouse, or position the text pointer, hold down the SHIFT key, and use the arrow keys to move the text pointer, selecting the text as you go.

Once you are done typing the text you want into the text box (or pasting it in using the clipboard), click outside the text box to automatically resize the text box to fit the contents. You can click and drag the sizing handles to change the shape of the text box. However, you cannot resize the text box to be too small to hold its contents, and the text box will normally resize to be just big enough to hold the contents. This is not a problem, because you can add items to the text box and it will automatically resize. To add more text to the text box, simply double-click inside the box and type or paste additional text.

Format the Text Box

You can apply formatting to the text box itself (as opposed to the text in the text box, covered later in this chapter). To format the text box, select it and make sure the Text Box tab (the left-most icon) is selected in the Text Properties panel.

 If you can see the text cursor in the text box (so that editing text is possible), the Text Box tab is the middle icon in the Text Properties panel. Select the Text Box tab and you'll see the same panel.

In addition to setting the Background color and Image (which works just as described for Layouts), you can set the following options:

- **Lock height**   If you don't want the text box to resize to be just large enough to hold the contents, select the Lock Height check box. This is helpful when designing your Layouts before all the text has been entered.
- **Size Layout to Text**   Selecting this check box resizes the Layout to match the selected text box size. Choosing this option typically shrinks the Layout and should not be used if you have placed more than one text box in the Layout (or added other objects to Layout besides the text box) because this will force the objects to overlap in the shrunken Layout. This also prevents you from resizing the text box.
- **Contents wrap to browser width**   This check box is only available if you choose the Size Layout To Text check box. The effect is to ensure that the contents of the text box wrap to the width of the browser, so you can see all the contents even when the browser window is narrower than the text box (and the Layout).
- **Text box is a form**   Designates the text box as a form, so you can add fields to collect data, as described in Chapter 13.

Format Selected Text with the Toolbar and Panel

To format text in a text box, the first step is to select it. Once you do so, several additional formatting tools become available. The first is the Text Format toolbar, from which you can set just about everything about the text, including the format, size, style, paragraph alignment, indent, background color and text color, word wrap, text position, and letter case, as shown in Figure 4-1.

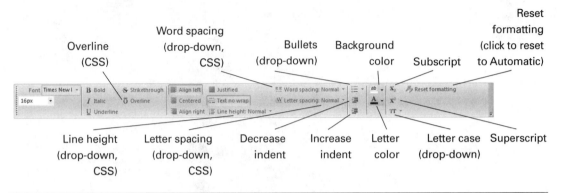

FIGURE 4-1   Use the Text toolbar to format selected text.

  As discussed later in this chapter (under "Select HTML or CSS Text Formatting"), many of these options (such as Word spacing) work only with CSS formatting. These are indicated by (CSS) alongside the callout.

Many of these same controls are available in the Text Properties panel under the Format tab, as seen in Figure 4-2.

  The buttons in the Options section of the Text Properties panel enable you to add hyperlinks to text. These are discussed in Chapter 9.

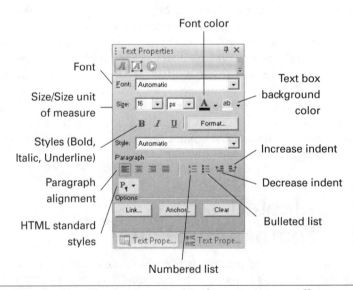

FIGURE 4-2   Use the Text Properties panel to format text as well.

The HTML Standard Styles button enables you to pick from, well, standard styles that have been used in HTML-based web sites since the beginning of the web. Clicking the button provides a drop-down list of styles, including standard paragraph (the first choice) and a bunch of different heading styles (H1, H2, H3, and so on).

Format Using the Format Dialog Box

You can also set the text format for the entire text box all at once. Realize, however, that setting the text format this way does not override any formatting you set for the text itself (as described in the section "Format Selected Text," earlier in this chapter). Thus, for example, if you format some of the text by setting the color and font, then format the entire text box with a different color or font, your previously formatted text will not change color or font.

The easiest way to set the formatting for the text in the text box is to click the Format button in the Text Properties panel. If you select the text box (but not the text in the text box), this opens the Object Format dialog box, which contains four tabs: Character, Paragraph, Borders, and Background.

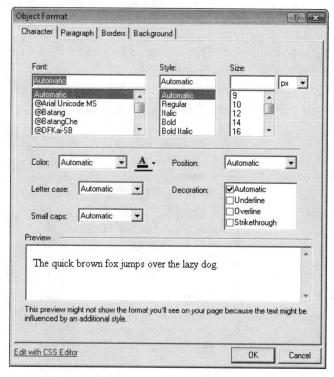

If you have selected some text (but not an entire paragraph), this opens the Span Settings dialog box, where you can format the Character, Paragraph, and Background properties of the text. If you have selected an entire paragraph, the dialog box is called Paragraph Settings. It looks just like the Object Format dialog box (with all four tabs).

The default tab in the Paragraph Settings dialog box is the Paragraph tab—but you can switch to any other tab to set the formatting.

Select HTML or CSS Text Formatting

Fusion supports two kinds of text formatting. HTML formatting will work in any browser, as it uses standard HTML tags to perform the formatting and thus results in a consistent look across many different browsers. HTML-supported options include font, size, style, color, paragraph alignment, bullets and numbered lists, and background color, image, and image position. However, there are many options that HTML does *not* support. These include most of options in the Paragraph tab (except for alignment), and all the options in the Borders tab. For example, borders that you set for text will not be visible if you format using HTML. The other formatting option is to use Cascading Style Sheets (CSS). This type of formatting enables you to format using much finer control and many more options. The problem with CSS, however, is that different browsers render the formatting differently because they interpret the style sheets differently. Thus, it is hard to tell what your web page is going to look like in a particular browser. And some browsers (especially early versions) don't support CSS at all. When you select CSS formatting, Fusion creates Cascading Style Sheet files and links them to the HTML generated for the site.

To choose which type of formatting to use, select Tools | Options | Current Site to open the Current Site Options dialog box.

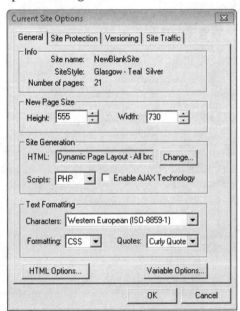

In the Text Formatting section, select either CSS or HTML from the Formatting drop-down list.

Regardless of what you pick for the formatting option, the Design view and Preview mode (both buttons are located at the bottom of the screen) will show the formatting as if CSS formatting were chosen. It is only if you publish the site or choose the Preview tool from the Views Bar that you'll see the results of formatting in HTML.

Set Character Formatting

The Character tab enables you to pick the Font, Style (Regular, Italic, Bold, etc.), and size from scrolling lists. You can also pick the following formatting options:

- **Text color**   Click the "A" button to display the ColorPicker, from which you can pick the color for the text.
- **Position**   The Position drop-down list enables you to choose whether to place the text normally (None), or as a subscript or superscript.
- **Letter case**   The Letter Case drop-down list enables you to control whether you exercise no special control over the letters (None) or force the letters to be all uppercase, all lowercase, or Capitalized (every word begins with a capital letter).
- **Small Caps**   The Small Caps drop-down list enables you to specify a font that uses large-size capital letters for uppercase, and smaller-size capital letters for lowercase.
- **Decoration**   The Decoration list enables you to choose various check boxes for "decorations": Underline, Overline, and Strikethrough. Overline works only with CSS formatting.

 You may have noticed that most of the formatting lists and options contain an "Automatic" setting. The special meaning of this setting is explained later in this chapter, in the section "Understand Automatic Formatting."

Set Paragraph Formatting

The Paragraph tab enables you to set the specifications for the paragraph where the text cursor is currently located. You do not need to select the paragraph beforehand.

Except for alignment (the four square buttons near the top of the dialog box) and first line indents, the balance of the options only work if you are using CSS formatting.

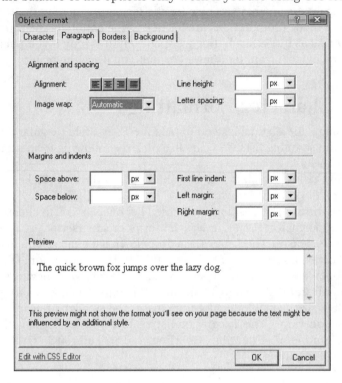

The options you can set for a paragraph are

- **Image wrap** This sets how text wraps around an image. You can locate the image on the left (Allow Left) with text wrapping to the right, (Allow Right), with text wrapping to the left, or both (Allow Both) with text wrapping on both sides.

It's much easier to adjust the properties of the image itself to specify text wrapping (see Chapter 5). That way, you can change the wrapping for each picture—and it works with HTML formatting. Paragraph formatting requires CSS.

- **Line height** This sets the amount of space between the lines of text. You can pick a unit of measure for this amount from the adjacent drop-down list. To return the line height to the default spacing, remove the quantity from this field.
- **Letter spacing** This sets the amount of space between letters in the text in the selected unit of measure.
- **Space above and Space below** These set the amount of space above and below the paragraph in the selected unit of measure.
- **First line indent** This sets the amount of the indent for the first line of the paragraph, in the specified unit of measure.

- **Left margin and Right margin** This sets the margin widths on either side of the paragraph in the selected unit of measure.

Set Border and Padding Formatting

The Borders tab enables you to specify the borders around the paragraph, as well as the distance between the text and border, known as the padding.

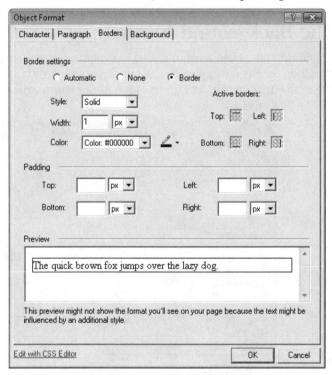

As with the Paragraph tab, all you need to do is place the text cursor in the paragraph for which you want to set the borders and padding. Realize also that you *must* use CSS formatting if you want anything on the Borders tab to work—these features do not work in HTML formatting. The options are

- **Border settings** Choose one of the radio buttons to set the border to use. Automatic applies the same border as the parent element (such as when one text box is embedded in another); None prevents any border from being applied; and Border enables the rest of the buttons and lists in this section to become available so that you can specify a border.
- **Style** Sets the style of the line that forms the border, such as solid, dashed, ridged, and inset.

- **Width**   The width of the line(s) that forms the border. Type the quantity into the field and select a unit of measure from the adjacent drop-down list.
- **Color**   Click the pencil button to choose a color from the ColorPicker.
- **Active borders**   There are four buttons available in this section. Click the button for the portion of the border you want—Top, Left, Bottom, and Right.
- **Padding**   Type in a quantity and pick a unit of measure for each side of the border to establish the padding for that side (Top, Bottom, Left, and Right).

Set the Background Formatting

The Background tab of the Format dialog box enables you to set the color, image, and image position for the background. Except for the color and image (which are also available in the Text Properties panel), none of the options on this tab work unless you are using CSS formatting.

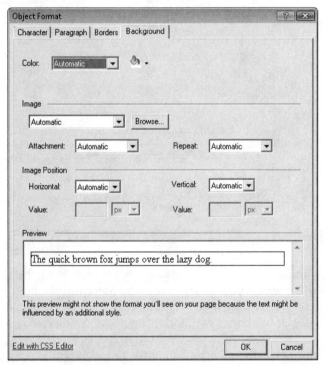

The options you can set are

- **Color**   Click the paint can button to choose the background color from the ColorPicker.
- **Image**   Pick an image by clicking Browse and choosing an image file (.jpg, .gif, .jpeg, and .png).
- **Attachment**   This setting determines whether an oversize image scrolls as you scroll the text (Scrolling) or the text scrolls over the fixed image (Fixed).

- **Repeat**   The Repeat drop-down list only applies if the image is smaller than the text box. If it is, you may choose how the image repeats:
  - **None**   The image appears once and does not repeat.
  - **Horizontal**   The image repeats horizontally in a row.
  - **Vertically**   The image repeats vertically in a column.
  - **Both**   The image repeats in both directions, tiling the entire background with the image.
- **Image Position**   This section of the dialog box enables you to set the position of the image relative to the text box. You can pick one of the options from the Horizontal or Vertical drop-down list, or pick Value from either list and fill in a value from the Value drop-down list, along with the associated unit of measure.
  - **Horizontal**   The values in the Horizontal drop-down list state what part of the picture aligns with the text box horizontally. For example, choosing Top aligns the top of the image with the top of the box. Choosing Bottom aligns the bottom of the image with the bottom of the box, and choosing Center centers the image in the text box.
  - **Vertical**   The values in the Vertical drop-down list state what part of picture aligns with the text box vertically. For example, choosing Left aligns the left edge of the picture with the left edge of the text box, whereas choosing Right aligns the right edge of the image with the right edge of the text box.
  - **Value**   The two Value drop-down lists (one for Horizontal and one for Vertical) determine the offset of the image relative to the text box. One very useful unit of measure is to use %. A 0% offset is the same as picking Left for Horizontal or Top for Vertical. A 50% offset centers the image in the text box.

Work with Lists

If you have a need to make lists on your web site, Fusion provides two different formats to do so. The first is bulleted lists (sometimes called "unordered"). These are useful for discussing points that don't have any particular order. This type of list places a bullet in front of each line of the list.

The second type of list uses some sort of number instead of bullet. These lists (sometimes called "ordered") are useful for step-by-step instructions where order is important.

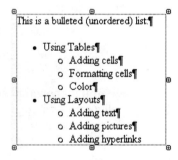

Create a New List

To create a list, start off by pressing the ENTER key to separate the list from any other text. Since lists actually format an entire paragraph, if you don't separate the list by creating a new paragraph, all of the text in the current paragraph will become a list—which is not usually what you want. Once the text cursor is on its own line in the text box, you can create the type of list you want in one of two ways. The first way is to make sure the Text tab is selected in the Text Properties panel, and select the list icon (either ordered or unordered) in the Paragraph section.

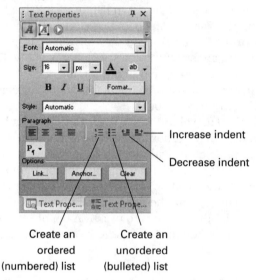

Create an ordered (numbered) list

Create an unordered (bulleted) list

An alternate way is to click the tiny arrow alongside the List tool in the Text Format toolbar and pick the type of list you want.

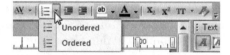

You'll know that you've successfully created the list because you'll see either a bullet or a number, depending on the type of list you created. Simply start typing in the text and do the following to build up your list:

- At the end of each line, press the ENTER key to start a new line with a new bullet or number.
- To indent a line in the list and thus create a sublevel in the list, press the TAB key or click the Increase Indent button in the Paragraph section of the Text Properties panel or in the Text Format toolbar.
- To decrease the indent of a line (thus moving it to a higher level in the list), press SHIFT-TAB or click the Decrease Indent button in the Paragraph section of the Text Properties panel or in the Text Format toolbar.

Change the Formatting of a List

Once you've built a list, you can change the list type (as discussed previously) as well as change some of the list format options. The easiest way to change the basic list format is to click the List tab in the Text Properties panel (which only appears if the

How to...   ## Change the List Type of Indented Lists

One of the things you'll notice when you increase the indent on a numbered list is that the indented line is bulleted, not numbered, as shown here.

If you try to correct this by selecting the bulleted line(s) and clicking the numbered list in the Paragraph section of the Text Properties panel (or choosing Ordered list from the Text Format toolbar), Fusion decreases the indent (returning those lines to the same level as the parent item) and renumbers the entire list to include the formerly bulleted lines. If this is not what you wanted, you'll need to adjust the list type of the indented lines using the following steps:

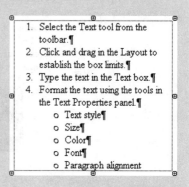

1. Select the indented lines and then click the List tab in the Text Properties panel. The List tab only appears if the text cursor is located within a list.
2. Change the List Type back to numbered by clicking the numbered list button in the List Type section. This causes the indented lines in the list to become numbered.

(continued)

3. If you want to use a different numbering scheme for the indented lines, pick the numbering scheme from the Bullet Type drop-down list. Here, I picked the i,ii,iii option from the list.

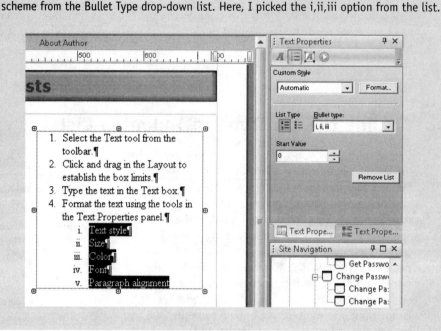

text cursor is in a list). To change the type of bullet, click the Bullet Type drop-down list and pick the type of bullet you want.

Keep in mind that if you choose a bullet type that implies a different type of list (such as picking the Square bullet while you have a numbered list selected), the list type for the line where the text cursor is located will change (from numbered to bulleted, in this example). In addition, *all other sublist lines of the same parent that are at the same level will also change to use the specified bullet.* To illustrate this, look at Figure 4-3. On the left side of Figure 4-3, there are five lines, which are indented under a single parent line (item 4). I placed the text cursor in the first subline (i) and chose the Disc bullet type from the Bullet Type drop-down list. On

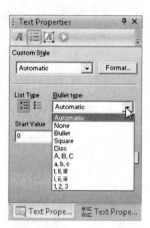

the right side of Figure 4-3, you can see what happened—all five sublines of item 4 changed to show the disc bullet. Note also that the bullets in the next level (the square bullets in this example) did *not* change.

For numbered lists, you can change the starting value by placing the text cursor in any line of the list and changing the value in the Start Value field.

Note   Changing the Start Value field when the text cursor is in a bulleted list has no effect on the list.

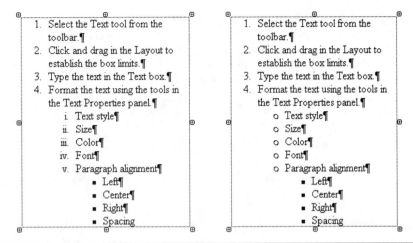

FIGURE 4-3   Before (on the left) all five sublines are numbered, After (on the right), all five sublines changed to bullets.

Another way to format lists is to click the Format button under the List tab of the Text Properties panel. This opens our old friend the Format dialog box, now called List Settings and sporting an extra tab: List.

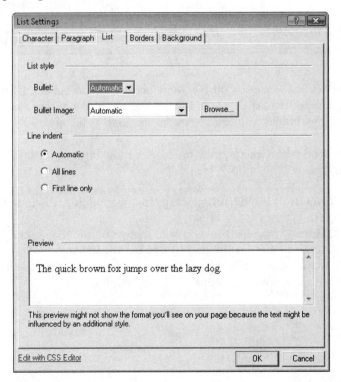

In addition to choosing a bullet from the Bullet drop-down list (which works just like the Bullet Type drop-down list discussed previously), you can choose an image to use as a bullet and set up the Line indent. To choose an image to use as a bullet, either choose Browse from the Bullet Image drop-down list or click Browse to open the Picture File Open dialog box. Pick the image you want to use and click Open.

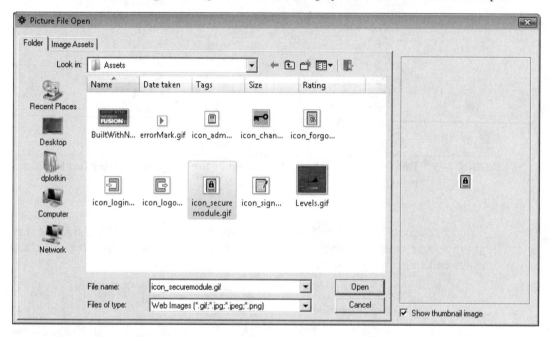

 Pick small images (.gif files work best) to use as bullets. If you choose large images, the list gets hard to read because of the huge bullets. And unlike with other images, you can't resize images used as bullets.

To set the line indent, pick one of the radio buttons in the Line Indent section of the dialog box. The options are

- **Automatic**   If the list line wraps to a second line, the indent is set by the parent object.
- **All lines**   If the list line wraps to a second line, the second line is indented by the same amount as the first line of the list item.
- **First line only**   If the list line wraps to a second line, the second line is indented to the same position as the line item bullet/number.

Understand Automatic Formatting

As you set text formatting for text, lists, the text box (such as background and color), and many other items in Fusion, you'll often see a value of "Automatic" as a selection. What "Automatic" means is that the property is inherited from the parent object in a hierarchy. For example, if a text box is located on a page, using "Automatic" as a format value means that the text box property (such as the background color and image) will be the same as the page. However, if the parent object doesn't have that property (for example, a page doesn't have a font property), the property is inherited from further up the inheritance chain. Figure 4-4 shows a good example using background color. The Layout has a yellow-brown background color (which sets the color for the whole page). If the embedded Layout Region background color was set to Automatic, it would have the same background color. However, the Layout Region background color was set to light blue. The embedded text box background color *is* set to Automatic and thus has the same light blue background color as the Layout Region.

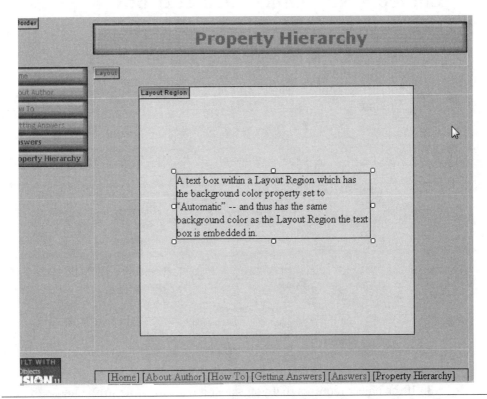

FIGURE 4-4   Automatic formatting of background color controls whether the object has the same color as its parent.

There is actually a hierarchy for this inheritance, which looks like

Browser | SiteStyle | Site | Page | Parent Object | Child Object | Selected Text

The SiteStyle (see Chapter 8) provides a value for almost all formatting properties, so if you leave most formatting properties set to Automatic, the entire site will have a consistent look and feel.

Note You can set some attributes to Automatic and others not. For example, you could set the font to be inherited (Automatic) but not the color.

Place an Object in a Text Box

A text box is very flexible. Not only can you type and format text, but you can embed other objects in a text box—including another text box or a picture. Once you do that, you can specify how the existing text wraps around the new object.

Embed a New Object in a Text Box

To insert an object into a text box, use the following steps:

1. Double-click in the text and place the text insertion point where you want to insert the object.
2. Choose Text | Insert Object and pick the object you want to insert from the submenu.

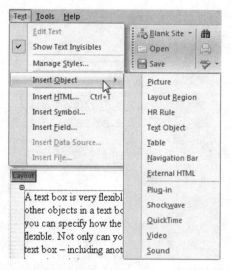

3. If the object requires that you select it (as with a picture), choose the item from the appropriate dialog box and click Open.
4. If the object is too large to fit in the text box (as many pictures will be) and would force the Layout to enlarge, you are offered the opportunity to crop or

resize the object using the appropriate tool—such as the Image Inspector for a picture. If you choose to do so, use the various tools to size or crop the object to the size you want, and click the appropriate button (the Done button in the Image Inspector) to finish.

5. The new object appears in the text box.

> A text box is very flexible. Not only can you type and format text, but you can embed other objects in a text box – including another text box or a picture. Once you do that, you can specify how the existing text wraps around the new object. A text box is very flexible. Not only can you type and format text, but you can embed other objects in a text box – including another text box or a picture. Once you do that, you can specify how the existing text wraps around the new object. A text box is very flexible. Not only can you type and format text, but you can embed other objects in a text box – including another text box or a picture. Once you do that, you can
>
> specify how the existing text wraps around the new object. A text box is very flexible. Not only can you type and format text, but you can embed other objects in a text box – including another text box or a picture. Once you do that, you can specify how the existing text wraps around the new object. A text box is very flexible. Not only can you type and format text, but you can embed other objects in a text box – including another text box or a picture. Once you do that, you can specify how the existing text wraps around the new object.

Set the Text Wrapping

Once the object is embedded in the text box, you'll see the Object's Property panel, if the Property Inspector is enabled. For example, if you embedded an image in the text box, you'll see the Picture Properties panel. Any embedded object has an extra tab: Align. Click the Align tab to see the options for aligning the object in the text box and specifying how the text wraps around the object.

There are eight possible options, though some may not be available, depending on the type of object you embedded and where you embedded it. The options (see Figure 4-5 for an illustration) are

- **Top**   A single line of text wraps around the object, and it is located at the top of the object.
- **Middle**   A single line of text wraps around the object, and it is located at the vertical middle of the object.
- **Bottom**   A single line of text wraps around the object, and it is located at the bottom of the object.
- **Left**   The object is located against the left margin. No text is wrapped around the object. The line that the object interrupts is located partly above and partly below the object.

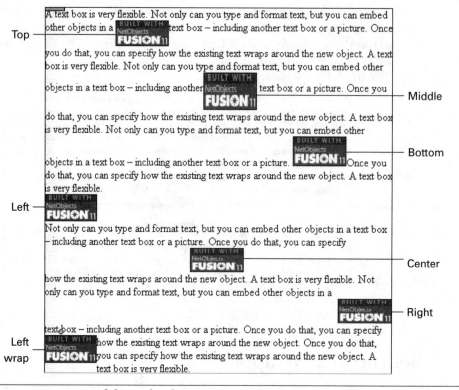

FIGURE 4-5 Seven of the eight alignment/wrapping options are shown here.

- **Center** The object is located in the center of the text box. As with the Left setting, no text is wrapped around the object.
- **Right** The object is located against the right margin. As with the Left setting, no text is wrapped around the object.
- **Left wrap** The object is located against the left side of the text box, and text is wrapped completely around it.
- **Right wrap** The object is located against the right side of the text box, and text is wrapped completely around it.

Note In addition to setting the wrapping and alignment, you can add some padding (space) around the object by specifying a quantity (in pixels) in the Horizontal and Vertical fields.

You can embed one text box in another. However, the Top, Middle, and Bottom alignment/wrap options are not available, and you can specify only a single quantity for the space around the object—and that distance is applied all around the text box.

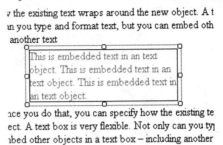

This is also true for embedded tables (see Chapter 6), Layout Regions, Navigation Bars (see Chapter 9), and HR Rules (see Chapter 5).

Insert Text Fields

You can add text fields to a page. These fields display a value that can change, such as the date and time the site was last modified, the site name, and so on. Some of the fields (such as the date the site was last modified) change automatically to reflect the most current information, saving you the trouble of manually updating them.

Insert a New Text Field

To insert a field, use the following steps:

1. Double-click the text in the text box and position the text cursor where you want to add the field.
2. Choose Text | Insert Field to open the Insert Field dialog box.

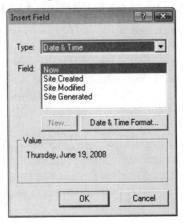

3. Choose the type of field from the Type drop-down list, and the field from the Field list. If the field you chose is a date & time field, click the Date & Time Format to specify the format from the long list of possibilities in the Date & Time Format dialog box.

4. Click OK to insert the field into the text box.

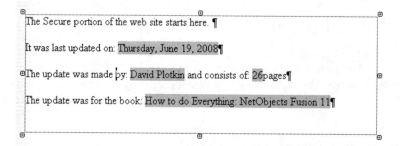

 Note Although you can't edit the *contents* of an inserted field, you can select the contents (text) and use the Text Properties panel to format the field text.

Understand the Text Field Types

You have three categories of fields to choose from. The first is the Date & Time category. Fields include the current date and time (Now), as well as the date on which the site was created, modified, and generated (published). The Site Modified and Site Generated are especially useful, as you can simply embed that information in the MasterBorder, which tells visitors how recently the site was changed.

The second category is called Site & General. This lists "internal" site information, such as the Site name, author, Number of pages, OS Platform, and the name of the software you built the site in (NetObjects Fusion 11, in this case).

By default, the Author field in the Site & General category is taken from the new site configuration and cannot be changed, but you can define a new one for yourself by setting a user-defined variable.

The last category is User-Defined Variable. Here you can define your own variables, which you can then insert into text anywhere you like.

How to... Create and Use User-Defined Variables

User-defined variables are handy because you can define any value you want, and then use it whenever you please. For example, you could define your contact information as a variable, since it will probably appear at multiple places in your site. If you then change the value of the variable (as described shortly), the new value will be used the next time you publish your web site.

To create a user-defined variable, select User-Defined Variable in the Type drop-down list of the Insert Field dialog box. Click New to display the New Variable dialog box.

Fill in the Variable Name and the Value you want to use, and then click OK to add the new variable to the list of User-Defined Variables.

To add the variable you just defined to the web site, select it and click OK, or double-click it in the list of fields.

To delete a user-defined variable or change its value, you must go to the Asset view, which shows you all the assets (files, images, links, objects, variables, etc.) used by your web site, grouped by type. To get to Asset view, click the Assets button

(continued)

(third from the right) in the Views Bar toolbar, or choose Go | Assets. Once in the Assets view, click the Variables tab.

To delete a variable, right-click it in the Assets view and choose Delete User-Defined Variable from the shortcut menu. To edit the value of the variable, double-click it to open the Edit Variable dialog box (which looks just like the New Variable dialog box), change the value, and click OK. The new value is reflected in the Assets view.

5

Add Graphics and Sound to Your Web Page

HOW TO...

- Add graphics to a web page
- Resize and optimize an image
- Flip, resize, and crop images
- Add dividing lines to a page
- Add a banner to a page
- Add sound to a page

Text is just fine for communicating information, but a web page that doesn't include any graphics and images is pretty dull. You can actually build an entire photo gallery using a special component (see Chapter 10), but you can also add and customize graphics and images individually on a page. That is what we're going to discuss next.

Add Graphics to a Web Page

You can add graphics—including photographs, simple shapes, drawings, illustrations, and more—to almost any place on a web page. As we saw in Chapter 4, you can insert a graphic into a text box (using Text | Insert Object | Picture) and then adjust how the text wraps around the graphic. But you don't have to have a text box on a page in order to add graphics. You can place graphics in a Layout or Layout Regions, and even in the MasterBorder (in which case it will appear on every page that uses that MasterBorder). And as we'll see in Chapter 9, you can even designate a portion of an image as a hyperlink to jump to another web page, giving you yet another reason to use graphics in your web site.

Comprehend File Types

There are a vast number of types of files you can use to create and edit graphics. However, most web browsers can only open three file types without help from "helpers" or "plug-ins": JPG, GIF, and PNG. As a result, I pretty much stick to these types of files when adding images to a web page.

Understand JPG Files

JPG (or JPEG) files are the most commonly used file type for digital camera images, though they are used for other purposes as well. JPG files do well for photographs because they contain millions of colors and you can choose to trade file size for picture quality. That is, you can pick the quality of the image—better quality results in a larger file, while lower quality results in a smaller file. This works because JPG uses compression to reduce the file size. At higher compression (lower quality and smaller files), more information is discarded, which eventually results in degradation in the picture that you can see as "jaggies" and pixilation. The amount of compression that a picture can stand depends on what the picture will be used for and how detailed the image is. An image with large blocks of the same color can be compressed quite a bit before showing much degradation. However, highly detailed pictures with a lot of high-contrast edges cannot be compressed as much. As we will see shortly, Fusion contains an optimization tool that enables you to adjust the JPG quality.

Understand GIF Files

GIF files are typically more useful for drawn diagrams, simple shapes, and icons/graphics that have limited complexity—like bullets, buttons, and page banners. This is because a GIF file can only contain 256 colors. Techniques to combine colors (called dithering) can simulate colors that are not available. You can do a surprisingly good job of simulating a photograph using a GIF file, but the equivalent JPG file does a better job and is actually smaller. On the other hand, GIF files are smaller than JPGs for simple files with limited colors. GIF files are also much better for page components (like buttons and banners) because unlike a JPG, part of a GIF file can be transparent, allowing the background page to show through. For a GIF file, you can adjust the color palette, as well as the algorithm used for dithering.

Understand PNG Files

The last (and least common) web file format is called PNG. The original PNG format (called PNG-8) worked much like GIF, in that it could handle 256 colors, dithering, and transparency. However, since it really didn't have any advantage over GIF, it wasn't used much. A newer format (PNG-24) handles millions of colors (like JPG) and transparency. But it isn't used much either.

Add Graphics from a File

To add a picture file to your web page, use the following steps:

1. Select the Picture tool from the Standard Tools bar.
2. Click and drag a rectangle on the web page approximately where you want the picture to be located. Don't worry too much about the size or shape of the rectangle, as you'll have an opportunity to adjust it later.
3. The Picture File Open dialog box opens. Navigate to the location of your picture. You'll be able to see small image icons of all the picture file types you can use in the dialog box. Click the image icon. If you have the Show Thumbnail Image check box selected, you'll be able to see a larger version of the selected image in the right panel of the dialog box.

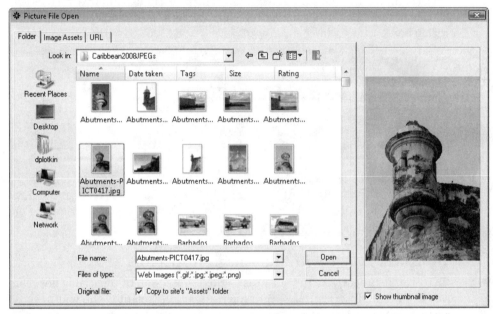

   Select the Copy To Site's Assets Folder check box if you want the image to show up as an Asset of the web site. This makes it easier to reuse the image later (just pick it from the Image Assets tab of the Picture File Open dialog box.

4. Click Open to add the image to the page.

If the image already exists in the site Assets, you'll be warned of that fact and given an opportunity to use the existing Asset. You can also copy the file to the Assets folder again with a different name, if the image is actually a different image from the one in the Image Assets, or you want to modify (crop) this image without changing (the shape of) the existing one. For example, if you crop an image and then click Done, the image will be also modified in the Assets folder. If you want to use the original (uncropped) image, you should open the original image and select the Copy To Site's Assets Folder check box and rename the image.

Fit an Image to the Page with the Image Inspector

Fusion adds an image to the page using the dimensions of the image. With large images, this could cause the Layout (and the page) to expand to a very large size. This is not usually what you want. Fusion warns you that this is about to occur with a dialog box.

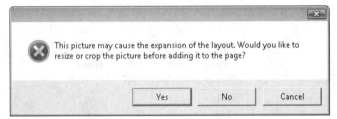

Choosing Yes opens the Image Inspector (see Figure 5-1), which enables you to resize or crop the image to fit the page. While the Image Inspector is open, you can see the picture at its actual size on the screen. This helps you preview the changes you are making.

Resize an Image with the Image Inspector

To resize the image, use the controls in the Size section of the dialog box. Normally, you'll want to preserve the aspect ratio (ratio of the height to the width) so that the picture doesn't get distorted, so select the Maintain Aspect Ratio check box. To directly adjust the size of the image, adjust the values in the Width and Height fields. You can adjust these quantities either in pixels (px) or percent (%) by choosing the unit of measure from the Unit drop-down list. As you make these adjustments, you'll see the image shrink (or enlarge, if you are going bigger).

Another way to resize the image is to use the slider at the bottom of the Size section. Drag the slider to the left to shrink the image, and to the right to enlarge the image. The slider works like it is spring loaded—the further you drag it to either side, the faster the image changes size. Release the mouse button to have the slider spring back to the middle and stop changing size.

Indicates that image
conflicts with other objects

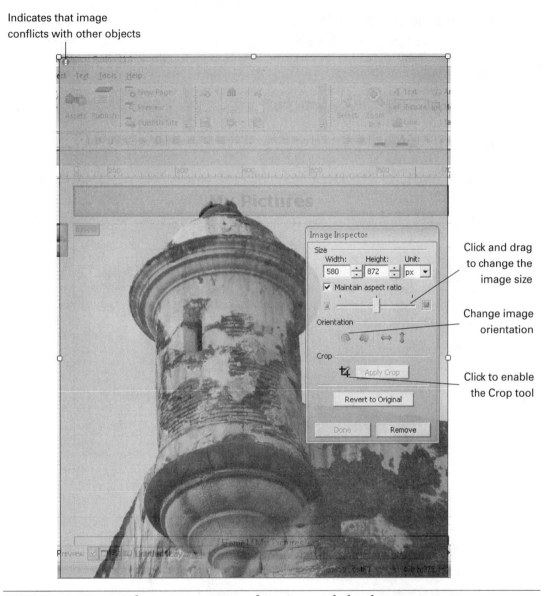

Click and drag
to change the
image size

Change image
orientation

Click to enable
the Crop tool

FIGURE 5-1   Ensure that your new image doesn't overwhelm the page it appears on.

You can click and drag the sizing handles to resize the image as well; though that is typically more useful for making small size adjustments after you have the image size fairly close to where you want it. And, if your mouse has a scroll wheel, you can roll it forward (enlarge) or backward (shrink) to adjust the picture size.

Change the Image Orientation

The controls in the Orientation section enable you to (from left to right) rotate the image clockwise, rotate the image counter-clockwise, flip the image right to left, and flip the image top to bottom.

Crop an Image to Make It Fit

If you'd rather crop the image (remove parts of it to make it fit the space), you can do that as well. Use the following steps:

1. Click the Crop tool in the Crop section and move the mouse pointer over the image.
2. Click and drag the pointer to define the section you want to keep (inside the rectangle).

3. After defining it, you can adjust the crop rectangle size and shape by clicking and dragging the sizing handles.
4. Once you have it the way you want it, click Apply Crop to remove the sections of the image outside the rectangle.

If you change your mind and want to start over, click Revert To Original. But make sure you do this before clicking Done, as you can't go back and revert to the original later. If you need to do that, you'll have to delete the image and start over.

Set the Graphics Properties

Once you have placed a picture on a web page, you can select it and adjust many of its properties in the Picture Properties panel. The simplest change to make is to fill in the Alt Tag text field. This is the text that appears while the image is loading, or is shown in place of the image if the browser is set to not show graphics. You can even change the image altogether by clicking the Browse button alongside the File field and picking another image.

 The alt tag text also appears when you mouse over the image/object.

Optimize the Picture for the Web

Modern digital cameras can take pictures that are much too large to be shown on a web page. Although you can shrink the size of the image using the Image Inspector (or the tools under the Geometry tab in the Picture Properties panel, as will be discussed shortly), you are not actually shrinking the file. That is, the entire file (which can be quite large) is still loaded to the web page, but it is then shown in a smaller size. Thus, a page full of high-resolution pictures can take a while to load, even with a broadband connection.

However, you can adjust an image to reduce its quality and size, especially if the image is a JPG. To do that, click Edit to open the Optimize Image dialog box, as shown in Figure 5-2.

 In addition to changing the zoom with the Magnifying Glass tool, you can pick the zoom level directly from the drop-down list. However, it is best to use 100% zoom—if you use a lower level, you won't be able to see the exact effects of reducing the quality or number of colors.

The first step in optimizing the image is to decide what type of image you want to use for the final result. This really breaks down to deciding whether to use GIF (PNG-8 has the same optimizing options as GIF) or JPG. PNG-24 does not support any optimization.

Optimize the Image Using GIF

To optimize your image using the GIF parameters, choose GIF (or PNG-8) from the Format drop-down list. The available fields (seen in Figure 5-2) are

- **Colors**   You can pick the number of colors in powers of 2 (2, 4, 8, etc.) up to a maximum of 256. As you reduce the number of colors, the image quality degrades because there are fewer colors available to render it. But the size also decreases.

Click and drag the image with this tool
to move the image around in the frame

Original

Preview of
optimized
image

Click the image
with this tool
to zoom in,
ALT-click to
zoom out

Click a GIF
to pick the
transparent
color

File name: Abutments-PICT0417.jpg

Format: JPEG, Millions of Colors

Image size: 203 x 396 Pixels

Settings: (Unnamed)

Format: GIF   Color Reduct.: Adaptive

Click to
create a
new setting
(that you
can reuse)

File sizes for
original and
optimized files

Size, loading time info on: Modem, 56K

Original: 783 KB, 1 min 50.79 sec

Optimized: 67 KB, 9.60 sec

Colors: 256   100   Dither: Floyd Steinb

Transparency   Add color

OK   Cancel

Click to pick
an assumed
download speed

FIGURE 5-2   Optimize your images so that they don't take forever to load into a web page.

Did You Know?

You Can Pick Settings from a Drop-Down List

You can pick from the prebuilt settings or settings you have created from either
the Settings drop-down list in the Picture Properties panel (just above the Edit
button) or from the Settings drop-down list on the right side of the Optimize
Image dialog box. To create a new setting, click the + button, fill in the setting
name in the Save Settings dialog box, and click Save. To discard an existing
setting, select it and click the – button.

- **Color Reduction**   As you reduce the number of colors, you can use various techniques to choose which colors to keep. The "best" technique will depend on the image; however, keep in mind that for photos, using different techniques will have an impact on the final file size.
- **Dither**   Dithering is a way to simulate colors by placing pixels of different colors in close proximity, fooling the eye into seeing an intermediate color. You can either choose the single dithering method available or None. Again, using dithering increases the file size, though not as much as adding colors.
- **Transparency**   To pick a transparent color, select the Transparency check box. You can pick the transparency color by clicking Add and choosing it from the ColorPicker, or by using the eyedropper tool to pick a color from the left (original) image. When you pick a transparent color, you can see the result in the right (optimized) image.

Tip   Transparent colors don't work very well with photographs because the transparent color has to match exactly the color in the image. Since a photo contains so many colors, picking one to be transparent typically only makes some very small areas transparent. Even when I reduced the number of colors to 16 (as in the last illustration), it wasn't possible to make the whole sky transparent.

Optimize the Image Using JPEG

To optimize your image using the JPG parameters, choose JPG from the Format drop-down list. The available fields (visible in the lower right corner of the Optimize Image dialog box, shown in the next image) are as follows.

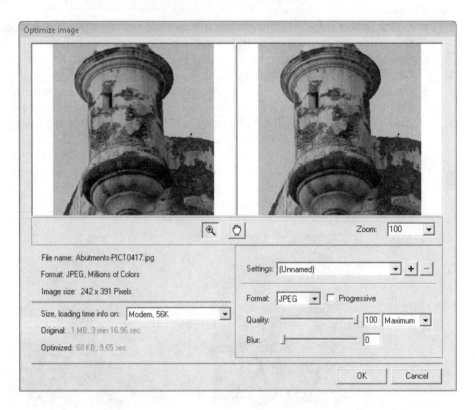

- **Progressive**   JPG images can be displayed in two ways. The more common way is to load the whole image and display it. If you do it that way, the person viewing the picture has to wait for the entire picture to be loaded in order to see what it looks like. The other way is to load a low-resolution image of the picture first; giving the viewer an idea of what the picture looks like while the higher-resolution version is loaded. This "progressive" load is what you get if you select the Progressive check box. It does make the file slightly larger but is considered the "polite" way to load large images.

- **Quality**   As mentioned earlier in this chapter, you can trade image quality for file size when working with JPG images. The Quality controls enable you to make that trade-off, with the optimized image showing the results. There are three ways to set the quality: choose a value (such as Maximum, High, Medium, or Low) from the drop-down list, type in a value between 0 and 100 in the text field, or drag the slider. In general, you don't have to reduce the quality much to decrease the file size considerably. In one example, I reduced it to 85, and the file size went from 276 KB to 50 KB. And I couldn't see any difference between the original and the optimized version.

- **Blur**   Another way to reduce the file size is to reduce the sharpness of the image, essentially blurring adjacent pixels together. To increase the blur, type a number into the field or use the slider.

I do not recommend trading sharpness for file size (using the Blur control). It is much less noticeable to adjust the Quality.

Flip, Resize, and Rotate an Image

The Geometry tab in the Picture Properties panel enables you to adjust the size of an image, as well as flip or rotate the image.

To resize the image, change the values in the Height and Width fields in either pixels or percent (choose the unit you want from the Unit drop-down list). Make sure to select the Maintain Aspect Ratio check box to avoid distorting the image.

Tiling the image provides yet another option. If you have shrunk the image to less than full size, clicking the Tile check box re-expands the image to its full size—but you can see only the portion of the image that fits in the specified image box.

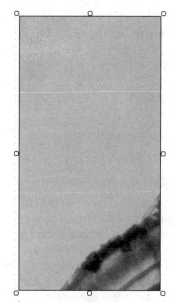

On the other hand, if the image is small, and you have expanded it to fit a larger area, then selecting the Tile check box returns it to its normal size and repeats the image across the image area (called "tiling"), as shown next.

You can rotate the image by making a selection from the Rotate drop-down list. Options include 90 degrees (quarter-turn) clockwise, 90 degrees counterclockwise, and 180 degrees (rotating the image upside down). To flip the image left-to-right, click the Horizontal button in the Flip section of the panel; to flip the image top to bottom, click the Vertical button.

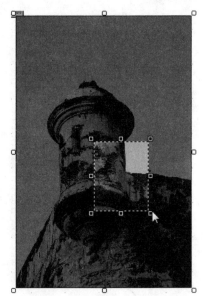

Crop an Image

To chop off portions (crop) of an image from the Geometry icon of the Picture Properties panel, click the Crop tool to place a resizable rectangle on the image.

To move the rectangle, click and drag inside the rectangle. To resize the rectangle, click and drag the sizing handles. This specifies the portion of the image you want to keep (inside the rectangle).

Once specified, click the Apply button in the panel. The image is cropped, and the image box is resized to contain just the remaining portion of the image.

Modify a Picture

Fusion is not an image editor, but it has a significant number of controls that enable you to modify a picture without resorting to another tool. You can change properties such as brightness and contrast, add borders to the image, fix red eye, and even embed text that becomes part of the image.

Adjust the Brightness, Contrast, and Color

Click the Adjustment tab in the Picture Properties panel to display a set of sliders/fields you can use to adjust the following quantities:

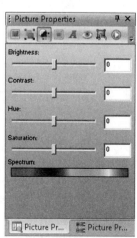

- **Brightness**   Makes the image brighter or darker. A small amount of change goes a long way; apply this change sparingly.
- **Contrast**   Increases or decreases the contrast. You can, to a small degree, increase the apparent sharpness of an image by increasing its contrast.

- **Hue** Shifts the entire spectrum of color for the image. For example, dragging the slider to the right turns yellow to green and red to yellow. You can get some pretty surrealistic effects with this one, but other than that, I'm not sure why you'd use it.
- **Saturation** Adjusts the amount of color in the image. Increasing the saturation (values greater than 0) can give the image more "punch," providing you don't overdo it. Decreasing the amount of saturation to –100 removes all color, converting a color image to black and white.

Add Borders to a Photo

You can effectively set off a photo from its background by adding borders to it from the Borders tab in the Picture Properties panel, as shown in Figure 5-3.

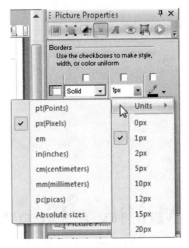

To add borders individually to each side of the image, click the left-hand column of buttons to turn on each border you want to use. Select the border style (such as a solid line, double-line, groove, etc.) from the drop-down list immediately to the right of the border buttons. The next drop-down list to the right enables you to select the border thickness from the drop-down list. You can also select the units from this list.

To set the color of each border, click the pencil icon button at the right end of each row to pick a color from the ColorPicker.

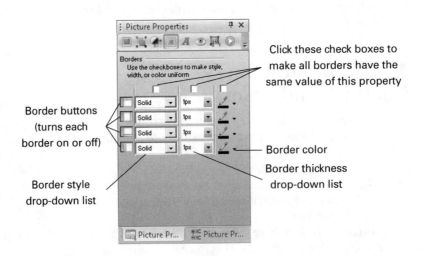

FIGURE 5-3 Add borders to a photo to make it more noticeable.

One common action you'll probably want to take is to make the properties of all the borders the same. Quite frankly, if you don't do that, the borders can get pretty "busy" and detract from the photo. The row of check boxes over each column enables you to do just that for the property the check box sits over. For example, if you click the left-most check box, all the borders will have the same style. As you can see here, selecting all the check boxes disables all the border property rows except the top one—the top row sets the properties for all four borders.

Add Text to a Photo

Fusion enables you to add descriptive text to a photo by clicking the Text tab in the Picture Properties panel.

It's actually fun to add text to a photo, and it can really help illustrate specific points about the picture. To add the text, simply type the text into the text box in the Picture Properties panel, and adjust the font, color, size, and style by using the various drop-down lists, which look very much like other text formatting tools (as discussed in Chapter 4).

To specify the position of the text in the picture, use the following adjustments:

- **Horizontal**   Specifies the left-to-right position. Middle places the text in the horizontal middle of the image, whereas Left or Right places the text against the left or right edge. However, if you choose Left or Right, the Offset field becomes available, and you can specify an offset from the selected edge to place the text exactly where you want it.
- **Vertical**   Specifies the top-to-bottom position. Middle places the text in the vertical middle of the image, whereas Top or Bottom places the text against the top or bottom edge. However, if you choose Top or Bottom, the Offset field becomes available, and you can specify an offset from the selected edge to place the text exactly where you want it.
- **Alignment**   This control only has an effect if you have two or more lines of text. If you do, it sets the alignment of the text lines to Left, Middle, or Right. For example, the following image shows an instance of three lines that are right-aligned.

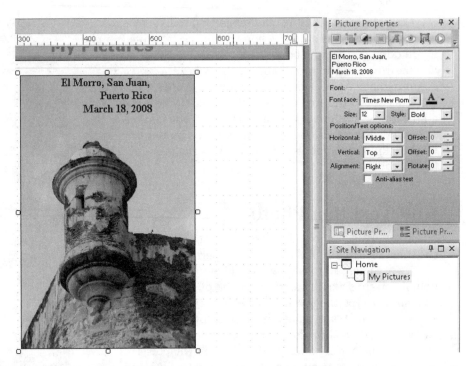

- **Rotate** If you want to rotate your text in the image, you can set the angle of rotation in the Rotate field. For example, here is an example of text that has been rotated 15 degrees.

- **Anti-alias text**   When you add text to an image, the edges of the text can look jagged, especially if there is a big color difference between the text and the image it is lying on top of, or if the text is rotated. To prevent this, select the Anti-Alias Text check box. This smoothes the edges by adding intermediate-color pixels along the edges. You can see the difference here when we turn on anti-aliasing (as compared to the last image).

Fix Red Eye

Red eye is a phenomenon that occurs when you take a picture of someone and the person's eyes appear bright red (see Figure 5-4). This phenomenon typically occurs when the photographic subject has light-colored eyes, the room is dark (so the pupils are dilated), and the flash is too close to lens—as is typical on most "point and shoot" cameras. While most photo adjustment software does a good job of removing red eye, you can remove it in Fusion as well, which is handy if you forgot to remove it elsewhere.

FIGURE 5-4   No, this beautiful bride is not devilish—my flash gave her red eye!

To remove red eye, click the Red eye removal tab in the Picture Properties panel.

Click the Eye button to place a rounded rectangle in the picture area. To move the rectangle, click inside the rectangle and drag it to the new position. To resize the rectangle, click and drag the sizing handles. This specifies the portion of the image containing the red eye. Adjust the strength of the effect you want to use using the Strength slider or the associated field, and pick the eye color that should be used from the Eye Color drop-down list. This list also has a Custom option, which opens the ColorPicker so that you can pick the exact color you want to use. Once you have all these quantities specified, click the Apply button in the panel to remove the red eye.

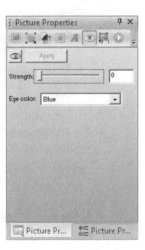

How to... Pick Exactly the Right Color to Correct Red Eye

To pick exactly the right color to use in Fusion, you'll need an image that actually has the correct color eyes—that is, an image where red eye did not occur. This might be a picture that was taken without flash, or perhaps an image that was taken by someone with a professional camera, where the flash is located far enough from the lens that red eye did not occur.

To correct red eye, use the following steps:

1. Place the picture that contains red eye on the web page.
2. Make a note of the size of the Layout that you have, because the next step is likely to enlarge the size of the Layout.
3. Add the second picture—the one that shows the correct eye color—to the page. Don't worry about it if you get the warning that the Layout will be resized. You *can* shrink the picture so that it fits easily onto the page, but make sure that the eyes are large enough to easily click on one to obtain the color you'll need.
4. Reselect the image with red eye, and choose the Red Eye Removal icon in the Picture Properties dialog box.
5. Click the Eye button and locate the rounded rectangle around the red eye portion of the image.
6. Click the Eye Color drop-down list and choose Custom to open the ColorPicker dialog box.
7. Move the mouse pointer outside the dialog box and notice that it turns into an eyedropper.
8. Move the eyedropper over the correct colored eyes in the second photo and click, selecting the correct color for the eyes.
9. Click OK in the ColorPicker dialog box, and then click the Apply button in the Picture Properties panel.
10. Click the second image (the one with the correct colored eyes) and delete it.
11. If the Layout size changed, click the Layout and fill in the values you noted in Step 2 to return it to the correct size.

Be careful with the Strength slider. You can actually apply too much correction—I tend to set the Strength slider to about 60 as a first pass, and if I don't like the result, I use undo (Edit | Undo or CTRL-Z) to try a different setting.

Add Simple Shapes to a Web Page

Simple shapes—such as rectangles, ovals, and lines—can be very handy for diagramming, making maps, even building an organization chart. Fusion provides a variety of these shapes that you can use and configure to your liking.

Draw the Simple Shape

In general, adding a simple shape to a web page is, well, pretty simple. The first step is to pick the shape you want from the shape list in the Standard Tools bar. The last shape you used shows in the bar, but you can click the tiny down arrow alongside the shape to display a list of available shapes.

From there, simply place the mouse pointer over the web page and click and drag to define the size of the simple shape.

The exception to this technique is the Polygon tool. With the Polygon tool, click the starting point, then move the mouse pointer to the next vertex, and click to set the vertex. Keep defining vertices this way until you reach the last one—at that point, double-click to set the last vertex and finish the polygon.

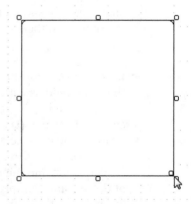

You can move a simple shape on the page by clicking the shape to select it, and then clicking inside the shape and dragging the shape to its new position. Clicking the shape also displays the sizing handles—click and drag a sizing handle to change the size of the simple shape. The sizing handles in a polygon also enable you to reshape the polygon by moving the vertices.

 You need to actually click the shape itself, *not* the bounding rectangle. That is, to select an oval, click the oval, not the rectangle around the oval.

Format the Simple Shape from the Properties Panel

You have a wealth of options you can set to customize simple shapes using the Properties panel. These include setting the line width and color, fill color, and more. The options are identical for the rectangle, rounded rectangle, oval, and polygon.

We'll cover these options first, and then discuss the minor differences for the line.

 You can attach hyperlinks and page anchors to simple shapes. This will be covered in Chapter 9.

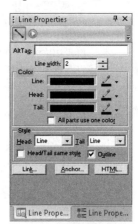

The options you can set for the Rectangle are as follows:

- **Alt Tag**   As with a photograph, the alt tag is text, which displays while the image is loading or instead of an image if your browser is set to not display images. Most browsers display the alt tag also as a screen tip when you roll the mouse over the image.
- **Line Width**   Use the Line Width field to establish the thickness of the line in pixels.
- **Fill Color**   To establish the fill color, click the paint bucket button alongside the Fill Color rectangle. Use the resulting ColorPicker to pick the fill color.
- **Line Color**   To establish the line color, click the paint bucket alongside the Line Color rectangle. Use the resulting ColorPicker to pick the color.

The line has different properties than the other shapes, primarily because a line has no fill color and has ends (both a head and a tail) that you can configure. Clicking the Line shape displays a new set of options in the Line Properties panel.

In addition to the alt tag, you can set the following options:

- **Line Width**   For the Line, you set the line width using the same field as with other shapes. However, you can also click and drag the sizing handle that appears in the center of the line (see Figure 5-5) to adjust the line width.
- **Color**   The color section of the Line Properties panel has three colors you can set: the line color, the starting point (Head) color, and the ending point (Tail) color. To set any of these colors, simply click the appropriate paint bucket button and choose the color from the ColorPicker. If you want to force all three colors to be the same, select the All Parts Use One Color check box. Once you do that, you can use any of the paint bucket buttons to set a color, and both of the other colors change to match.

 You can't actually see the line end colors (Head or Tail) unless you specify a Style other than "Line" for the Head and Tail.

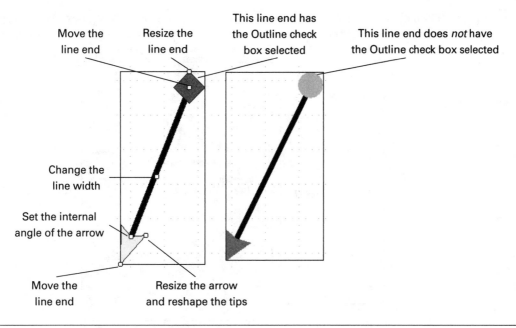

FIGURE 5-5   Line ends without the outline (on the right) and with the outline (on the left).

- **Style**   You can apply a style (such as an arrow, diamond, circle, etc.) to the Head and the Tail by using the two drop-down lists in the Style section. If you want to ensure that the Head and Tail use the same style, select the Head/Tail Same Style check box. You can then select the style from either Style drop-down list, and the other one changes to match. You can also choose the Outline check box to outline each line end with a thin line that has the same color as the line (see Figure 5-5).
- **Line end size and shape**   For all styles, except the arrow, you can click and drag a sizing handle (see Figure 5-5) to enlarge or shrink the shape. The arrow is a little more complicated—it has two sizing handles. The sizing handle at the lower back tip (see Figure 5-5) adjusts the size of the arrow as well as the location of the back tips. The sizing handle at the interior angle (where the arrow meets the line) adjusts the sharpness of the interior angle.

Add Text to a Simple Shape

Except for the Line shape, the simple shapes can have text associated with them. To enable the text, select the Enable check box in the Text In Element section of the panel. Then click Settings to open the Text In Element Settings dialog box. As you type text into the text field at the top of the dialog box, that same text appears in the shape.

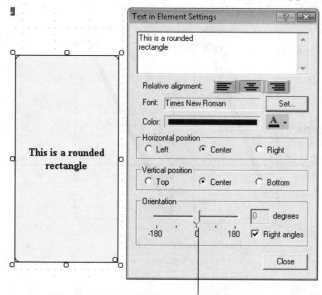

This is a rounded rectangle

Drag this sizing handle to adjust
the radius of the rounded corners

Adjusting the text properties works the same as with other text dialog boxes and panels—use the various controls to pick the text color, horizontal and vertical positions of the text relative to the shape, and rotation angle. To adjust the rotation angle, use the slider or type a value into the associated field. To make the field available, make sure to deselect the Right Angles check box. The relative alignment (left, center, or right) adjusts how multiple lines of text align to each other—it has no effect for a single line of text.

Setting the font, size, and style does work just a little differently. To set these quantities, click the Set button alongside the Font field to open the Font dialog box. Pick the Font, Font Style, and Size from this dialog box and click OK.

Note When adding text to a polygon, the text is originally centered in the bounding rectangle, which may place some of the text outside the polygon itself. In addition, the positioning of the text (Horizontal Position and Vertical Position) is relative to the bounding rectangle.

Add Horizontal Rules or SiteStyle Lines

On occasion, it can be handy to place lines across your web page, perhaps to offset different sections. Fusion actually provides two types of lines you can use: the HR Rule and a SiteStyle line. The HR Rule tool and the SiteStyle tool are grouped together under a single button in the Standard Tools bar.

Add an HR Rule

To add an HR Rule to the page, pick the HR Rule tool from the Standard Tools bar. Then, click and drag to create the horizontal line on the page.

To adjust the properties of the HR Rule, you can do the following:

- **Resize the HR Rule**   Use the sizing handles at each end to click and drag that end, effectively sizing or shrinking the line.
- **Move the HR Rule**   Click and drag inside the HR Rule to relocate it on the page.
- **Change the line width**   Use the Thickness field in the HR Rule Properties panel to adjust the thickness of the line.
- **Change the line to shaded**   The HR Rule seen previously shows a thick, heavy line—which is what you get if you leave the Shaded check box unselected. If you select the Shaded check box, you get a narrow line at the top of the rule, with a lighter area below.

Add a SiteStyle Line

A SiteStyle line is a line that is governed by the SiteStyle you have chosen for the web site or the page (see Chapter 8). These lines tend to be colorful and fun to use.

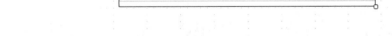

To place the SiteStyle line on the page, select the SiteStyle tool from the Standard Tools bar, then click and drag on the page to create the line. You can use the sizing handles to resize the line. Click and drag the sizing handles in the middle of the top or bottom to adjust the line thickness. You can change the image file used for the line (.gif file) from the SiteStyle Line Properties panel.

To adjust the image, you can do the following:

- **Choose another image to use** Click Custom Image to open the Picture File Open dialog box. You do need to be careful about the image you pick—wide, short images work best, and they should be patterns (not photos) so that they can be stretched or shrunk without showing noticeable distortion.
- **Choose the SiteStyle Line from another SiteStyle** If you have made several SiteStyles "active" (added them to your list of active SiteStyles as detailed in Chapter 8), those SiteStyles will show up in the Other drop-down list. Click the Other radio button and pick the SiteStyle whose line you want to use from the list.

Add a Banner to Your Page

Although all of the SiteStyles you can use to tailor the look and feel of your web site have a page banner (located in the top portion of the MasterBorder), you can, if you wish, add another banner. The new banner can be added either to a page (by placing it in the Layout) or to all the pages that use that MasterBorder (by placing it in the MasterBorder).

You can use the information in the next few sections to adjust the properties of the default page banner (which appears in the top margin of the MasterBorder) as well. For example, you can change the banner to use a different active SiteStyle.

Add a New Banner

To add a banner to a page, select Banner from the button that also includes Navigation Bars in the Standard Tools toolbar. Click on the page where you want to place the banner to add it to the page.

 If you are wondering why you only click on the page (and not click and drag), it's because you can't actually set the size of the banner when you place it on the page. The initial size of the banner is set by the banner built into the current SiteStyle. You can move the banner by clicking and dragging it to a new location.

Adjust the Banner Style

To change the style of the banner, use the drop-down lists in the Display section of the Banner Properties panel.

The items you can change are

- **Site Style**   You can pick the SiteStyle that defines the banner choices from the Site Style drop-down list. The options include Current SiteStyle (whatever the current SiteStyle that is defined for the site), as well as a list of all active SiteStyles (see Chapter 8 for information on how to make a SiteStyle appear in this list).
- **Banner Set**   Each SiteStyle may have multiple available banners you can use. At a minimum, they have the Default banner (which is what appears when you click to place the banner on the page) and a Flash banner. Pick the banner you want to use from the Banner Set drop-down list.
- **Orientation**   Choose Horizontal or Vertical from the Orientation drop-down list to position the banner either across the page (horizontal) or up and down (vertical).

You Can Change the Text of the Banner

The text of the banner normally is the same as the Page Name. However, you can easily change that by deselecting the Use For Banner Title check box. This makes the Banner title field available. Simply type in the text you want in the Banner Title field.

Configure a Flash Banner

A "Flash" banner enables you to implement many additional properties, such as the banner size, animation effects, and much more. To choose a Flash banner (assuming that the selected SiteStyle includes one), pick it from the Banner Set drop-down list. The result might look like this.

After you select the Flash banner, you can use the sizing handles to resize the banner. You'll also see a new Style tab appear in the Banner Properties panel. Click the Style tab to display the available properties for the Flash banner.

The list of properties depends on how the Flash component was designed. However, you can usually adjust the colors, animation (pick one from the Effect drop-down list), alignment, border color and thickness, and Fill Type by clicking the appropriate field and picking a value from a drop-down list, the ColorPicker, or a dialog box. The Font field uses such a dialog box, which actually enables you to change the font, size, style, alignment, and color.

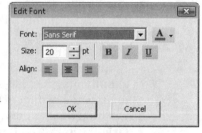

How to...   ## Get a Flash Banner to Work

Any Flash component (such as a Flash banner) must be "played" by the browser to see the component. You must have a Flash player installed on your computer for this to work. If you don't, you'll be prompted to download and install the Flash player from the Adobe web site. If you don't do that, you won't be able to see the Flash component. Since there are quite a large number of Flash components you can use on your web site (there is an entire panel of them), you will at least need the Flash player to test your web site. In addition, Internet Explorer "sees" Flash components as potential security threats and won't play them without showing you the infamous "yellow bar" warning at the top of the page. You'll have to click in the yellow bar (which then turns blue) and choose "Allow Blocked Content" from the menu that appears.

To help protect your security, Internet Explorer has restricted this webpage from running scripts or ActiveX controls that could access your computer. Click here for options...

Allow Blocked Content...

What's the Risk?

More information

Banner F

Add Playing Sound to Your Page

We've already seen how to add an annoying background sound to your web page (Chapter 3). You can also add a sound to the page in a way that your site visitor can control when to play it. To accomplish this much more polite way of playing a sound, use the following steps:

1. From the Custom Components panel, click the Plug-ins heading to display a list of available plug-ins.
2. Click the Sound plug-in, and then click and drag an area on the web page to locate where the sound icon will be shown. This opens the Open dialog box.
3. Navigate to the location of the sound you want to use, select it, and click Open to place it on the page. The default icon appears on the page.

    You have a wide range of sound files you can choose from, including .wav, .mp3, .mid, and many more.

4. Set the properties of the sound and how the icon is displayed from the Sound Properties panel.

To play the sound in a browser, simply click the sound indicator (icon, picture, or inline icon).

You can set how the sound file is displayed on the page. Your options are

- **Inline**   Displays an inline player on the page. Clicking the Play button in the player plays the sound, although you may have to (in Internet Explorer) click the yellow bar warning to allow this control to work. You also have a Stop button, a Pause button, and a slider to control what part of the sound plays.
- **Icon**   Pick one of the three icons available in the panel. To play the sound in a browser, click it to open the default player for that type of sound file.
- **Picture**   Pick the Picture option and then choose the picture to use by clicking Browse and picking the picture. As with the icon, to play the sound in a browser, click it to open the default player for that type of sound file.

6

Work with Tables

HOW TO...

- Create a table from scratch
- Import a file as a table
- Add contents to cells
- Adjust the dimensions of the table, rows, columns, and cells
- Format the background and text contents

Before the advent of Fusion, tables were just about the only way you had to easily align and lay out text on a web page. This is because HTML (the underlying language of web pages) doesn't lend itself to the specification of exact positioning of text on a page. Fusion gives you other tools to exactly position your text and other content, such as Text boxes and Layout Regions. However, tables are still an excellent method to place your content in a grid and format the background color, borders, and text formatting for the grid.

 Fusion is still using tables to align and position your text, though it cleverly hides that fact. For example, Layouts, Layout Regions, and Text boxes are actually tables! Check the HTML on the page if you don't believe me.

Understand Basic Table Concepts

In essence, a table is a grid, much like a (limited) spreadsheet. As shown in Figure 6-1, a table has rows that stretch across the width of the table, and columns that run up and down. At the intersection of each row and column there is a rectangular *cell*. The cell is where you place information, such as text, a picture, a plug-in, or even an entire new table.

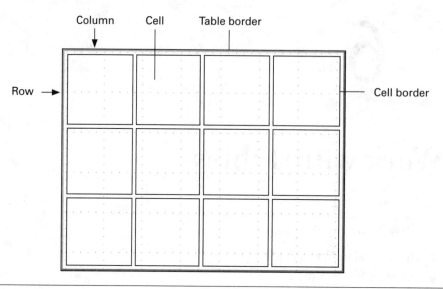

FIGURE 6-1   Put a grid of information into a table.

You have considerable freedom when formatting a table. For example, you can specify a background color or image for the entire table—then override that in specific cells by specifying a background color or image just for that cell. You can change the border style, color, and thickness for the table, and again, override that for individual cells.

Create a Table

There are quite a few ways to create a table in Fusion, including embedding a table in a Text box, adding a table to a Layout or Layout Region, and even creating a table with data already in it.

Create a Table Using the Table Tool

To create a table in a Layout, Layout Region, or MasterBorder, use the following steps:

1. Click the Table tool in the Standard Tools bar to display a grid of cells.
2. Move the mouse over the cells to define the initial size of the table. The selected cells are shown in blue.

3. Click and drag to define the size and position of the table on the web page.

Embed a Table in a Text Box

You can also embed a table in a Text box. To do so, double-click in the text box to show the text cursor, and move the cursor to the point in the text at which you want to insert the table. Then choose Text | Insert Object | Table. This opens the Create Table dialog box.

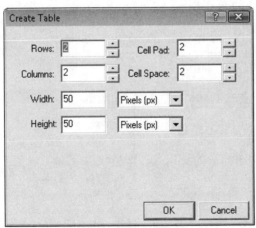

From this dialog box, you can define the following items:

- **Number of rows and columns**   Select the number of rows from the Rows field, and the number of columns from the Columns field. Remember that the number of rows and columns also defines the number of cells—for example, a 2 x 2 table (2 rows and 2 columns) provides four cells. The initial cell size is set to divide the table dimensions evenly among the cells.

- **Table width and height** Set the overall width and height of the table using the Width field and the Height field, along with the units you prefer, selected from the drop-down list alongside each field. The default units are pixels, but you can also use Percentage or Auto. The Percentage unit is the percentage of the size of the text box in which the table is embedded, and cannot be set higher than 100 (you get an error message if you try). If you choose Auto, the Width and Height fields are blanked out and unavailable—Fusion sets the table size according to what is specified in the SiteStyle.
- **Cell Pad** The distance between the cell border and any content in the cell, measured in pixels.
- **Cell Space** The distance between the cells (interior of the table) or between the cell border and the table border (cells along the edges of the table).

Click OK to create the table embedded in the Text box. Once you have done so, you can set how the text wraps around the table by clicking the Align tab in the Table Properties panel and choosing one of the available options (Left, Center, Right, Left Wrap, and Right Wrap). The details of using the wrapping options were discussed previously in Chapter 4 (under "Embed a New Object in a Text Box").

Convert a Layout Region or Layout to a Table

If you have already defined a Layout Region, you can create a table by converting the Layout Region to a table. To do so, select the Layout Region and choose Convert Layout Region To Table from either the Object menu or the Layout Region shortcut menu. This opens the Convert Region To Table dialog box, which has you specify how you want to handle empty cells.

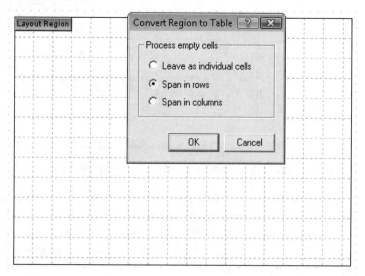

The options are

- **Leave as individual cells**   Don't merge any unused cells in the new table—leave them as individual (empty) cells.
- **Span in rows**   Merge unused cells in each row, giving you some wider cells.
- **Span in columns**   Merge unused cells in each column, giving you some taller cells.

You can also convert an entire Layout to a table by choosing Object | Convert Layout To Table. The Convert Layout To Table dialog box gives you the same options as those discussed for the Layout Region, as well as two additional options:

- **Place table in text box**   Creates a text box the size of the original layout, and embeds the Layout contents in the text box.

You won't be able to see the text box because the table is exactly the same size and hides it. However, if you shrink the table a bit by clicking and dragging a table sizing handle, you can see the text box. If you click the text box outline, you can configure the text box in the Text Properties panel. One very handy option is to choose the Size Layout To Text check box, which is available in the Text Box tab. The effect of this is to make the page only as large as necessary to hold the text.

- **Size table to browser window**   Changes the size of the resulting table to match the site visitor's browser window. This option is only available if you choose the ZeroMargins MasterBorder and select the Place Table In Text Box check box. Essentially, this option wraps the contents of the Layout (which in this case represents the entire page) to the site visitor's browser window.

Create a Table from a Data File

If you have a data file that you want to display on a web page, you can import the file as a table. The contents of the file are treated as text, and you have to specify a text character or other "delimiter" so that Fusion can tell where each data field starts and ends. To import a data file into a table, use the following steps:

1. Select the Table (Import Data) tool from the Standard Tools bar.

2. Click and drag in the web page to define the dimensions of the table. The Import Table dialog box opens.

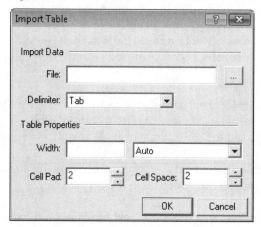

3. Specify the file that contains the data by either typing the full path into the File field or clicking the browse (. . .) button alongside the field and specifying the file from the Import Table dialog box. You can import either a text file (.txt) or a comma-delimited file (.csv).

Spreadsheets can export their contents as comma-delimited files. Thus, the easiest way to create a file to import is to use a spreadsheet and export the file as a .csv file.

4. Specify the "delimiter" (the character that separates the fields in the file) by choosing it from the Delimiter field. If you pick Custom from the Delimiter drop-down list, another field appears into which you can type the delimiter character.

5. Choose the table width by either typing a value into the Width field and selecting Pixels or Percent from the adjacent drop-down list, or picking Auto—which will automatically size the table to fit the data.

6. Specify the Cell Pad (pixels between the cell contents and the cell border) and the Cell Space (pixels between the cell borders) using the appropriate fields.

7. Click OK to create the table and import the data, as shown in Figure 6-2.

Header row ——

Name	Street	City	State	Zip	MemberSince
David Plotkin	1969 Christina Ln	Walnut Creek	Ca	94597	03-16-1967
Joseph Smith	44 Golf Ct	Teaneck	NJ	23490	02-12-1978
Maria Parker	344 1st Avenue	San Francisco	Ca	96790	11-05-1951
Jacob Parker	344 1st Avenue	San Francisco	Ca	96790	12-12-1991
Mark Manning	4545 Guidotti Ct	Salinas	Ca	93908	08-04-1988
Norman Smith	2020 Twin Oaks Dr	Monterey	Ca	93940	09-08-1994
Marta Ivanson	309 Buck St	Santa Barbara	Ca	91209	04-01-2004
Hattie Pinkerton	3209 Malta Ave Apt 3	Los Angeles	Ca	90932	05-22-1954

FIGURE 6-2   Your data is imported into a table.

How to...   Sort the Contents of a Table

You can sort the information in your table to put it in order. You should plan ahead if you intend to do that. For example, if you want to sort on the last name, that field has to be in its own column. If your data has only a single column for the whole name, you won't be able to sort on last name.

To sort the data in the table, select the table and choose Object | Table | Sort Table to open the Sort Table dialog box.

Sort Table		
Sort By		
	Column 1	Ascending
☐	Column 1	Ascending
☐	Column 1	Ascending
Options		
☐ Exclude cell headers	☐ Ignore initial whitespace	
☐ Sort selected cells only		
	OK	Cancel

(continued)

Configure how the sort is going to work with the following controls:

- **Sort column** Choose which column to sort on from the uppermost drop-down list in the Sort By section of the dialog box. If you want to sort on more than one column (you can use up to three), select the check box alongside the next drop-down list and pick the column to sort on from that list. The table is sorted first by the column specified in the uppermost drop-down list. If anywhere in that column the values are identical, those rows are sorted by the column specified in the next drop-down list.
- **Sort order** The drop-down list alongside each sort column specifies the order in which the rows are sorted. Ascending sorts the rows from lowest value to highest value, while Descending sorts them in the opposite order—from highest value to lowest value.
- **Exclude cell headers** As discussed later in this chapter, you can designate cells as "header cells." These are typically the cells in the top-most row in the table and describe the contents of the cells in that column. For example, the header cell might contain "City", and the rest of the cells in that column contain the City portion of an address. To exclude the header cells from the sort (so they don't end up somewhere in the middle of the table), select the Exclude Cell Headers check box. Note that if you *do* designate header cells and exclude them, the drop-down lists in the Sort By section reflect the column name as given by the header cells (instead of Column 1, Column 2, etc.):

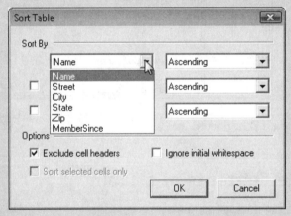

- **Ignore initial whitespace** Select this check box to ignore spaces at the beginning of the data when sorting.
- **Sort selected cells only** This check box becomes available if you select entire rows before starting the sort. Only the selected rows are included in the sort. If you select individual cells that do not form complete rows, this check box is not available.

Because of the way selecting rows and cells works, you can't select non-adjacent rows. This is actually a good thing when it comes to sorting, as it would be pretty confusing to try and sort non-adjacent rows!

Add Contents to Cells

The main reason to use tables in a web site is to provide structured data laid out in rows and columns. To add text to a table cell, simply double-click in the cell to select it and provide a text cursor. Then start typing. The cell expands vertically as you type to make room for the text.

You can format the text in a table cell just as you would text in a Text box. (Remember, a Text box is really just a table with cells!) If you select the cell, the Cell Properties panel contains a Text tab (at the far left of the toolbar)—complete with all the standard text formatting tools, including font, size, style, color, alignment, and paragraph controls.

Adjusting any of the formatting tools applies the change to all the text in the cell.

Double-clicking in the text to show the text cursor also displays the Cell Properties panel with its Text tab. Now, however, you can select text and apply the formatting to just the selected text.

Select Parts of a Table

Before you can adjust the formatting and size of parts of a table (like a row or a column), you need to know how to select just that part.

- **Select entire table**   Click anywhere inside the table boundaries to select the entire table. A selected table displays a blue border around it, complete with sizing handles you can click and drag to resize the table. Clicking and dragging inside the table enables you to change its location on the page. Once the table is selected, the rest of the selection options in this section will be functional.

- **Select one or more cells** To select a single cell, click in the cell. You can click and drag across cells to select multiple cells, including an entire row or column. You can also click in a cell, and then use the SHIFT-arrow keys to select cells. Finally, you can select all the cells in the table by choosing Object | Table | Select All Cells.
- **Select a row** To select an entire row, move the mouse pointer over the left border of the table until it turns into a right-facing arrow. Click to select that row. Once the mouse turns into the arrow, you can click and drag the mouse up or down to select additional adjacent rows. You can also select a cell and choose Select Row from the cell shortcut menu.
- **Select a column** To select an entire column, move the mouse pointer over the top border of the table until it turns into a down-facing arrow. Click to select that column. Once the mouse turns into the arrow, you can click and drag left or right to select adjacent columns. You can also select a cell and choose Select Column from the cell shortcut menu.

Work with Rows and Columns

Although a table is made up of cells, you'll often want to work with larger chunks of the table to adjust the number of columns and rows, as well as adjust the size of the group of cells that together form a row or column.

Add Rows and Columns

To add a row, select the row adjacent to (either above or below) the row you want to add. In the Table Row Properties panel, select the Row tab (the farthest to the right). Then choose either the Insert Row Above button or the Insert Row Below button in the Adjust section (see Figure 6-3). You can also select these commands from the row shortcut menu or the Object | Table menu.

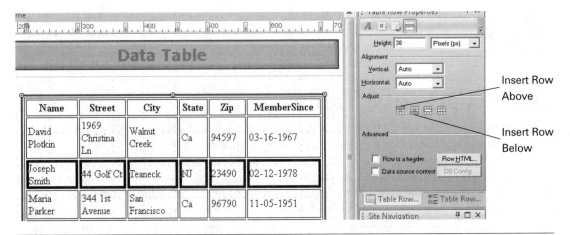

FIGURE 6-3 Configure rows and add them with the Row Properties panel.

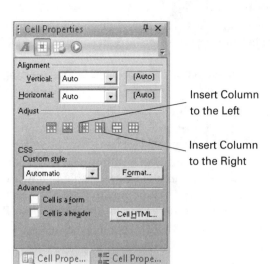

FIGURE 6-4   Add rows and columns with the Cell Properties panel.

 If you select multiple rows before inserting rows, the number of rows inserted is equal to the number of rows selected. For example, if you select three rows, three rows will be inserted above the top-most selected row or below the bottom-most selected row.

Another technique for inserting rows is to select at least one cell. This causes the Cell Properties panel to appear. Click the Cell tab to display the same two controls (Insert Row Above and Insert Row Below), as well as additional controls to Insert a Column to the Left and Insert a Column to the Right (see Figure 6-4). These controls are also available from the cell shortcut menu or the Object | Table menu.

You can select an entire column to display the Table Column Properties panel and then click the Column tab (see Figure 6-5). From there, you can click the Insert Column

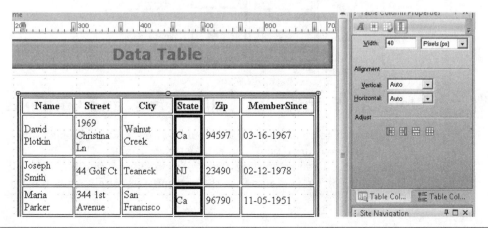

FIGURE 6-5   Add columns and adjust properties with the Column Properties panel.

To The Left or Insert Column To The Right button. As with the row commands, these options are available from the column shortcut menu or the Object | Table menu.

As with rows, if you select multiple columns before inserting, multiple columns will be inserted.

Delete Rows and Columns

If you change your mind about a row or column, you can delete it. To do so, select the rows you want to get rid of and choose Delete Table Row from the shortcut menu or Delete Row from the Object | Table menu. To discard columns, select the columns and choose Delete Column from the shortcut menu or Delete Table Column from the Object | Table menu.

Size Rows and Columns

The default row and column sizes may well not fit your needs, but you can easily change them. The easiest way is to select the row or column and click and drag the row or column border.

Name	Street	City
David Plotkin	1969 Christina Ln	Walnut Creek
Joseph Smith	44 Golf Ct	Teaneck
Maria Parker	344 1st Avenue	San Francisco
Jacob Parker	344 1st Avenue	San Francisco
Mark Manning	4545 Guidotti Ct	Salinas

Did You Know?

You Can Empty Out Cells, Rows, and Columns

If you just want to empty the contents out of a cell, row, or column, simply select the cell, row, or column, and choose Object | Table | Clear Table Cells. Alternatively, you can select Clear Cell Contents, Clear Table Row Contents, or Clear Table Column Contents from the appropriate shortcut menu (Cell, Row, or Column).

When you adjust the column width or row height, it also changes the column width or row height of the adjacent column or row. For example, if you increase the width of a column by dragging the left border to the left, the column on the left has its width decreased by an equal amount. If you decrease the column width by dragging the left border to the right, the column on the left has its width increased by an equal amount.

An alternate way to adjust the column width is to select the column, choose the Column tab in the Table Column Properties panel, and adjust the Width field.

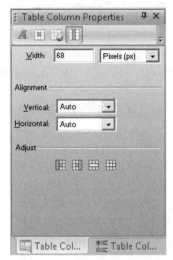

The same technique works for row height, using the Height field after choosing the Row tab in the Table Row Properties panel. You can adjust the width or height units by using pixels, percentage (of the overall table width or height), or Auto.

Designate a Header Row

As discussed earlier in this chapter (and shown in Figure 6-2, previously), a "header row" is a row of cells that describes the data in the column. To designate a header row, choose the row and select the Row Is A Header check box in the Table Row Properties panel under the Row tab.

There are a couple of things to keep in mind when designating header rows. First of all, you can designate more than one row as a header row, though I can't think of a good reason to do that. In fact, if you *do* designate multiple rows, you get some odd behavior when you sort and exclude the header rows. Basically, all the rows between the two row headers (and between the last row header and the bottom of the table) are sorted independently of each other.

You can also click a single cell and designate it as a header cell by selecting the Cell Is A Header check box under the Cell tab in the Cell Properties panel. If, however, you select cells in different rows, each row that contains a cell that has been designated as a header will behave like a header row during a sort. Again, pretty confusing and not particularly useful.

Set Row and Column Protection

You can protect specific aspects of the table from being changed. To specify these protections, use one of the following methods:

- Select a column and choose Table Column Protection from the shortcut menu.
- Select a row and choose Table Row Protection from the shortcut menu.
- Select a cell and choose Cell Protection from the shortcut menu.
- Select the table and choose Table Protection from the shortcut menu.

Regardless of which technique you choose, the dialog box you get is the same (except for the title)—and the protections apply to the entire table, *not* to the row, column, or cell selected.

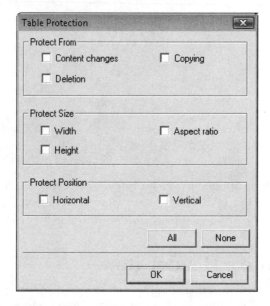

This bears repeating: no matter what dialog box you use (Table Protection, Cell Protection, Table Row Protection, or Table Column Protection), the protection applies to the entire table, not to the cell, row, or column. For example, if you choose the Deletion check box from the Row Protection dialog box, it stops you from deleting the table. You can delete the row, as confusing as that sounds.

Choose the protections you want by selecting the check boxes in the dialog box. The moment you add any protections, all of the property panels (Table Properties, Table Row Properties, Table Column Properties, and Cell Properties) show a lock icon at the left end of the tabs. In addition, the table itself displays a lock icon in the upper-left corner.

Name	Street	City	State	Zip	MemberSince
David Plotkin	1969 Christina Ln	Walnut Creek	Ca	94597	03-16-1967
Joseph Smith	44 Golf Ct	Teaneck	NJ	23490	02-12-1978
Maria Parker	344 1st Avenue	San Francisco	Ca	96790	11-05-1951
Jacob Parker	344 1st Avenue	San Francisco	Ca	96790	12-12-1991
Mark Manning	4545 Guidotti Ct	Salinas	Ca	93908	08-04-1988
Norman Smith	2020 Twin Oaks Dr	Monterey	Ca	93940	09-08-1994
Marta Ivanson	309 Buck St	Santa Barbara	Ca	91209	04-01-2004

Each section of the dialog box sets a different type of protection. The Protect From section includes the following options:

- **Content changes**   Locks the contents of the cells so that you can't adjust them. In addition, this locks the background color and image, disables adjustment of row height and column width, stops you from adding or removing rows and columns, and disables all text formatting controls. In fact, after applying this protection, you can't even select a row or column. About all you *can* do is to adjust the overall dimensions of the table and move it around on the page. If you try to select a cell by double-clicking it, you'll get a warning flag.

Name	Street	City	State	Zip	MemberSince
David Plotkin	1969 Christina Ln	Walnut Creek	Ca	94597	03-16-1967
Jo Sl	The current protection options do not allow the execution of this command.				
Maria	344 1st	San			

- **Deletion**   Prevents deleting the table.
- **Copying**   Prevents copying the table. You *can* select and copy the contents of a cell, even if you choose this command from the Cell Protection dialog box.

The Protect Size section includes the following options:

- **Width**   Stops you from changing the width of the table. If you move the mouse over the sizing handles in the right or left side of the table, a lock icon shows and you can't click and drag the table borders.
- **Height**   Stops you from changing the height of the table. If you move the mouse over the sizing handles in the top or bottom of the table, a lock icon shows and you can't click and drag the table borders.
- **Aspect ratio**   Stops you from changing the ratio of the width to the height of the table. Clicking and dragging one of the table borders adjusts both the width and height to maintain the aspect ratio.

The Protect Position section has two options, Horizontal and Vertical. Selecting the Horizontal option prevents you from dragging the table left or right, while selecting the Vertical option prevents you from dragging the table up or down.

 To select all the protection options at once, click All. To deselect all the options, click None.

Work with Cells

As we've already seen, you can configure a table's contents by adjusting the rows and columns—including adjusting the width and height and inserting new columns and rows. You can also change how a table handles its data by adjusting individual cells, including splitting cells and combining them together (merging). You can also configure the cells to size automatically to the cell contents.

Split and Merge Cells

If you only need a table with a regular arrangement of cells in rows and columns, you won't need to worry about splitting and merging cells. However, if you need more flexibility in your table design, you have that option as well. For example, here is a table that has more cells in the first row than in any other row. It also has an area with one very large cell—perhaps a good place to put an image.

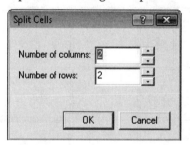

To split cells, select all the cells you want to split and choose Split Cells from the cell shortcut menu or the Object | Table menu. Alternatively, you can click the Split Cells button (far right icon in the Adjust section) in the Cell Properties panel under the Cell tab. In all cases, the Split Cells dialog box opens.

Set the number of columns and rows you want to split the selected cells into and click OK to execute the split.

Tip If you converted a Layout Region into a table (which may result in a one-cell table), this is an easy way to split the table into more cells.

To merge cells together, select the cells you want to merge. Note that you can only select a rectangular group of cells, as shown here.

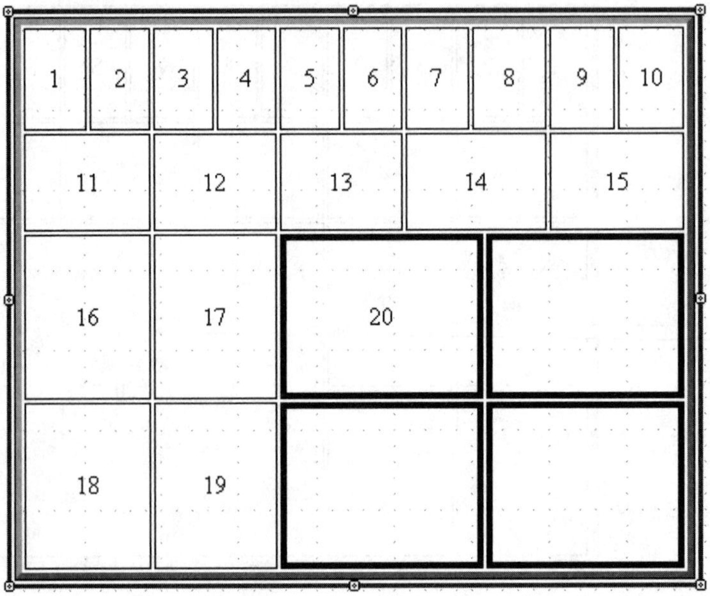

Choose Merge Cells from the cell shortcut menu or the Object | Table menu, or click the Merge Cells button (second icon from the right in the Adjust section) in the Cell Properties panel under the Cell tab. The cells are merged into a single cell.

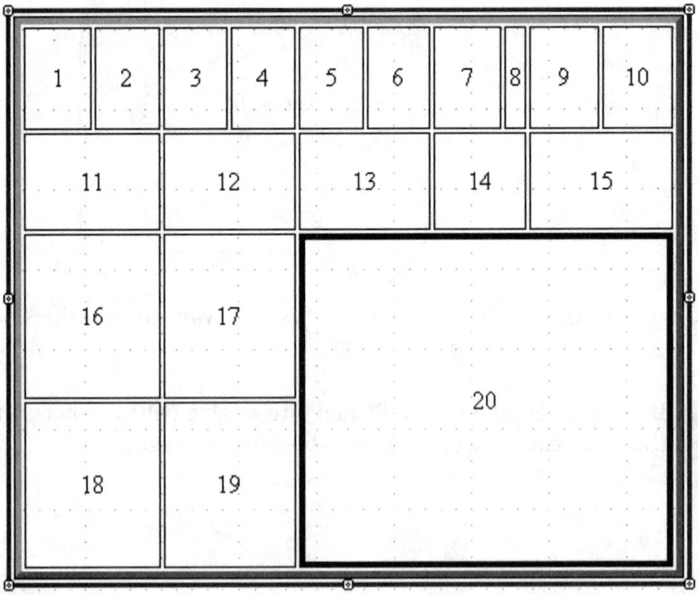

Fit Cell Size to the Contents

As you adjust the width of cells (which adjusts the width of all the cells in that column), you may find that you have cells that are overly wide. To shrink cell widths, select the cells and choose Fit Cells from the shortcut menu or the Object | Table menu. Here is what happens when you choose Fit Cells:

- **If you select a single cell or multiple cells in a given row**   The cell widths shrink to fit the contents of the selected cells. This will cause other cells in the same column to shrink to the same width—potentially making them very tall in order to fit the cell contents.
- **If you select multiple cells in a single column**   The width of the column is decreased to the size allowed by the cell with the widest content.

Format the Table

You can adjust the properties of a table over and over, tweaking them until the table looks just the way you want—and displays the content effectively. The Table Properties panel provides a lot of power to make these changes.

Set the Basic Table Properties

The Table tab in the Table Properties panel provides the ability to adjust the overall Width and Height of the table (in the units selected from the adjacent drop-down list), set the number of Rows and Columns, as well as set the Cell Pad (distance in pixels from the content to the cell border) and Cell Space (space in pixels between cells in the table).

Setting the border width is especially handy. The Border field sets the border of the entire table, shrinking the cells as needed to make room. You can also pick the border color by clicking on the pencil button and picking the color from the ColorPicker. Here is a table with a wide border.

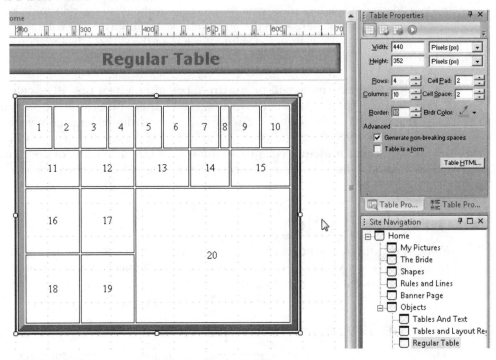

 Did you notice the two-tone border? This is a feature of the SiteStyle. Be careful though—if you change that color, you'll lose the two-tone effect, even if you switch the color back to Automatic.

The Advanced section offers two additional options:

- **Generate non-breaking spaces**   Generates an HTML "non-breaking space" in empty table cells. Without this option, rows that don't contain any content will collapse to zero height.
- **Table is a form**   Designates the table as a form so that you can collect data using fields embedded in the cells (see Chapter 13 for more information on forms).

Set the Background Color and Image

To set the background color and image, switch to the Background tab in the Table Properties panel. This panel should look very familiar—the controls for setting the background color and image works exactly the same for tables as they do for Layouts and Layout Regions. Even the Cell Properties, Table Row Properties, and Table Column Properties panels have this same tab to configure the background color and image for a cell, row, or column. The results are a little different for tables (and rows, columns, and cells) than they are for Layouts, however. Unlike with Layouts, you aren't given the chance to resize the image before using it. The image is added to the background full-size, and you'll only see as much of the image as fits in the table (or row, column, or cell). Further, if the table style or cell uses a background color, the image will not be visible except in the tiny spaces between the cells, if you do not click the Clear button displayed on the Table Style tab in the Table Properties panel.

 So how do you get around these limitations if you want to display an image as a background for a table or a cell? The trick is to size the table or cell and note the dimensions in pixels. Then use an imaging program (such as Photoshop Elements, Picasa, or PaintShop Pro Photo) to resize the image to the dimensions of the table or cell.

There is one more tab in the Table Properties panel that enables you to set the table style—the Table Style tab.

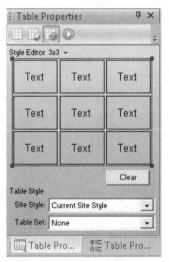

You can select a Site Style (see Chapter 8) and a table style (from the Table Set drop-down list) from the selected SiteStyle.

With the Style Editor, you can specify various portions of the table and specify the color (or mixture of colors) for that section. The instructions for configuring the Style Editor are discussed in Chapter 8, because it actually makes more sense to go through the work (and it *is* a lot of work) when customizing SiteStyles. If the new table style is added to the SiteStyle, it is reusable for any page or site that uses the SiteStyle by simply picking the style from the Site Style drop-down list in the Table Style tab.

Format a Cell

In addition to setting the background color and image of a cell, you can set quantities that affect how the contents of the cell are displayed. These properties include the content alignment and the text properties.

Set the Content Alignment

To set the alignment of the cell contents, switch to the Cell tab of the Cell Properties panel.

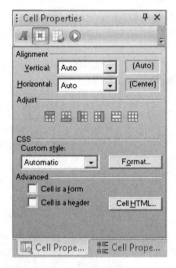

Select the vertical alignment from the Vertical drop-down list. The options (in addition to Auto) include Top, Middle, and Bottom. One thing to keep in mind is that the alignment applies to the entire contents of the cell, including blank lines (inserted by pressing ENTER). Thus, if you change the alignment value and the contents don't move, look for blank lines that cause the contents to fill the cell—so that the contents can't move to adjust the alignment.

Select the horizontal alignment from the Horizontal drop-down list. The options (in addition to Auto) include Left, Center, Right, and Justify (makes all the lines of text in the cell the same length except for the last line).

Format the Text Contents

As with text boxes (which are actually tables with cells), you can format the text in a cell. Either select a cell (to format all the text in the cell) or double-click in the cell and select the text you want to format. Make sure the Format tab is selected in the

Cell Properties panel, and set the text formatting as discussed previously for text boxes (Chapter 4).

Export a Table

If you've gone to the trouble of filling out a table of data, you can export the table as a data file (which you could import into another site as described earlier in this chapter). To export the table, select the table and choose Export Table from the shortcut menu or the Object | Table menu. This opens the Export Table dialog box.

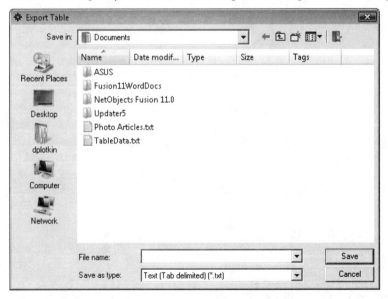

Fill the filename into the File Name field and choose the type of file (tab delimited or comma delimited) you want to use for the export. Click Save to create the exported file.

7

Work with Objects

HOW TO...

- Align objects
- Arrange the stacking order of objects
- Group objects
- Size the Layout and MasterBorder to fit the objects they contain

You've already seen many of the types of objects you can place on a page—text boxes, tables, shapes, Layout Regions, and images. Farther along in this book you'll see many more objects, including some sophisticated components. This chapter discusses the tools that enable you to arrange objects on a page and bring some semblance of order from the chaos that can result as you add items.

Align Objects with Each Other

If you enjoy items neatly lined up with each other on the page, you can align selected objects with each other. The first step is to select all the objects to include when performing the alignment. To select multiple objects, click the first object, hold down the SHIFT key, and continue clicking other objects.

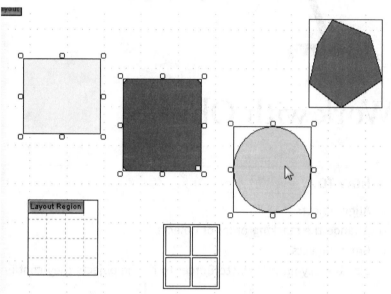

 Tip   You can also click and drag a rectangle on the page. Any object that falls at least partially inside the rectangle will be selected. If, on the other hand, you decide you want to exclude an object you've selected, simply click it again (with the shift key still held down) to deselect it.

To align the objects, make a selection from the Object | Align Objects menu. The various options (see Figure 7-1 for examples) are

- **Left**   Aligns the left edges of the objects to the left edge of the left-most object.
- **Right**   Aligns the right edges of the objects to the right edge of the right-most object.
- **Top**   Aligns the top edges of the objects to the top edge of the top-most object
- **Bottom**   Aligns the bottom edges of the objects to the bottom edge of the bottom-most object.
- **Vertical Center**   Aligns the vertical (up/down) center line of all the selected objects.
- **Horizontal Center**   Aligns the horizontal (left/right) center line of all the selected objects.

 Note   If the alignment causes objects to overlap, you'll see a red exclamation mark to warn you about that. You can leave them that way if you want; in fact, if you intend to stack objects for effect (discussed later in this chapter), you'll need to overlap them (otherwise, you won't actually see the effects of the stacking). However, if you have overlapped objects, you need to select the Fixed page layout as the HTML output in the Layout Properties panel.

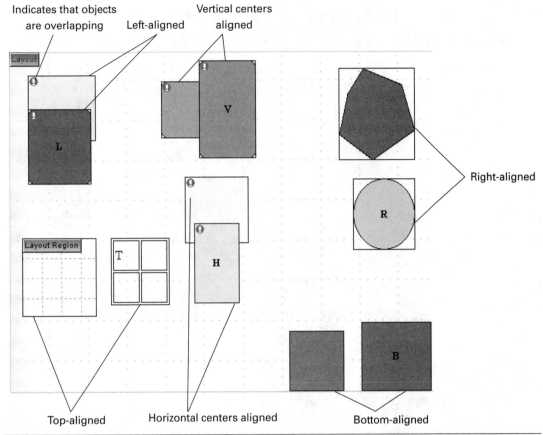

FIGURE 7-1   Aligning objects enables you to line up the selected edges or centers.

Distribute Objects Across the Page

Another way to bring order from chaos is to evenly distribute your objects across a web page. To do so, select the objects and make a selection from the Object | Distribute Objects menu. You have only two options (see Figure 7-2):

- **Vertically**   Distributes the objects across the page from top to bottom. The uppermost and lowermost objects remain in place, and the other objects are distributed vertically between them, maintaining the same vertical order they were in originally. That is, if object A was higher than object B prior to the distribution, it will still be higher.
- **Horizontally**   Distributes the objects across the page from left to right. The leftmost and rightmost objects remain in place, and the other objects are distributed horizontally between them, maintaining the same horizontal order they were in originally.

Align and Distribute Objects with the Multi-Object Properties Panel

In addition to the menu options discussed previously, you can align and distribute objects using the Multi-Object Properties panel. This panel appears whenever you select more than one object. Click the Position tab to display the buttons you'll need.

Normally, the Position tab is the only one visible in the Multi-Object Properties panel. However, if all the selected objects are of the same type (such as all pictures, or all shapes), you'll also get the other controls you'd expect for that type of object. For example, here is what the Multi-Object Properties panel looks like if all the selected objects are images.

The Position tab is still there, but now it is all the way at the right end of the panel toolbar. As you have probably guessed by the fact that all the standard tabs (with their controls) are present in the panel, you can adjust the properties of all the selected objects at once. For example, you can click the Adjustment tab and bump up the brightness for all the selected images at once.

The buttons work just like the menu options discussed previously—but now there is a new option: the Relative To Layout check box. Selecting this check box performs all the actions relative to the Layout. For example, if you choose to align the objects Left (click the Left button in the Horizontally section), all the objects will align to the left edge of the Layout.

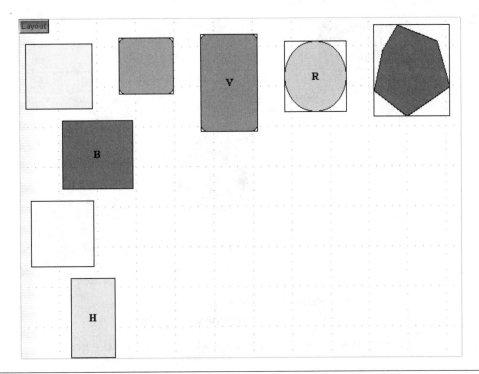

FIGURE 7-2   Objects distributed evenly vertically (on the left side) and horizontally (across the top).

Set the Stacking Order of Objects

You can overlap objects on a page to achieve some interesting effects (see Figure 7-3). All objects have a stacking order—although you can't see the order if the objects don't overlap. Each time you create a new object, it receives an assigned stacking order that is higher than the object created before it. That is, the new object is one layer higher (closer to the front) than the object created before it. Thus, if you add an image to a page and then add another image, the second image (which is on a higher layer) will appear on top of the first image if you overlap them.

If you don't like the stacking order, you can change it by selecting an object and making a selection from the Object | Arrange Objects menu. The options available are

- **Bring Forward**   Brings the object one level up (higher). Thus, if the object was on layer 5, it is moved to layer 6, and the object that formerly was on layer 6 changes to layer 5. Note that you may not see the change between overlapping objects if they are more than one layer apart. For example, if the objects on layer 5 and layer 10 overlap, bringing the object on layer 5 forward (so that it is now on layer 6) does not cause it to be on top of the object on layer 10.
- **Bring to Front**   Brings the object to the "front," or top layer. It will overlap any other object on the page.

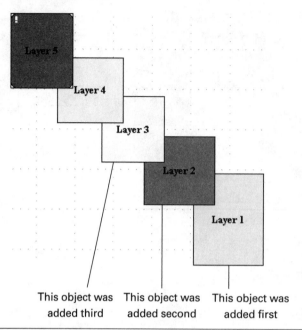

FIGURE 7-3   The initial stacking order depends on when you added the item.

- **Send Backwards**   Sends the object one level down (lower). Thus, if the object was on layer 6, it is moved to layer 5. The object that formerly was on layer 5 changes to layer 6.
- **Send to Back**   Sends the object to the back, or bottom layer. It will be overlapped by any other objects on the page.

Group and Size Objects

If you have a lot of objects, it can be a tedious process to move them around on the page, especially if you want to keep the same distance and layout relative to each other. You can select multiple objects and click and drag them at once, but you have to reselect them all each time you want to do that.

To make things a little easier, you can group objects to create a group that can be manipulated together. To do that, select all the objects you want to have as part of the group. Then choose Group from either the Object | Group Objects menu or the shortcut menu. Once you do this, clicking any of the objects in the group selects them all.

You can also see the group (with its component parts nested beneath it) in the Object Tree panel.

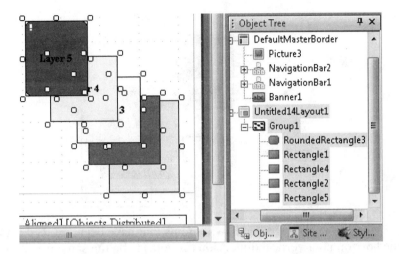

Once you've created the group, you can move it around the screen. Simply click any of the objects in the group and drag to a new location. A transparent version of the group shows you where the group will be when you release the mouse button.

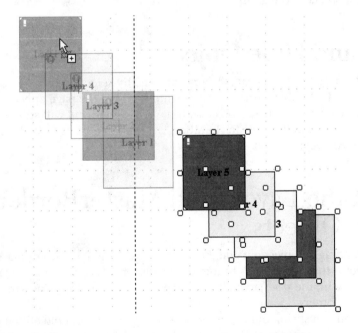

Interestingly, if you click (to select the group) and then click an individual object in the group, you can drag the object to a new location.

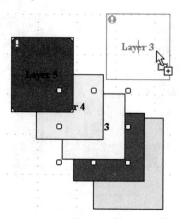

Another trick you can pull with items that have been grouped is to set either the horizontal or vertical dimension (or both) to be the same for all the items in the group. Simply click the group and select Object | Size Objects | Width or Object | Size Objects | Height. If you choose the Width, all the objects take on the width of the widest item in the group. If you choose Height, all the items take on the height of the tallest object in the group.

Show and Hide Objects

You can make objects vanish from the page by selecting the objects and choosing Object | Hide Object (CTRL-H). This simply makes the page appear less "busy" while you are designing it. The objects aren't really gone and will still be visible if you preview or publish the site. To return the hidden objects to visibility, select Object | Show All Objects (CTRL-SHIFT-A).

Adjust the Layout and MasterBorder Size to Objects

If you drag an object outside the boundaries of the Layout—or place an object (like a photo) that is too big to fit into the Layout, the Layout automatically expands (along with the page) to be big enough to hold the object. The same is true for the MasterBorder.

You can shrink the Layout to be just big enough to hold all the objects it contains. To do so, simply select Object | Size Layout To Objects (CTRL-SHIFT-L). Here is how the Layout looked before resizing.

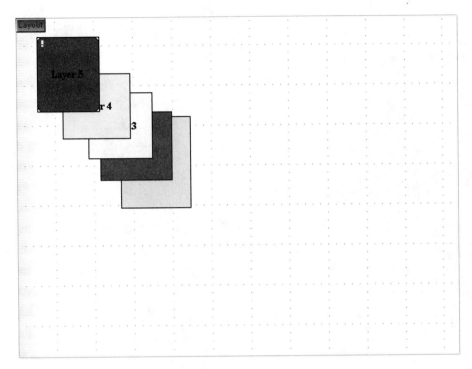

And here is how it looked after being sized to hold the objects.

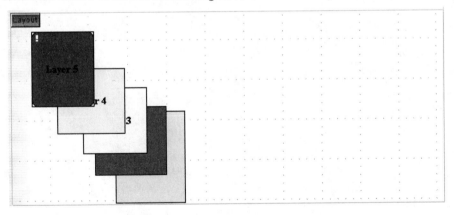

You can also resize the MasterBorder to be just big enough to hold the objects it contains by selecting Object | Size MasterBorder to Objects (CTRL-SHIFT-M).

PART II

Customize the Look and Navigation

8

Establish Look and Feel with SiteStyles

HOW TO...

- Change the style of a web site
- Customize banners and buttons in a site style
- Customize table styles in a site style
- Change the page background for a site style
- Configure text styles for a site style

One of the problems with early web sites (and even some web sites today) is that they lack a common look and feel from one page to another. Color schemes, buttons, table styles, and fonts vary, and the whole effect is jarring. And unprofessional. To help you build more of a professional-looking site, Fusion provides "SiteStyles."

Understand SiteStyles

A SiteStyle is a matched set of colors, fonts, buttons, banners, bullets, Flash elements, and other objects and settings that all work together to provide a common and consistent look and feel for the web site. Each SiteStyle also includes a set of text styles, such as the font and size for the body of the page, and various combinations of text attributes for the different headings. You can preview a SiteStyle in Style view by clicking the Style button in the Views bar (see Figure 8-1). Fusion comes packaged with a large number of SiteStyles. However, if none of the included ones suit your taste, you can build your own SiteStyle or purchase additional SiteStyles online.

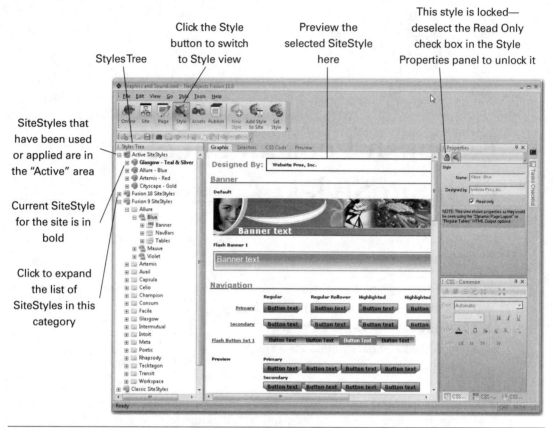

FIGURE 8-1 View the objects and colors in Style view.

View Available SiteStyles

In addition to the graphic elements (seen in the Graphic tab, shown in Figure 8-1), the Table and Text styles are also parts of the Graphic tab (see Figure 8-2). The Selectors tab shows all of the different components used by a SiteStyle for such things as e-mail, tables, and form handling controls. To look at the controls associated with the SiteStyle, pick the control you want to see from the Other Selectors list on the left side of the screen, and then view the results on the right side of the screen (see Figure 8-3).

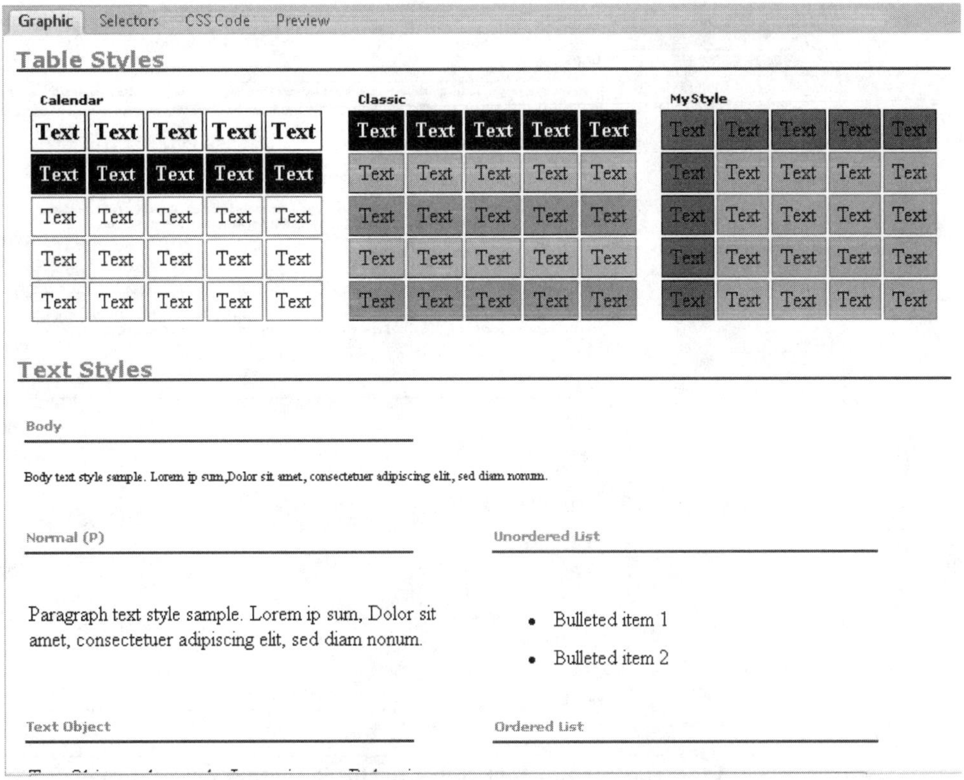

FIGURE 8-2   View the text styles and component controls in the Graphic tab of the Style view.

You can also get a quick sample of what a page might look like on your web site by clicking the Preview tab (see Figure 8-4). However, this preview is somewhat limited in that it uses only the Default banner, the Primary navigation buttons, and so on. There is no way to specify that you'd like to use (say) the Flash version of the banner (called Flash Banner 1 in most SiteStyles) when viewing in the Preview tab.

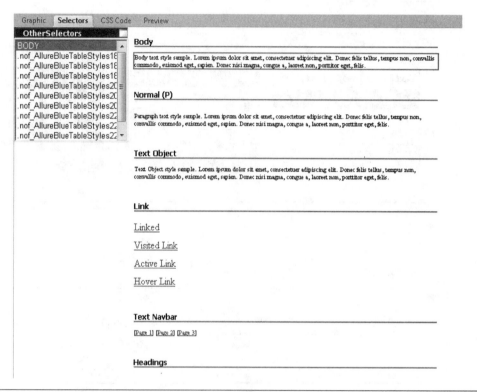

FIGURE 8-3 View the various text styles in the Selectors tab.

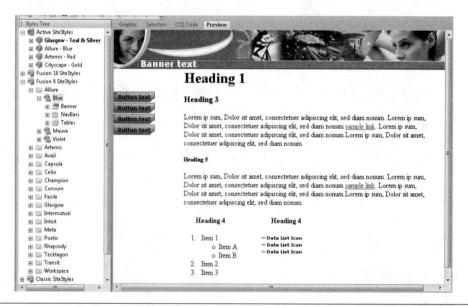

FIGURE 8-4 The Preview tab shows a simple rendering of your page with the default elements in a SiteStyle.

Change the Style of a Site

When you first create a site, it has a default SiteStyle. To change to a different SiteStyle, switch to the Site view (seen previously in Figure 8-1). At this point, the default SiteStyle is the only one listed in the Active SiteStyles section of the Styles tree on the left side of the screen.

 You can expand the subitems of a SiteStyle (such as Banner, NavBars, and Tables) to see a list of the types of banners, NavBars, and tables included with that SiteStyle. This gives you a quick way to check for a particular type of element, such as a Flash banner or a Calendar table style.

To pick another SiteStyle, expand one of the categories (such as Classic SiteStyles) to show the list of included SiteStyles in the Styles Tree. If you see the SiteStyle icon, you can click the icon to display the contents of the SiteStyle in the tabbed section (Graphic, Selectors, etc.). If, instead, you see a folder (as in the Fusion 9 SiteStyles), you'll need to click the folder to expand it further and see the SiteStyles.

 You can click a category (such as Fusion 10 SiteStyles) and get a list of SiteStyles (or folders) on the right side of the Style view, replacing the tabbed previews. To expand a folder, double-click it to show the SiteStyle contents. To preview a SiteStyle, double-click it. However, this is more work than just using the Styles Tree, so I never bother with this technique unless I want to quickly scan through a big list of SiteStyles.

Once you've decided which SiteStyle you'd like to use for your web site, select it and choose Set SiteStyle from either the shortcut menu or the Style menu. This copies the selected SiteStyle into the Active SiteStyles section at the top of the Styles Tree and converts your entire web site to use the new SiteStyle.

 You can also just double-click the SiteStyle to make it the SiteStyle for your site.

 Specifying the SiteStyle for Your Site Should Be Done First

Specifying the SiteStyle for your site is really the very first thing you should do—before adding lots of pages and designing your content. This is because changing SiteStyles later can wreak havoc on your pages and cause you to have to make lots of little corrections. For example, one SiteStyle might use a default Navigation Bar that is located in the left margin of the MasterBorder and is oriented vertically (the buttons are stacked in a column). A different SiteStyle, however, might use a horizontal Navigation Bar, which could cause the MasterBorder to expand, trashing your layout. If you switch, you might have to change the Navigation Bar orientation, reposition it in the MasterBorder, adjust the MasterBorder width, and resize the page (guess how I know all this?).

Make the SiteStyles Easily Available

SiteStyles can be buried in long lists. If you want to make one easily available so that you can pick it for your web site, choose the SiteStyle and select Add To Active SiteStyles from the shortcut or Style menu. This copies the SiteStyle you selected into the Active SiteStyles section at the top of the Styles Tree. The name of the SiteStyle is selected so that you can rename it if you wish. When you are done typing in the new name (or leaving it alone), just press ENTER.

You probably noticed that when you choose to use a SiteStyle for your web site (as described in the previous section "Change the Style of a Site"), the selected SiteStyle is added to the Active SiteStyles in addition to being made the SiteStyle for the site. This points out something that is very important: in order to customize an object (such as a table, page banner, or button set) by choosing its style from the SiteStyle drop-down list that appears in many properties panels, the SiteStyle must be in the Active SiteStyles section of the Styles Tree. You can use the techniques discussed here to move all the SiteStyles you want to use into the Active SiteStyles portion.

One thing to keep in mind is that all the files necessary to support the use of a SiteStyle are published to your web site. Thus, if you move a bunch of SiteStyles to the Active SiteStyles area, those files will be published whether you use them or not. This takes up more space on the web server and causes your publishing operation to take longer. Thus, you may wish to select Style | Remove Unused Active Styles to remove any SiteStyle you didn't use in your site from the Active SiteStyles section of the Styles Tree—and thus not publish those files.

You can also remove a SiteStyle from the Active SiteStyles section by selecting Delete SiteStyle from either the shortcut menu or the Style menu. For Fusion-provided SiteStyles that exist elsewhere in the Styles tree, this doesn't actually delete the SiteStyle; it just removes it from the Active SiteStyle section of the Styles Tree. Note that you can't remove the default SiteStyle for the web site (the one whose name is shown in bold print) without first making another Active SiteStyle the default for the site by picking Set SiteStyle from the shortcut menu for that SiteStyle.

For SiteStyles you create yourself (either starting with a blank SiteStyle or from a copy), deleting the SiteStyle actually does delete it from Fusion because it doesn't exist elsewhere in the Styles Tree. If you don't need one of these SiteStyles in the Active SiteStyle section but don't want to discard it, click and drag it to one of the categories in the Styles Tree (such as Fusion 10 SiteStyles). This copies it to that category, so you can now delete it from the Active SiteStyles and still have a backup copy. You can also add a new SiteStyle folder (from the context menu) and drag your custom SiteStyle to the new folder.

Customize a SiteStyle

If none of the existing SiteStyles quite meet your needs, you can design your own. There are a couple of things to keep in mind, however. First of all, building a SiteStyle "from scratch" is a *lot* of work. The "blank" SiteStyle isn't completely blank—you do get defaults for all the objects (banners, buttons, table styles, text styles, and so on)—but they are pretty non-descript, so you'll end up customizing everything. What is more important, however, is that unless you are a professional designer, the results may not be especially aesthetic. So exercise care when doing your customizations.

Start with a Blank SiteStyle

If you really want to start with a "blank" SiteStyle, either choose Style | New Blank SiteStyle or right-click an existing active SiteStyle or the Active SiteStyles heading (in the Styles Tree) and choose New Blank SiteStyle from the shortcut menu. This displays a new, blank line in the Active SiteStyles section of the Styles Tree. Fill in the name and press ENTER to create the SiteStyle with its default objects.

 This menu option is *not* available from the other categories, such as Fusion 10 SiteStyles. Instead, you can add a new folder to these categories by right-clicking them and choosing New Site Styles Folder from the shortcut menu or from the Style menu.

Create a Copy as a Starting Point

The best way to customize a SiteStyle is to start by duplicating an existing one. You *can* actually change one of SiteStyles provided with Fusion by simply de-selecting the Read Only check box in the Style Properties panel, but I don't recommend it, as you will never have access to the unmodified version if you do it that way. Note also that you can't change the name of the SiteStyle even if you make the SiteStyle editable.

To create a copy of an existing SiteStyle, select the SiteStyle and choose Duplicate SiteStyle from either the shortcut menu or the Style menu. The SiteStyle is copied and the name becomes editable. Type in the new name and press ENTER to create the duplicate SiteStyle in the same category (including Active SiteStyles) the original was in.

Work with Banners

Banners are blocks of text or graphics that you'll often see located at the top of a page (in the MasterBorder), though you can actually put them anywhere. There are three types of banners: text, image, and Flash. To create any of these banners, right-click in the Graphic tab in Style view and choose the type of banner you want to create from the shortcut menu.

Create and Customize a Text Banner

A text banner is just what you think—a text block that, since it is defined as a banner, you can pick from the Banner Set drop-down list in the Banner Properties panel. To create a new text banner, choose New Banner (text) from the shortcut menu. This creates the new banner with a default name and text properties.

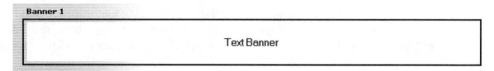

The new banner has two tabs in the Banner Properties panel. The first is Configure, which enables you to pick the font, size, background color (Bg color), font color (Color), and Horizontal and Vertical alignments.

The second tab (Properties) enables you to change the name of the banner by typing it into the Name field. You can also do the following:

- **Duplicate the banner** After you have gotten the text banner just right, you can duplicate it by clicking Duplicate. This creates a copy of the banner with the default name, which you can then customize further. Note that you can also simply right-click the banner in the preview and choose Duplicate from the shortcut menu.
- **Delete the banner** To delete the banner, click Delete. Note that you can also right-click the banner in the preview and choose Delete from the shortcut menu.
- **Create a new banner** To create a new banner, choose the type (Text, Image, or Flash) from the Type drop-down list and click Add Banner. This duplicates the functionality in the Graphic tab shortcut menu, discussed earlier.

Create and Customize an Image Banner

A graphic banner is a banner that uses an image as a background and overlays text on that image. To create a new image banner, choose New Banner (image) from the shortcut menu. This creates the new banner with a default name and text properties.

The new banner has two tabs in the Banner Properties panel. The Properties tab is identical to the text banner, but the Configure tab is quite different.

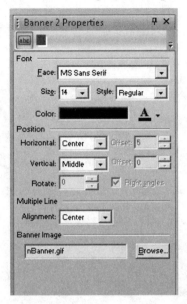

In addition to choosing the font (from the Face drop-down list), size, style, text color, and horizontal and vertical positions, you have the following options available:

- **Rotate**   You can rotate the text by specifying the angle (in degrees) in the Rotate field. If you select the Right angles check box, your choices are limited to 90, 180, –90, and –180 degrees.

Both 180 and –180 settings for Rotate simply flip the text over and reverse it. The 90 and –90 settings aren't very useful because only a few letters are visible in the horizontal banner box when the text runs vertically. When you place a banner on the page, all you can see are those few letters, and, in case you're wondering, changing the orientation of the banner to vertical doesn't help.

- **Multiple Line Alignment**   If the banner contains more than a single line of text, the Alignment drop-down list enables you to specify how the words on multiple lines align with each other.
- **Banner Image**   Click Browse to pick the image file that will serve as the background for the banner. This file not only sets the image, but the size of the banner as well. Since the background is completely specified by the chosen image, you'll notice that an image banner does not have a control for setting the background color.

How to... # Create or Edit a Banner Image

If you're not happy with the image used for the graphic banner, you can create your own. To do so, right-click the Banner and choose Edit Image from the shortcut menu. This opens the Paint accessory or the program you specified for editing GIF files in the Program tab of the Application Options dialog box (in this case, Adobe Photoshop Elements).

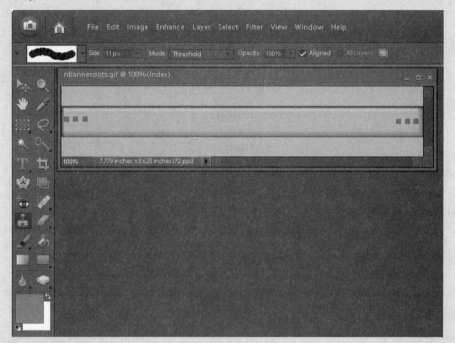

You can edit the existing image and save it or create a new image. Just save it to the same directory as the original banner image, and the next time you browse for a banner image, your new image will be available.

Create and Customize a Flash Banner

A Flash banner is a banner that uses Adobe (formerly Macromedia) Flash to provide animation. As with other Flash components, a page with a Flash banner may not display the banner until you allow it to run by clicking the yellow warning bar in Internet Explorer.

To create a new Flash banner, choose New Banner (Flash) from the shortcut menu. This creates a banner with the default name and properties.

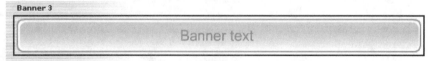

The new banner has two tabs in the Banner Properties panel. The first is the General tab, where you can change the name, duplicate or delete the banner, and create a new banner, much like on the Properties panel for text or image banners. You can also pick a different Flash file (which controls how the banner looks and what animation properties it has) by clicking the button alongside the File field (which has ... on it).

The second tab (Style) is where things get interesting—this is where you can configure the properties of the banner. Exactly what you can change depends on the .swf file, but for most banners in Fusion (which use the banner.swf file), you can change the background and fill colors, font, alignment, the Corner Type and Corner Radius (for the rectangle containing the text), border color and thickness, and the animation effect (Effect).

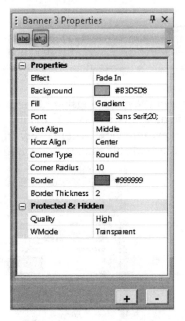

Here are some pointers when configuring the Flash banner:

- **Background and Border color**   Clicking in the boxes alongside these entries displays the ColorPicker so you can choose a color.
- **Font**   When you click in the box alongside Font, you get another dialog box that enables you to set font, size, style, and alignment. When you're done, just click OK. While the dialog box is open, a drop-down arrow appears alongside the Font

face in the Banner Properties panel, but it is only accessible if you click OK, and clicking it then simply reopens the Edit Font dialog box.

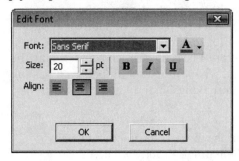

- **Corner Type and Corner Radius** You have three choices for Corner Type: Normal (square corners), Rounded, and Diagonal (triangular corners). Corner radius controls how large the corners are. At a value of zero, the corners are square; as you increase the value, the rounded or diagonal corners get larger and larger. For example, here is a set of rounded corners with a radius of 20.

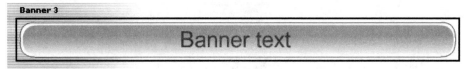

- **Effect** Clicking in the box alongside Effect provides a drop-down list that controls the type of animation used to display the text. For example, Fade In slowly fades the text into view, whereas Fly In moves the text in from the side. Here is a list of the available effects in the banner.swf file.

Find Images to Use When Building a SiteStyle

As you go about building or customizing your SiteStyles, you may decide you'd like to use different images than those included in the SiteStyle you made a copy of (or the Blank SiteStyle). For example, you might decide you'd rather use the image for a banner or the images for buttons included in another SiteStyle. The issue, of course, is finding those images so that you can use them.

The easiest way to accomplish this is to move any SiteStyle you want to purloin an image from into the list of Active SiteStyles. If you do that, Fusion copies the SiteStyle—and all its images—into the directory given by

C:\Documents and Settings*Username*\My Documents\NetObjectsFusion 11.0\User Sites*Site name*\Styles*Style name*\ (for Windows XP)

Or

C:\Users*Username*\Documents\NetObjectsFusion 11.0\User Sites*Site name*\Styles\ *Style name*\ (for Windows Vista)

The images are grouped into folders added to these paths. They are

- **Images**   Contains the images for the non-flash banner, bullets, lines, non-Flash Navigation Bars, buttons, and various other graphical items.
- **Flash**   These are not really images, but the .swf file that defines the banner and Navigation Bar Flash options *are* in this directory, assuming the SiteStyle contains Flash-based items (many do not).

Once you have this information, you can pick a different image by using the following steps:

1. Select the banner in the Graphical tab of the Site view, and click the Browse button in the Banner Image section of the Banner Properties panel.
2. In the Picture File Open dialog box, click the Up One Level button (the folder with the arrow on it) until the Look In field displays "Styles".
3. Double-click the SiteStyle name from which you want to grab the image file.
4. Double-click the folder containing the type of image you want—for example, the Images folder for the banner.
5. Choose the image and click Open.

Fusion displays the new image banner in the preview.

Work with Buttons

Buttons are very useful on a web page. You can click a button to submit information on a form, use buttons as part of a Navigation Bar (see Chapter 9), and add hyperlinks to a button to send you to another page or web site. Each SiteStyle contains at least a primary set and an alternate (secondary) set of buttons, and many contain a Flash button set as well.

Site View enables you to create three types of button "sets" from the shortcut menu: text, graphical, and Flash. A button "set" contains four buttons—one for each button state. They are

- **Regular**   This is what the button looks like as long as the mouse is not over the button, and the page that the button links to (or one of the child pages) is not currently being displayed.
- **Regular Rollover**   This is what the button looks like when you move the mouse over a Regular button. Typically, the button background or font/font color changes. Not all button sets respond to a rollover—if you make the Regular button and the Regular Rollover button the same, then the button doesn't change when the mouse rolls over it.
- **Highlighted**   This is what the button looks like if the page that the button links to (or one of the child pages) *is* being displayed.
- **Highlighted Rollover**   This is what the button looks like when you hover the mouse over a Highlighted button.

 Basically, there are two main types of buttons: Regular and Highlighted. The Regular buttons are displayed if the button's corresponding page (or a child of that page) is not currently being viewed. The Highlighted button is displayed if the button's corresponding page (or a child of that page) is being viewed.

Each set of buttons appears twice in the Site View preview (see Figure 8-5). The individual button sets appear in the top part of the Navigation section. Below the button sets is a second set, labeled "Preview". Move the mouse over these buttons to see how they respond. This is helpful when designing your button sets.

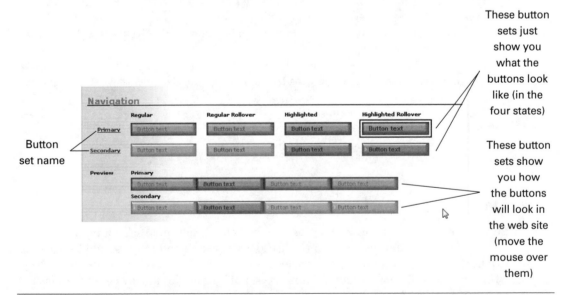

FIGURE 8-5   View the button sets in the Style view.

What is shown by the buttons in the Preview section is a bit confusing. The left-most button shows the Regular button. Move the mouse over it to see a preview of the Regular Rollover button. The second button from the left is a preview of the Highlighted button. Move the mouse over the second button to see a preview of the Highlighted Rollover button. The other two buttons simply duplicate the functionality of the left-most (Regular) button.

Under the Style View Preview tab, there's a sample structure where you can test the NavBar (Navigation Bar) appearance, and it shows you how the NavBar looks and behaves. The first button is the active button (the Highlighted button), the other three are Regular buttons. The second Regular button has two secondary Regular buttons, and one of those has a child page button, too.

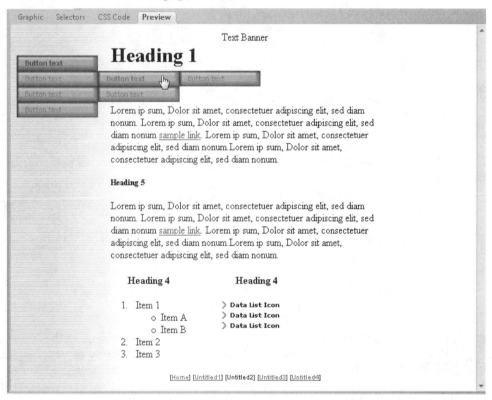

Set the Button Set Properties

You can set properties for the button *set* (as opposed to the buttons contained within the set). To do so, select the name of the button set (e.g., "Primary") located to the left of the button set. This action displays the NavBar Sample panel (prefaced by the name of the button set). If you're confused by this naming convention, remember that in Fusion, the SiteStyle buttons are primarily used for Navigation Bars (see Chapter 9).

For a set of text or graphical buttons, the Sample panel enables you to set the thickness of the Border (in pixels) around the entire button set, as well as the spacing between the buttons (the width of the border between the buttons). Here is an example of a text button set with a wide border and spacing.

In the Selected Button Set section of the panel, you can change the name of the button set by typing a new name into the Name field. You can also duplicate or delete the button set using the appropriate buttons, which you can also do by choosing Duplicate or Delete from the button set's shortcut menu. And as with the banners, you can create a new button set by choosing the type from the Type drop-down list and clicking the Add New Set button.

Note You can't delete either the Primary or Secondary button sets, as the Delete entry in the shortcut menu and the Delete button in the Property panel are unavailable. You can, however, delete the Flash Navbar button set that comes with many SiteStyles. You also can't rename the Primary or Secondary button sets, as the Name field in the Property panel is locked.

Add End Caps to a Button Set   For text and graphical button sets, you can choose to add End Caps and Section Titles by selecting these check boxes (these are not available for Flash button sets). End caps are graphical elements that can be added both above (End Cap 1) and below (End Cap 2) each Navigation Bar. End Caps can be merely decorative or can be linked to their adjoining navigation button. You make the specification for this behavior when you use End Caps in Navigation Bars (see Chapter 9) by making the appropriate selection in the Navigation Bar Property panel.

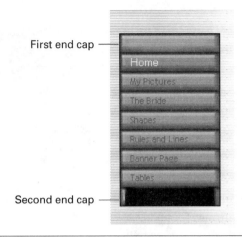

First end cap

Second end cap

FIGURE 8-6   End caps add a little more pizzazz to a Navigation Bar (if done right!).

You will actually have to add them to the Navigation Bar (as described in Chapter 9) in order to see what they look like (see Figure 8-6 for a sample), as the preview in the Style view does not show the end caps.

 If the End Caps look like they are part of the button, you should link them into the button so that clicking either the navigation button or the end cap executes the link and sends you to the destination page.

To add End Caps, use the following steps:

1. Select the button set name and select the End Caps check box in the Sample panel. This displays buttons to specify a pair of end caps for each of the four button states (regular, regular rollover, highlighted, and highlighted rollover).

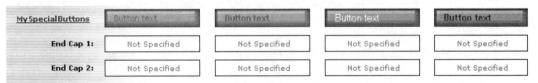

2. Select each End Cap button (which initially say "Not Specified") and click the Browse button in the Button Properties panel. You can also double-click the End Cap button.
3. Pick the image to use for the End Cap from the Picture File Open dialog box. Click Open to complete picking the file and display the image in the End Cap box (in place of "Not Specified").
4. Continue picking the images to use from the other End Cap buttons.

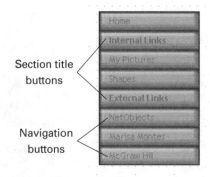

Section title buttons

Navigation buttons

FIGURE 8-7 Separate buttons in a custom Navigation Bar with "section title" buttons.

You can use a different picture file for each End Cap. However, if the End Cap images are very different (especially in size), the effect can be quite jarring when used, as the Navigation Bar may move around on the page to make room for the larger file. I build my own End Caps (using a graphical editing program) by starting from one of the button images. This technique ensures that the end caps are approximately the same size as the buttons in the Navigation Bar.

Add Section Titles to a Button Set A "Section Title" is a static button that can be placed between other buttons in a custom Navigation Bar (see Chapter 9 for details). They can be used to divide the Navigation Bar into sections. You can add text to the section buttons so that they can serve as "headings" for groups of buttons in the Navigation Bar (see Figure 8-7).

As discussed in Chapter 9, Navigation Bars come in two types. The first is based on the structure of the web site (Site) and the buttons are provided automatically by Fusion. The second type is called "Custom"—you specify which buttons you want, the button text, and where the buttons link to. You can use Section Titles only for the second (Custom) type.

To add Section Titles, click the Section Titles check box in the Sample panel. This action adds two buttons to the Button Set: a Regular button and a Regular Rollover button. These buttons look initially like the buttons in the Button Set, but you can customize them just like any other button by clicking them and making changes in the Properties panel.

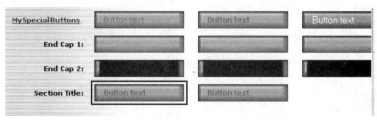

Create and Customize a Set of Text Buttons

Text buttons are just what you think—text that Fusion treats as buttons. To create a
text button set, click the Graphic tab, move the mouse into the area below the tab, and
choose New Button Set (Text) from the Style view shortcut menu. This creates a new
text button set with a default name.

Button Set 1   Button text   Button text   Button text   Button text

You can duplicate an existing set of text buttons by clicking the button set name
and choosing Duplicate from the shortcut menu. This also works for graphical and
Flash button sets, discussed later in this chapter.

You can configure each of the four text button states (Regular, Regular Rollover,
Highlighted, and Highlighted Rollover) by clicking it and using the Button Properties
panel. In the panel, you can use the same techniques as described for text boxes to
set the font face, size, style, background color, font color (Color), alignment, and offset
(for values of alignment other than Center and Middle). You can also set the Width
and Height of the button by using the two fields in the Button Size section.

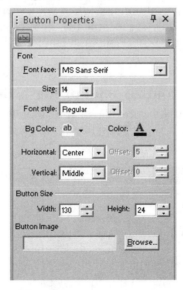

One pretty slick feature you can use for
text button is that you can use an image as a
backdrop. To do so, click the Browse button
alongside the Button Image field and choose an
image. The image will be truncated to the size
of the button.

If you use one of the button images included in the SiteStyle, it will be right size
for the text button.

Create and Customize a Set of Graphical Buttons

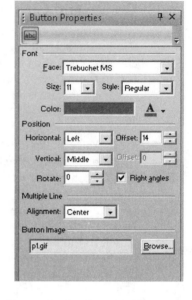

Graphical buttons use an image as a background and then overlay text on the button. To create a new set of graphical buttons, choose New Button Set (Graphical) from the Style view shortcut menu. To configure the graphical button set, use the Button Properties panel.

The configuration options for graphical buttons have very few differences from those for text buttons. They are

- The font drop-down list is called Face (as opposed to Font Face for a text button).
- You can't set the background color, since the background is determined by the image you use.
- You can't set the button size, as this too is determined by the image you use. In fact, that is the most important difference between text buttons and graphical buttons. When you use an image as the background for a text button, you only see as much of the image as would be visible for the given-size button. On the other hand, the graphical button size is set by the image—you can't set it independently.

Create and Customize a Set of Flash Buttons

Flash buttons use Flash to provide an animation when you roll over them or click them. To create a new set of Flash buttons, choose New Button Set (Flash) from the Style view shortcut menu.

Unlike when configuring individual buttons in the text and graphical buttons, you set the properties for the entire Flash button set at once. Click either the Flash button set name or the Flash button set itself to display two different tabs on the property panel. The first enables you to choose the Flash file (.swf); name, duplicate, or delete the button set; or create a new button set.

The Style tab is where you configure the properties for the buttons in the buttons set.

The properties you can set are

- **Background**   This is the background color for the Regular button. To change this (and all the other colors), click the color rectangle, and then click the drop-down arrow to open the Color Picker to choose a color.
- **Rollover**   The background color when you roll the mouse over the button.
- **Rollover Font**   The color of the font when you roll the mouse over the button.
- **Font**   Opens the Edit Font dialog box so that you can set the font, font color, size, style, and alignment for the regular button font.
- **Flyouts**   Select this check box to enable "flyout" menus (menus that fly out from the menu button) for any page button, which contains child (or sub) pages below it in the site structure. Here is a sample.

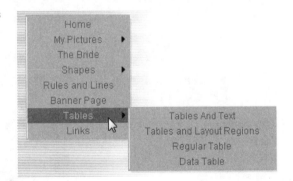

Create a New Table Style

A table style sets the color of the cells in the table. By dividing up the table into well-defined areas, you can specify what those areas look like, and then apply the table style to any table on a web page from the Table Style Properties tab of the Table Properties panel. To create a new table style, choose New Table Style from the

Style view (Graphic tab) shortcut menu. This displays a 5x5 table in the Table Styles section, which will display a preview of the style as you build it.

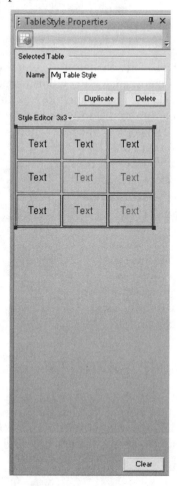

The real work of designing a table takes place in the Style Editor, which is visible in the Table Style Properties panel.

The default 3x3 Style Editor essentially breaks the table up into nine areas: the four corners, the sides between the corners (left, right, top, and bottom), and the middle region. The middle region is actually defined by the blue rectangle. When you first create a new table style, the entire table is the "middle" because the blue rectangle includes the entire table (as seen on the left side of Figure 8-8). However, you can click and drag the rectangle to define the "middle" as any portion of the table you want. For example, you can stretch the middle region to cover a corner or side, effectively blotting out the ability to format those regions independently (see the right side of Figure 8-8). Once you have specified the various sections, you can select the colors in each section and they will be used. To set the color of a section, click a cell in the Style Editor and choose the color from the ColorPicker.

In essence, you can select the cells inside the blue rectangle and apply color to them, thus setting the colors of the cells corresponding the position of the blue rectangle in the table. You can also set the color of the cells outside the blue rectangle, which sets the colors of the cells in those positions of the table. Here is an example

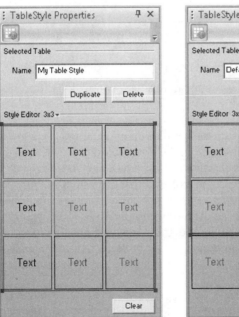
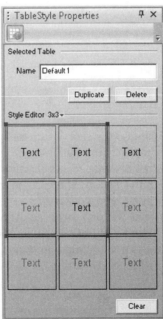

FIGURE 8-8   The entire table is the "middle" (left) and multiple sections in the table (right). The blue center area (not visible in this black and white screen shot) is the section inside the selected rectangle (which is visible).

that shows how the colors within the blue rectangle and outside the blue rectangle line up with the table style itself.

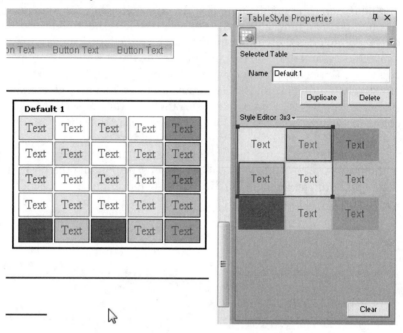

If a 3x3 grid doesn't suit your needs, you can pick a different size grid by using the following steps:

1. Choose the size of the middle region by clicking and dragging the blue rectangle. You should do this first, especially if you want to reduce the size of the grid, as you can't pick a grid that is smaller than the middle region.
2. Click the tiny down arrow alongside the Style Editor heading to display the grid. The dark blue section is the middle region.

3. Slide the mouse over the grid. As you do, new cells light up in light blue—these will be included in the new style editor grid when you click to complete the operation.

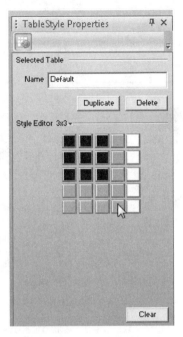

Some samples should help illustrate the kinds of things you can do with table styles. Here is a table with a 1x3 grid with a row of white, a row of black, and a white "center" (which is actually at the bottom row).

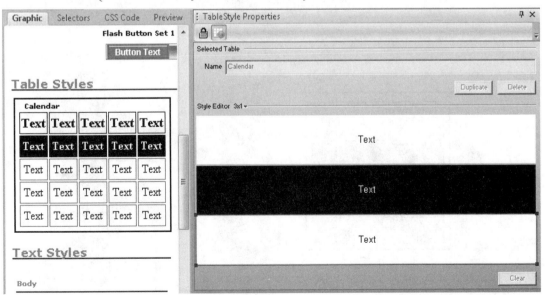

And here is a table with a 2x2 grid with the "middle" section actually located in the lower-right corner (in baby blue) with a row of medium blue cells around that.

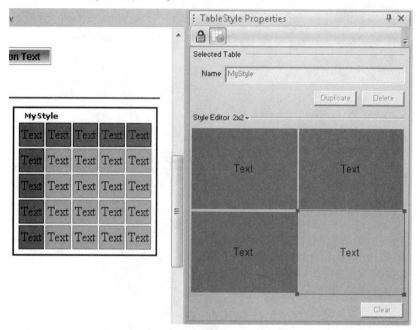

Finally, here is a table that has different colors for the sides, and an alternating candy stripe for the center. The possibilities are endless!

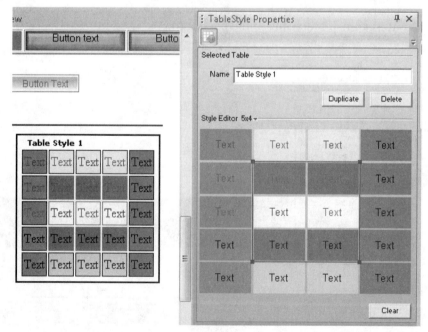

Adjust the Page Background

If other page elements (like a background image) don't hide the page background, you can adjust the background style. To do so, scroll down the Graphic tab of the Site view and click the Page Background area.

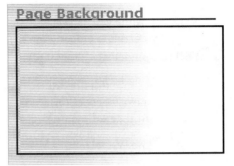

Use the Page Background Properties panel to adjust the Color and Image, just as you would the Layout, the Layout Region, or any other object that has a background color and image.

Adjust the Data List Icons

The Data List icons set the default picture bullet for bulleted lists. To specify the image to use, select the Data List Icons section and then click the Browse button in the Bullet Properties panel to pick the image.

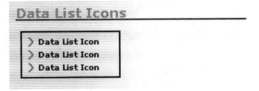

Adjust the Styled Line

The Styled line is the line you get when you pick the Styled Line tool from the toolbar. Click the item and then click the Browse button in the Properties panel to pick an image to use.

Adjust the Text Properties

The text styles used on the page (such as Body, Normal, Text Navbar, Headings, and Links) are controlled by the CSS-Common panel.

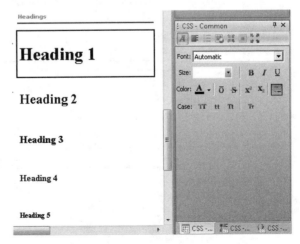

To configure any of the text-based elements, click the item in the Text Styles section and adjust the properties in the CSS-Common panel. Most of the tabs should look familiar. For example, the first tab (Character) enables you to set the font, size, style, font color, special styles (such as overline and strikeout), super and subscript, and the case (uppercase, lowercase, capitalized, and small caps)—pretty much just as you would format text.

Note   While you can set the properties for individual headings in the Headings section, setting a property for any item in the Unordered List or Ordered List sets the properties for all entries in that type of list.

The functionality of the rest of the tabs is covered in the next few sections. Most of the tabs should look very familiar—they are very similar to the controls for text boxes, Tables, Layouts, Layout Regions, and MasterBorders.

Configure the Paragraph Tab

The Paragraph tab enables you to set the alignment (left, center, right, and justified), increase or decrease the indent, and adjust the line height, word spacing, and letter spacing from the three drop-down lists.

Configure the List Tab

This tab is active only if you choose either the Unordered List or the Ordered List. You can pick a type of bullet from the Bullet drop-down list or click the browse button (...) and choose an image to use as a bullet. To make sure that all lines in a bulleted item are indented to the same level as the first line, select the Indent Wrapped Lines check box.

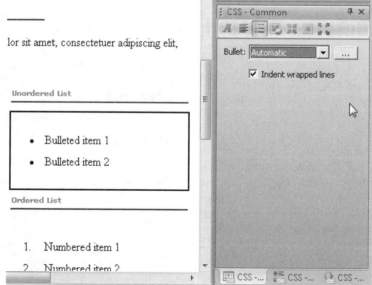

Configure the Background Tab

The Background tab enables you to specify an image (click the ... button to open a dialog box to choose one), pick a background color from the paint can icon, and decide whether to allow the background to scroll if you scroll the page. Select the Fix Background Position check box if you don't want the background to scroll with the page. If the image is smaller than the overall background, you can specify how you want the image to repeat to fill in the space—either Horizontally or Vertically. If you don't select either check box, the image will be shown only once and may leave blank space in the background.

Finally, you can specify the offset of the image horizontally and vertically using the drop-down lists in the Position section. You can specify this offset using a long list of units (click the Units entry in the drop-down list to see the list, which includes %, pixels, inches, cm, and more).

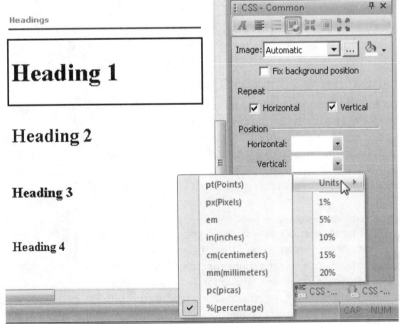

Configure the Padding Tab

"Padding" is the space between the edge of the text area and the text it contains. This area is invisible unless you have set background properties (such as the color or image) that make this area visible. Set the padding for the top, right, bottom, and left from the drop-down lists. You can specify the padding using a long list of units—click the Units entry in the drop-down list to see the list.

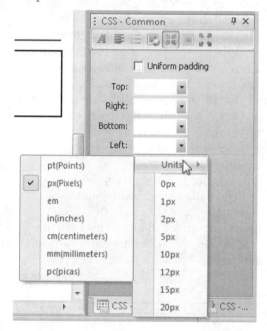

Configure the Borders Tab

The Borders tab enables you to turn on a visible border for each side of the text element by clicking one or more of the buttons in the left color. Once you activate a border, you can set its style (such as Solid, Double, Groove, and so on), its thickness, and its color by using the two adjacent drop-down lists and the Pencil icon (which produces the ColorPicker).

 The three check boxes enable you to easily create uniform borders. Select them to use the top margin row specifications for (from left to right) the style, thickness, and color. Realize, however, that you still have to activate a border (using the buttons in the left column) in order to make a border visible.

Configure the Margins Tab

The margins measure the space between the box containing the text and any other object. The Margins tab enables you to specify the top, right, bottom, and left margins. You can pick the top, right, bottom, and left margins by picking a quantity from the appropriate drop-down list. Choose the units to use from the Units drop-down list. You can also establish uniform (all the same) margins by selecting the Uniform Margins check box and then picking a value from the Top drop-down list—which will be used for all the margins.

How to... Define Your Own CSS Styles

To build your own CSS (Cascading Style Sheets) styles, you must use the Style view and click the Selectors tab.

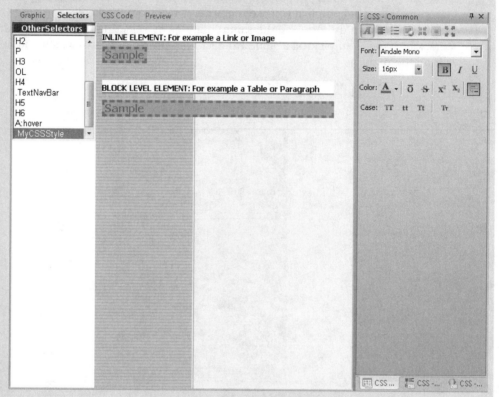

Then use the following steps:

1. Right-click in the scrolling list of Other Selectors and choose Add CSS Rule from the shortcut menu. This opens the Add CSS Rule dialog box.

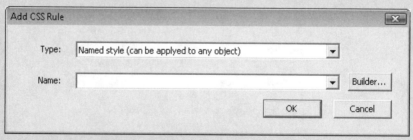

2. Leave the Type set to the default (Named style) and type in the name for the rule. Click OK to create the new Rule (Style).

3. Specify the initial properties from the CSS—Common panel. This is the first of the three nested panels (click the left tab at the bottom of the nested panels). As you make changes in these panels, the sample text shows you what the style looks like. The CSS—Common panel includes the tabs you've seen before for text boxes (Character, Paragraph, List, Background, Padding, Borders, and Margins). Use these tabs to set the properties for your new CSS style.

4. If you wish, specify additional detailed properties (such as Background, Box, Font, and so on) in the CSS—Property Sheet panel. This is the second of the nested panels (click the middle tab at the bottom of the nested panels).

If you'd like to see what the CSS code actually looks like (and modify it if you wish), you can view it in the CSS—Code Editor. This is the third of the nested panels (click the right tab at the bottom of the nested panels).

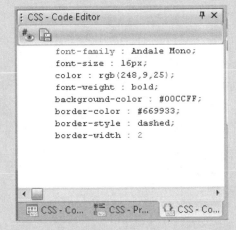

9

Set Up Site Navigation and Build Hyperlinks

HOW TO...

- Add Hyperlinks to pages
- Create local hotspot hyperlinks for graphics
- Create Navigation Bars based on the site structure
- Customize your Navigation Bars to change the look and function
- Have hyperlinks open exactly where you want

It doesn't do you much good to have lots of pages in your web site if you don't have a simple mechanism to navigate from one page to another. And there will also be times that you need to link to destinations on the Internet. The mechanism for linking to other web pages (either within your site or outside) or to specific points within a web page is called *hyperlinks*. Hyperlinks can be embedded in text, hooked up to buttons, and mapped onto specific areas of an image (called "hotspots"). Hyperlinks should be planned carefully, or areas of your web site may be inaccessible unless you know the specific URL (web address) of the page.

 Sometimes you *want* to hide pages this way. This is especially true for administrative pages, like the sort you'll need for some of the advanced components like FAQ and the Guestbook.

Understand and Build Different Link Types

Fusion supports four basic kinds of hyperlinks, and adding each one is a bit different, as we'll discuss later in this chapter. The four kinds of links are

- **Internal hyperlinks** Internal hyperlinks link to another page within your site, including to a specific place on the page denoted by an "anchor."

197

- **External hyperlinks** External hyperlinks link to destinations outside your web site. These are often other web pages but may also be links to files, for sending e-mail, and of many other types. You can even create a JavaScript link, which will execute the script you place into the link field when you click the link.
- **File links** File links link to a file stored on the web site. Normally, clicking this type of link will prompt users to open or save the file to their computer. An exception is when the browser has a plug-in or other enhanced functionality (like Adobe Acrobat), which recognizes the file so that it opens automatically in the browser window.
- **Smart links** Smart links are normally built automatically by specific components, such as the Photo Gallery. Smart links work with special features. For example, in the Photo Gallery, there is only a single visible page that displays photos, but there are actually multiple instances of this page that are "stacked" in the order of the photos in the gallery. Smart links enable you to step through the stacked pages (and back). The Smart links you can build yourself enable you to navigate through the site structure based on the Site view. For example, you can create a button to navigate to the next page to the left or right in the structure. If you plan to use this feature, you'll need to plan your site structure to take advantage of Smart links.

 You can add HTML to a Smart link and the HTML will execute when you click the link.

Add an Anchor to a Page

Anchors are a slightly different take on an internal link. Most commonly, an internal link simply points to a web page, given by the URL (page address) of the page. However, you can add anchors to a page that are attached to a specific point on the page, such as the first cell in a table or the first word in a text box. Once you have built an anchor, you can specify it as part of an internal link so that clicking the link jumps right to the specified point on the page.

To add an anchor to a page, use the following steps:

1. Select the point on the page where the anchor will be located. This can be an image or a text insertion point (but not selected text). But it can also be almost any type of object, such as a table, table cell, Navigation Bar, page banner, text box, Layout Region, and so on.
2. Click either the Anchor tool in the Standard Tools toolbar or the Anchor button in the Properties panel. Only a text insertion point or an image has this button, however. This opens the Add Anchor dialog box. Filling it out is simple—just add a name.

Anchors in the Layout section of the page are listed separately from anchors in the MasterBorder. That is, if you add a target to an object in the MasterBorder, you won't see it listed in the Add Anchor dialog box for an object in the Layout—and vice versa.

3. Fusion adds an anchor icon to the anchor location on the page. This anchor icon is not visible in a browser, but it serves as a useful marker to remind you where the anchors are located.

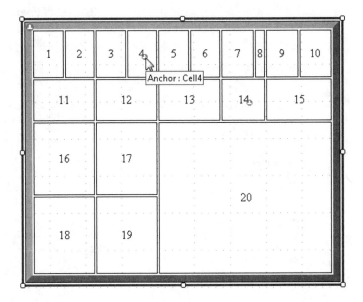

Hover your mouse over the anchor icon to see a tooltip that displays the name of the anchor.

Renaming an anchor is a bit tricky. To do so, click the anchor and then select the Anchor tool in the Standard Tools toolbar. This displays the Change Anchor dialog box with the selected anchor already in the Name field. Type in the new name and click OK to change it.

Tip You can remove anchors from the page with the Add Anchor dialog box as well. Select the anchor from the Anchors On Page list and click Remove.

Add an Internal Link

To add an internal link, the first step is to select the item that will carry the link, that is, the hyperlink. Then, click either the Link button in the Properties panel (if there is one) or the Link button in the Standard Tools toolbar. This opens the Link dialog box, where you can select Internal Link from the Link Type drop-down list.

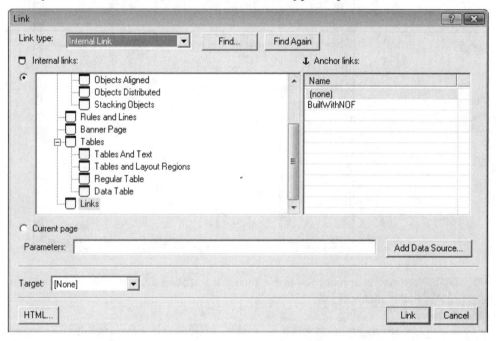

 Note If the Link button is unavailable, it means you can't add a link to the object. For example, you cannot add a link to a text box. However, you *can* select the text in the text box and add a link to the selected text.

On the left side of the dialog box (Internal Links) the site structure is displayed. Pick the page you want to link to by clicking it in the structure. If a given page has anchors, the anchors are listed on the right side in the Anchor Links list. To link to a particular anchor, pick it from the list. Use "None" if you just want to link to the page. Click the Link button to complete building the hyperlink. If the hyperlink is text, you'll see the familiar blue underlined text to indicate the presence of the hyperlink. If the hyperlink is an image, however, you'll see a special hyperlink icon on the image. Like the anchor icon, the hyperlink icon won't be visible in a browser, though hyperlinked text will be.

Indicates hyperlinked image   Hyperlinked text

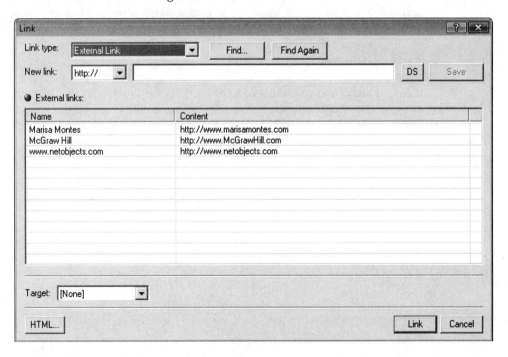

 Note You can also add multiple hyperlinks to an image using "hotspots," as discussed later in this chapter.

To remove a link, select the hyperlink and then click the Link icon in the Standard Tools toolbar to reopen the Links dialog box. You'll now see an Unlink button. Simply click it to remove the hyperlink. To select a text hyperlink, double-click in the text and make sure the text insertion point is within the hyperlink text. Selecting an image hyperlink is easier—just click the image.

Add an External Link

To add an external link, select the hyperlink and open the Link dialog box just as with an internal hyperlink. Choose External Link from the Link Type drop-down list to see the new version of the dialog box.

Pick the type of link (such as http://) from the New Link drop-down list and enter the URL into the field immediately to the right of the list. Alternatively, you can pick an external link you have used before from the list of External Links in the lower portion of the dialog box. To finish up, click Link. As with internal links, you'll see the familiar blue/underlined text or an icon to call out the presence of the hyperlink.

 You can add a bunch of hyperlinks into the External Links list when you have the Link dialog box open. Just pick the type of link, type in the hyperlink itself, and click Save.

The list of link types in the Link Type drop-down list is pretty complete, though many of the links are specialized—and if you don't know what they mean, you probably don't need them. However, there are a few exceptions to this observation, so here is an explanation of the most common link types:

- **http://** A "normal" web page, that is, a page out on the Internet, such as http://htdenetobjectsfusion.com.
- **https://** This is a secure web page, information transmitted back and forth is kept secure using encryption. Banks and other major institutions often use secure web pages for handling payments.
- **ftp://** A "file transfer protocol" site, used primarily for transferring files back and forth. It is, in essence, a set of directories on a server somewhere with (optionally) security and passwords to limit access.
- **mailto:** This type of link indicates an e-mail address, such as dplotkin@pacbell.net. You must type the e-mail address into the adjacent field. When someone clicks this link, it opens the default e-mail application (rather than navigating to an Internet destination).

Once you add a link to the list of External Links, you can change the link name by clicking in the Name column and typing in a new name. It's best to keep the name short because the name is used in places (such as DynaButtons, described later in this chapter) where a long name can be unwieldy.

Add a Smart Link

To add a Smart link, select the hyperlink and open the Link dialog box as described previously. Choose Smart Link from the Link Type dialog to see the types of available Smart links.

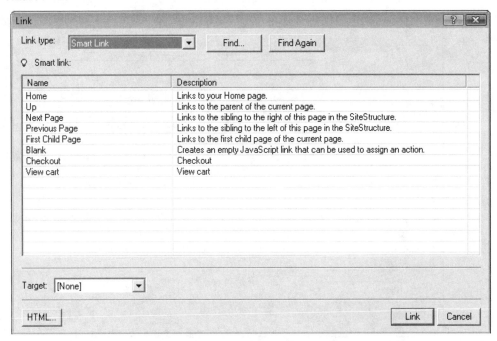

As mentioned previously, most of the available Smart links enable you to navigate through your site structure. For example, if you place a "Next Page" link, clicking it sends you to whatever page is immediately to the right of the current page in the site structure.

 Note   One special type of Smart link is the "Blank" link, which creates an empty JavaScript call (see Chapter 12 for more details). If you know your way around JavaScript, you can write a script and link it into the HTML so that it runs when you click the link.

Add a File Link

To create a File link, select the hyperlink and open the Link dialog box as described previously. Choose File Link in the Link Type drop-down list and pick the file by clicking Browse or typing the full path to the file in the File Path field.

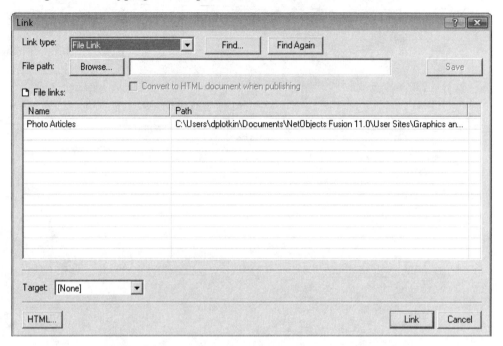

If you want to convert the document to HTML when it is published (uploaded to the site), select the Convert To HMTL Document When Publishing check box. If you do convert the document, it will appear in the user's browser when the link is clicked. Otherwise, the user will get the standard dialog box prompting him or her to either save the file or open it.

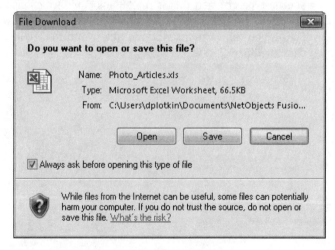

Find a Hyperlink

After you've added a bunch of hyperlinks to a site, it can be difficult to track down a specific one, perhaps so you can reuse it. To find a link, open the Link dialog box as described and use the following steps:

1. Select the type of link you want to hunt for from the Link Type drop-down list.
2. Click Find to open the Find dialog box. The dialog box title includes the type of link you are looking for, so if you are hunting for an external link, it will be called Find External Link.

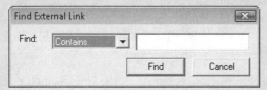

3. Choose the comparison term from the Find drop-down list. Choices include Begins With, Contains, and Ends With.
4. Type the comparison term into the adjacent field and click Find.

Fusion both locates and highlights the link (if a match is found) or displays an error dialog box informing you that no match was found. Note that there are no "wildcards" in this search, so you can't use a symbol like "*" to do a wildcard match.

 To just find the next occurrence of the searched term, click Find Again.

Note Only a limited set of file types can be converted to HTML. These include: mcw, doc, xls, and rtf files.

Add Hyperlinks to Images

In addition to attaching a link to an entire image (as discussed earlier), you can create "hot spots"—areas of an image that link to different destinations. For example, say you had a picture of a state map. You can add hot spots to the major cities, and clicking a city would then bring up a map of that city (or anything else you wanted to show). Another excellent use for this technique is to display a screen shot of a software package. Clicking any of various areas of the screen would then open another web page that explains how to use that section.

The Hotspot tools are in the Standard Tools toolbar. You can only see one at a time—to pick a tool other than the one that is visible, click the tiny down arrow to show the list.

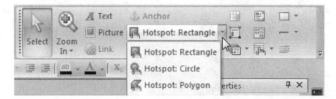

To add a hotspot to an image, first select the tool you want to use. For the Rectangle and Circle tools, simply click and drag on the image to define the hotspot area. When you release the mouse button, the Link dialog box opens, where you can define the link as described earlier in this chapter.

 If you click the Cancel button in the Link dialog box, the dialog box closes, and the hotspot disappears.

The Polygon tool works just a little differently. Click once to establish the first point of the polygon, and the mouse cursor turns into a pencil. Continue clicking to define the sides of the polygon. Then, double-click to finish the polygon and open the Link dialog box.

Any hotspots you have added are visible in the image, though you won't see them in a browser or preview.

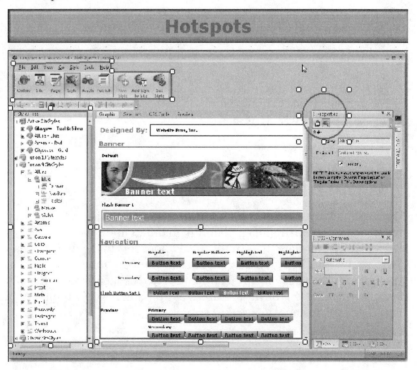

I selected all the hotspots in the previous illustration to make them easier to see.

You can adjust the hotspot location and size, much as you would with simple shapes (see Chapter 5). To move the hotspot, click the line to select it (the sizing handles appear). Then click inside the hotspot and drag it to a new location. To resize (or in the case of the polygon, reshape) the hotspot, click and drag one of the sizing handles.

Add Hyperlinks with DynaButtons

One of the neatest ways to add hyperlinks to a Fusion web page is to use "DynaButtons." DynaButtons produce a set of buttons for which you can configure the behavior. DynaButtons are one of the Custom Components, available from the NOF Standard Components panel. Here is what a DynaButton might look like.

 You have to publish your site (at least locally) in order to preview DynaButtons. You also must have Java on your machine—which might mean a quick trip over to Java.com to install it, as it doesn't come with the current versions of Windows.

To start the process of defining DynaButtons, select the component from the panel and click on the page. This displays the DynaButtons icon, which you can move by clicking and dragging inside of it.

To configure the DynaButtons, make sure the Properties tab in the DynaButtons Properties panel is selected.

The items you can configure are

- **Orientation**   You can set the orientation of the buttons as Horizontal (the buttons are laid out next to each other) or Vertical (the buttons are laid out up and down).
- **Number of Buttons**   Since a DynaButton actually consists of a set of buttons, you can specify the number of buttons that will be in the set. The DynaButton icon on the page adjusts its size automatically as you add or remove buttons. Each button gets two lines in the DynaButtons Properties panel, where you can configure the individual buttons.

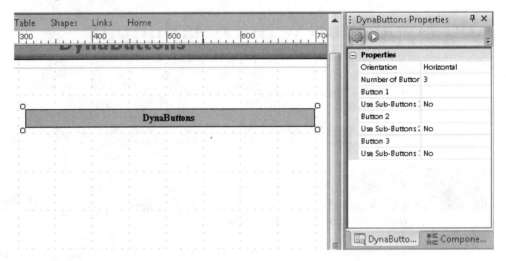

- **Hyperlink**   To specify the target hyperlink (where to go when the DynaButton is clicked), double-click the button name or click the button name and then click the … button. This opens the Link dialog box so you can specify the link, as described earlier in this chapter.

If you choose to use sub-buttons (as described in the next item), you cannot attach a hyperlink to the main button. Instead, you can type text in the field alongside the button name. The text is displayed on the DynaButton.

- **Use Sub-buttons**   Sub-buttons are buttons that appear when a site visitor clicks the main DynaButton (as shown in Figure 9-1). To establish sub-buttons, set the Use Sub-Buttons drop-down list to Yes. This action makes another field available: Number Sub-Buttons. Pick the number you want, and a list of Sub-Buttons appears. Simply choose the hyperlink for each sub-button as you did with the main button.

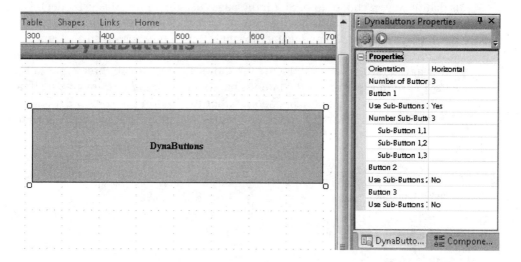

 As you can see from Figure 9-1, the button names are hard to see because they butt right up against the left edge of the button. Unfortunately, you don't have any control over this. What you *can* do is add underscores or other characters to the beginning of the name to push the name to the right (blanks won't work; they are ignored). For buttons that have sub-buttons, you change the name in the DynaButton Properties panel. For links, you must change the name in the Link dialog box.

FIGURE 9-1   Click a DynaButton to show its sub-buttons.

Build Navigation Bars from the Site Structure

As noted in Chapter 2, Fusion builds a web site using a structure that looks like an organization chart. You control this structure using the Site view. A "Navigation Bar" built from this site view is a construct that provides hyperlinks (as either buttons or text) to navigate through the site. The nice thing about this type of Navigation Bar is that once you choose to put it on the page (usually in the MasterBorder), Fusion maintains it for you, adjusting the buttons or text to show hyperlinks according to the options you specify, and using the labels that you choose. And as you adjust the structure of the site, Fusion keeps the Navigation Bar in synch with the structure—you never have to worry about it. Figure 9-2 shows a page with all three types of Navigation Bars (the third type creates the buttons based on Flash rather than graphic images).

To create a Navigation Bar, choose either the Button Navigation Bar tool or the Text Navigation Bar tool (they are grouped together under a single icon) in the

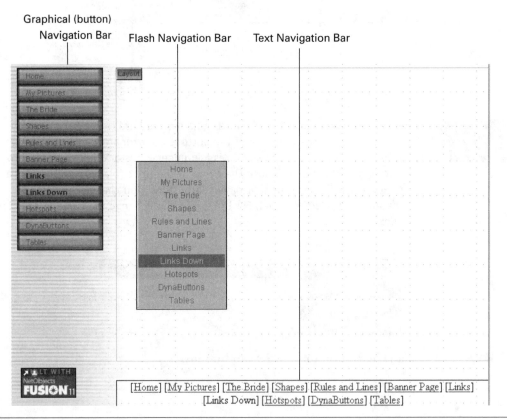

FIGURE 9-2 Three, three, three kinds of Navigation Bars!

Standard Tools toolbar. Click and drag on the page to define where the Navigation Bar will go, and it appears, using the default properties for a Navigation Bar.

Use the General tab in the Navigation Bar Properties to configure the structure of the Navigation Bar.

Set the Structure to Use

The Structure section contains two radio buttons—Site and Custom. Obviously, if you want the Navigation Bar to be based on the site structure, leave this set to Site. We'll see how to build a custom Navigation Bar later in this chapter.

The Display drop-down list provides choices on what level of the structure should be shown in the Navigation Bar. Your options are

- **First Level**   This level links to all the child (one level down) pages of the Home page.
- **Parent Level**   This level links to all pages in the level above the current page in the site structure.
- **Current Level**   This level links to the current page and all other pages that share the same parent page.
- **Child Level**   This level links to the children of the current page.
- **Breadcrumb Trail**   This option displays the current page as the last level of a tree, and all the parent pages in succession. For example, if P1 is a child of the

home page, and C1 is a child of P1, this option would produce a Navigation Bar on page C1 that looks like this.

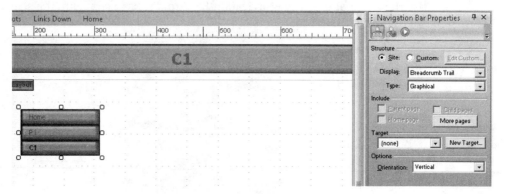

The options in the Include section of the Navigation Bar Properties panel are unavailable when you choose Breadcrumb Trail.

- **All Pages** Displays all the pages in the web site. You'll rarely want to use this one—it can produce a huge Navigation Bar.

Add Additional Pages

The Include section of the Navigation Bar Properties panel enables you to add pages to the Bar even when they wouldn't normally be included by the selection you made in the Display drop-down list. Select the appropriate check boxes to add the Parent page, Home page, and/or Child pages to the Navigation Bar.

The Child Pages check box actually adds buttons for the child pages of the level selected in the Display drop-down list. For example, if the Display drop-down list is set to First Level, selecting the Child Pages check box displays pages at the second level down from the Home page.

You Can Change the Type of the Navigation Bar

Regardless of the type of Navigation Bar you pick originally, you can change to a different type. This is accomplished by using the Type drop-down list in the Navigation Bar Properties panel. Just pick Graphical, Text, or Flash from the list to switch the type of Navigation Bar.

If you want to add more pages to the Navigation Bar, click the More Pages button to display the More Pages dialog box.

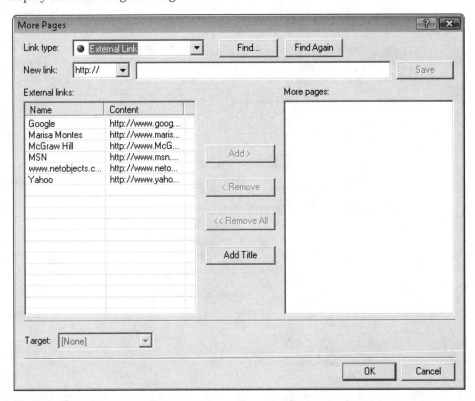

From this dialog box, you can choose the type of link (Internal, External, or File), which displays a list of links in the left pane. Simply click the link and then click Add to move the link to the right (More Pages) pane. Except for the first link you add, each link is placed just below the selected link in the More Pages pane. For external links, you can create a new link just as you would with the Link dialog box, described earlier in this chapter.

You can also simply click and drag a link from the left side to the right side. A red line appears where the link will be placed, enabling you to put the links in the order you want in one step.

You can break up groups of pages in the More Pages dialog box by clicking the Add Title button. This inserts a new button that doesn't actually do anything—it breaks up the list of buttons for visual effect. Here is what it looks like in the More Pages dialog box.

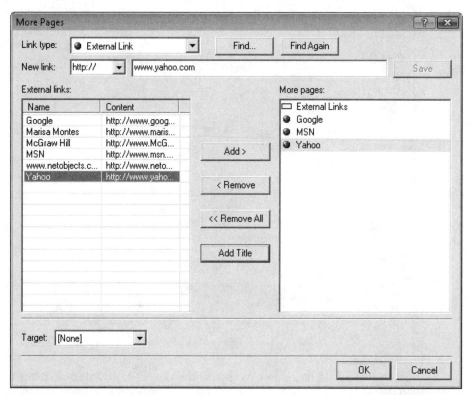

And here is the result in the Navigation Bar. Unfortunately, the "Title" button looks just like any other button, so visitors to your site may be frustrated if they click it, though they should notice that the mouse does not turn into the "hyperlink pointing hand" icon when it is over this button.

You aren't limited by the order of the pages in the More Pages dialog box. You can click and drag any pages in the More Pages pane to rearrange them. As you drag, a red line appears where the page will appear when you release the mouse button.

Build Custom Navigation Bars

A custom Navigation Bar is one that you essentially build "from scratch," specifying exactly what will appear, independent of the structure of the site. To create a custom Navigation Bar, create a Navigation Bar as described earlier, but pick the Custom radio button in the Navigation Bar Properties panel. Then click the Edit Custom button to open the Custom Navigation Bar Structure dialog box. It looks *exactly* like the More Pages dialog box described earlier, and you pick pages to include the same way—select the link in the left pane, and click Add to add it to the custom Navigation Bar (right pane).

Unlike when using the More Pages dialog box, however, you can build a structure in the Custom Navigation Bar Structure dialog box. Each link you select in the left pane becomes a child of the selected link in the right pane. However, you can rearrange the links as follows:

- **Rearrange the order**   You can reorder the links within a given level (and attached to a given parent page) by clicking and dragging as you did in the More Pages dialog box.
- **Move a child link to a different parent**   You can take a link and make it the child of another link by clicking and dragging the link on top of the parent link. As you do, you'll see a tiny "+" sign but *not* the red line that indicates that you've changed the order.
- **Promote a link**   You can promote a page to another level by clicking and dragging the page *almost* on top of another page at the level where you want it. As you do this, a tiny "+" symbol appears, the page at the new level is highlighted, and you'll see the red line. This is key: if you don't see the red line, the link will not be promoted. Here is what it looks like.

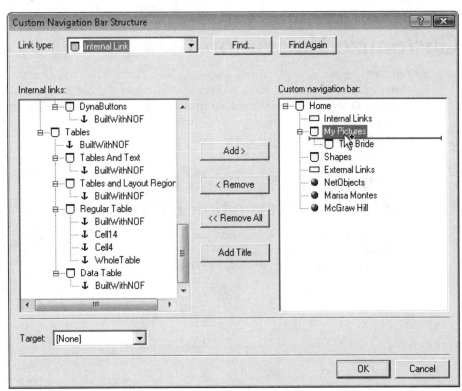

Another important difference between a custom Navigation Bar and a structure Navigation Bar is that the "title" buttons use the Section Title style from the SiteStyle. Thus, if you formatted the Section Title style to look different from "regular" buttons (as described in Chapter 8), the title buttons will be easily distinguishable from the navigation buttons.

There are a few important things to remember when building a custom Navigation Bar. First of all, you can have multiple pages at the same level as the Home page. However, if you do, the page at the top of any particular "tree" of pages is considered the Home page. For example, if you are on a page that is in the tree below one of these top-level pages, the only way to get the top-level page to show up is to select the Home Page check box in the Include section (which does *not* display the actual Home page, but instead the top page of the tree). In addition, the only way to get all of these "top-level" pages to show up in the Navigation Bar is to use the Parent Level value for the Display drop-down list, enable the Include Child Pages option, and deselect the include Home Page check box if the parent level includes the Home page.

You don't even have to include the Home page if you don't want to, though you get many of the same results described in the previous paragraph. Typically, I start with the Home page and build a structure of pages below that one to avoid all this.

Finally, it is important to realize that the rest of the items in the Navigation Bar Properties panel are still fully functional. You can still set the Display level and pick the Include check boxes. You can even add more pages with the More Pages button.

Customize Navigation Bars

You have a great deal of control over how Navigation Bars look and how they respond to the mouse. First of all, you can set the orientation (either Horizontal or Vertical) from the Orientation drop-down list in the General section of the Navigation Bar Properties panel. The rest of the options depend on whether you're working with a graphical, text, or Flash Navigation Bar.

Configure the Look and Behavior of Graphical Navigation Bars

To configure a graphical Navigation Bar, click the Style tab in the Navigation Bar Properties panel. You can configure the Button Style, how the buttons respond (Options), and some display choices (Display).

The Button Style section enables you to specify what SiteStyle and button set within that SiteStyle are used for each of the levels in the site structure. What you see in the Level drop-down list depends on what page you are on. For example, if you are on the Home page, you'll see options for Current, Child, and then numbered levels.

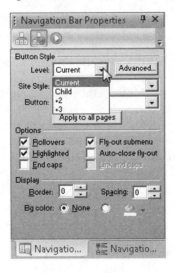

However, if the page is further down in the structure, you'll see references to the Parent, levels above that (with a negative number), Children, and levels below that. You get the idea.

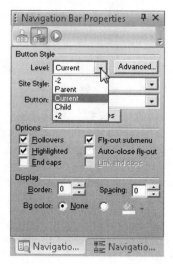

What you need to remember here is that you can set the rest of the style formatting options individually for each level in the site structure. For each level, here is what you can do:

- **Choose the Site Style**   Pick the SiteStyle you want to use for the buttons on that level from the Site Style drop-down list.
- **Choose the Button Style**   Once you've picked the SiteStyle, you can pick the button style (such as Primary or Secondary) from the Button drop-down list.
- **Rollover option**   Selecting the Rollovers check box displays the image for the Rollover button state when the mouse is over the button.
- **Highlighted option**   Selecting the Highlighted check box displays the image for the Highlighted button state.
- **End caps option**   Select this check box to display the end cap graphics associated with a button style. As discussed in Chapter 8, end caps are graphics that are placed at both ends of a Navigation Bar. That is, for a horizontal Navigation Bar, the end caps are placed at the left and right ends, and for a vertical Navigation Bar, the end caps are placed at the top and bottom.

Unless you apply the Site Style and button style to all the levels in the site (by clicking the Apply To All Pages button) and thus making all the buttons in the Navigation Bar look the same, the end caps will not be visible even if you specify them.

- **Fly-out submenu**   Select this check box to display buttons for child pages not included in the current Navigation Bar when the site visitor moves the mouse pointer over the button for the parent link. Here is a sample.

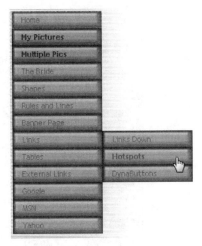

- **Auto-close fly-out**   Select this check box to have the fly-out menu close automatically when the site visitor moves the mouse pointer away from the button for the parent link. If you don't select this check box, the fly-out menu remains visible until something else is clicked.
- **Link end caps**   If you enable end caps, selecting this check box links the end caps to the adjoining button in the Navigation Bar. What this means is that if the site visitor clicks an end cap, it produces the same result as clicking the adjoining button. If you don't select this check box, the end cap is just a graphic decoration, and clicking it produces no result.

The Display section enables you to set the following items:

- **Border**   Set the width of the border around the entire Navigation Bar in pixels. The border starts outside the spacing area (see Figure 9-3), and the style is specified by the Navigation Bar style for the current SiteStyle.
- **Spacing**   Select the width of the spacing between the buttons and around the whole button set in pixels. That is, in addition to space between the buttons, this control sets the spacing between the buttons and any specified border. You can select a background color by clicking the radio button alongside the paint bucket. Pick the color you want by clicking the paint bucket button and choosing the color from the ColorPicker. To turn off the background color, click the None radio button.

Use the Advanced Button Style to Configure Your Buttons

It can be hard to visualize the various levels of your web site when using the Level drop-down list in the Navigation Bar Properties panel to specify the button styles. For example, which level is –2? What pages are on that level? Fortunately, there is an easier way, and oddly, it is hidden under the Advanced button! Click the Advanced button to open the Advanced Visual Style Settings dialog box (see Figure 9-4). This dialog box shows the structure of the web site. It also provides drop-down lists to set the Site Style and Button Set, and a preview area to show what the button looks like.

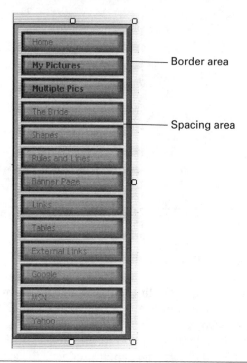

FIGURE 9-3 The Border and Spacing combine to add contrast to a Navigation Bar.

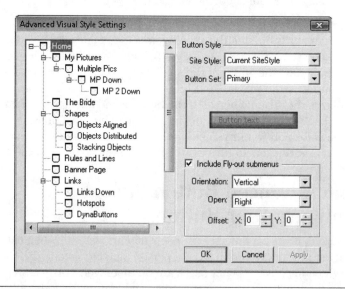

FIGURE 9-4 The Advanced Visual Style Settings dialog box enables you to pick levels visually and set the button properties.

Using the dialog box is pretty simple. The first step is to choose a page in the left panel (site structure). Clicking on any page selects that page as well as all the other pages on that level.

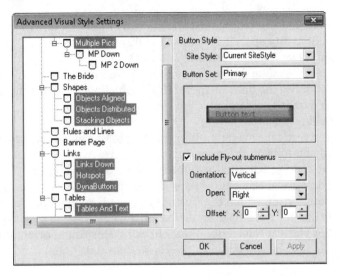

After that, you choose the Site Style and Button Set to use from the drop-down lists. This dialog box also provides far more options for using fly-out submenus. To include these submenus for a specific level, select the Include Fly-Out Submenus check box and set the parameters as follows:

- **Orientation**   Choose Horizontal or Vertical. This specifies the geometry of the fly-out buttons. Vertical buttons are stacked up and down; Horizontal buttons are laid out side to side. You've seen a few examples of Vertical orientation; here is a sample of Horizontal orientation.

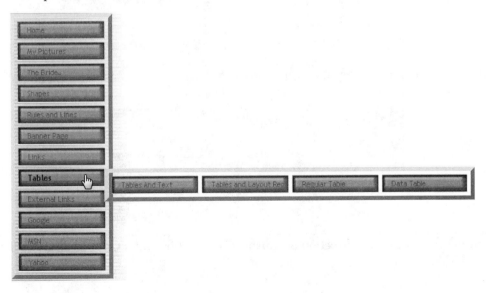

Tip If you are going to use fly-out menus, you can shrink the main Navigation Bar by not selecting the Child Pages check box. Just hover the mouse over the parent page and the buttons for the child pages will "fly out."

- **Open** This drop-down list specifies the direction in which a fly-out appears, as well as any special effect used to display the buttons. The directions include Right, Left, Top, and Bottom, and the special effects include Slide and Fade (see Figure 9-5). Slide draws the buttons in the direction specified; for example, Slide Right draws the buttons from left to right. Fade displays the buttons faintly at first, then darker and darker. When choosing a direction, there are some things you should remember:
    - For vertical Navigation Bars in the left MasterBorder, choosing Left places the buttons off the page unless you have a very wide left margin between the Navigation Bar and the left edge of the MasterBorder.
    - For vertical Navigation Bars, choosing Vertical orientation and Top hides the button from which the fly-out originated. You can partially compensate for this using the Y-offset (described shortly).
    - For vertical Navigation Bars, choosing Horizontal orientation and Bottom hides the next button down in the Navigation Bar.

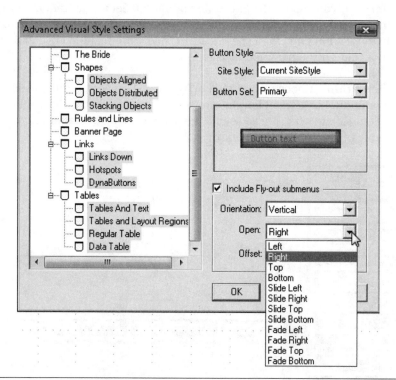

FIGURE 9-5 Choose a direction and display an effect from the Open drop-down list.

- Realistically, combining Horizontal and Vertical orientations and various directions can be tricky, so it is actually best to keep things simple. For vertical Navigation Bars, you can't go wrong using Vertical orientation and Right for all levels, and for horizontal Navigation Bars, you are best off using Horizontal orientation and Top (for bars in the bottom MasterBorder) or Bottom (for bars in the top MasterBorder) for all levels. You don't have to do that, but almost any other combination hides buttons on some levels. You have been warned!

- **Offset**   The X offset moves the starting point of the fly-out buttons to the left and right, while the Y offset moves the starting point up and down. You can set either of these fields between –30 and 30. Choosing a positive number moves the starting point in the same direction as the direction chosen from the Open drop-down list. For example, if you choose Right, a positive value of X moves the starting point to the right, while a negative value of X moves the starting point to the left. On the other hand, if you choose Left, a positive value of X moves the starting point to the left, and a negative value of X moves it to the right. For Y, a positive value moves the starting point up (for Top) or down (for Bottom), and a negative value moves the starting point in the opposite direction (down for Top and up for Bottom).

For Right and Left, a positive value of Y moves the starting point down and a negative value of Y moves the starting point up. For Top and Bottom, a positive value of X moves the starting point right, and a negative value moves the starting point left.

How to... Configure Individual Buttons in a Navigation Bar

Up until now, we've been setting how buttons look by choosing a SiteStyle and a Button (set). However, you have more controls than that—you can configure each button individually if you wish. To do so, click a Navigation Bar, and then double-click an individual button to place a selection box around the button.

(continued)

What you see next depends on whether the button is an internal link (to one of the pages in the web site) or an external link. If the link is internal, the Navigation Button Properties panel looks like this.

The default button text is given by the Page name, but you can override that by deselecting the Use Page Name In Button check box and then typing the button text into the Button title field.

If the link is external, the Navigation Button Properties panel is a little simpler—Button Title specifies the text for the button, so just type in what you want to use.

 Tip This panel is available for "Titles" you may have added (such as the "External Links" button) when adding more pages to the Navigation Bar.

Either way, you can pick the specific Button Image and Rollover Image (the image used when the mouse pointer is over the button) from the two fields near the bottom of the panel. To pick a different image, click the ... button and choose a picture file.

So why would you want to go to all this trouble? One reason might be to use a special graphic button for a special page, which would call attention to that page in the Navigation Bar. Another reason might be to make the Title buttons stand out so they don't look *too* much like buttons you can actually click on. Just be careful not to make them too garish!

Configure the Look and Behavior of Text Navigation Bars

You can configure a text Navigation Bar from the Style tab of the Navigation Bar Properties panel, which looks considerably different than for a graphical Navigation Bar.

The options you can set are

- **Background color**   Set the color behind the Navigation Bar from the Color drop-down list or by clicking the paint bucket button and picking a color from the ColorPicker. Choosing "Transparent" sets the background color to the same color as the parent object, so that the bar appears transparent.
- **Background image**   You can place a background image behind the Navigation Bar by choosing either Automatic, None, or Browse. Choosing either Browse or clicking the ... button enables you to pick the image from the Picture File Open dialog box. Only as much of the picture as will fit inside the Navigation Bar will be visible.

- **Delimiters** Delimiters are text symbols, such as (, [, or {, which are placed at the ends of each text hyperlink. Type the text symbol you want to use for the left side of the text hyperlink into the Start field, and the symbol you want to use for the right side of the text hyperlink in the End field. If you want the hyperlink to extend to include the delimiters as well as the text, select the Include Delimiters In Link check box.
- **Alignment** Select Left, Center, or Right to align the set of text hyperlinks inside the area of the Navigation Bar.
- **Constrain to a single line** Normally (if this check box is unselected), the Navigation Bar will spill over to multiple lines (as shown here) if all the text hyperlinks won't fit on a single line. If you select the Constrain To Single Line check box, however, the Navigation Bar will extend as far to the right (for horizontal) or as far down (for vertical) as necessary to show the hyperlinks—which may force the page size to increase to make room.

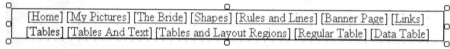

[Home] [My Pictures] [The Bride] [Shapes] [Rules and Lines] [Banner Page] [Links] [Tables] [Tables And Text] [Tables and Layout Regions] [Regular Table] [Data Table]

- **Link current page** A text Navigation Bar does not normally show a hyperlink for the page you are on. This is actually kind of handy—you can glance at the bar and see which hyperlink is the current page. But if you'd rather that the current page have a hyperlink as well (not sure why you'd want to do that), select the Link Current Page check box.

Configure the Look and Behavior of Flash Navigation Bars

Configuring a Flash Navigation Bar (from the Style tab of the Navigation Bar Properties panel) works much like configuring other Flash components.

After picking the Site Style to use and the button set from the Button drop-down list, you can configure the following properties:

- **Colors**   Click Background, Rollover, or Rollover Font and then click the small down arrow at the right end of the field to set the color for those items from the ColorPicker. The Rollover and Rollover Font colors are used for the button indicating the current page until you roll the mouse over a different button.
- **Font**   Specify the font, style, alignment, and size to use for both the regular and rollover fonts, as well as the color of the regular font. This is all done from the Edit Font dialog box, which opens when you click the color rectangle or Font name in the right side of the Font property.
- **Flyouts**   Select this field (which shows a check mark when activated) to allow fly-out menus for parent pages that have child pages that are not visible in the Navigation Bar.

Set the Target Frame for Hyperlinks

Fusion offers the option to set a "target" for a hyperlink. When you click a hyperlink in your web site (including the buttons in graphical, text, and Flash Navigation Bars), that link has to know where to open the linked material. Fusion's default behavior (when the link Target is set to "None") is to replace the entire page with the target page. For internal links (pages within your web site) this works well because you can use the Navigation Bar in the MasterBorder of the new page to navigate to other pages in the web site.

 This assumes that you don't set the MasterBorder to ZeroMargins and that you place a Navigation Bar in the MasterBorder.

But there are other times that you might not want to replace the entire page with the new page. For example, if the link is to a site outside your web page, the MasterBorder (and its handy navigation buttons) disappear, and you have no easy way to find your way back to your site, except by using your History list or Favorite/Bookmark that you set. In cases like that, you might prefer to have the new window open in the Layout section of the page (leaving the MasterBorder intact and visible) or even in a new window altogether. You can achieve both of these results, though you do need to configure the Target parameter for a hyperlink or Navigation Bar in order to do so.

Targets are set in one of three ways. For Navigation Bars based on the site structure, you choose the target from the Target drop-down list in the Navigation Bar Properties panel. For all other types of links except custom Navigation Bars, you set the target from the Link dialog box. For custom Navigation Bars, the Target drop-down list is actually visible in the Properties panel, but it is grayed out and unavailable. To set the Target for a custom Navigation Bar, you must click the Edit Custom button and select from the Target drop-down list in the Custom Navigation Bar Structure dialog box.

The options that are available for setting a target depend on whether you have established frames for the MasterBorder or not. We'll take the simpler case first—where you have *not* established frames for the MasterBorder.

Establish a Link Target with No MasterBorder Frames

For Navigation Bars based on the site structure, only the default targets are available in the Target drop-down list of the Navigation Bar Properties panel.

In addition to the default value of "(None)," which opens the link by replacing the existing window, the values are _blank, _parent, _self, and _top. The value _blank opens the link in a new window with same name as the page name; the rest of the values open the link in the current window, just as (None) does.

You also have the option to open the link in a new window, which you can name. To establish the existence of the new window, click New Target to open a simple dialog box where you can type the name of the Window into the Target Name field.

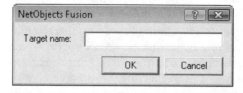

Once you have done so, this target is available in the Target drop-down list. If you choose this new window as the target, the Navigation Bar links are opened in a window labeled with this name.

When you specify a Target in the Link dialog box (for all links except Navigation Bars), you have three options in the Target drop-down list: (None), Existing, and

Pop-Up Window. (None) works just as it does for a site-based Navigation Bar: the link opens in the current window. Existing displays a new Name drop-down list. This list includes all the default target values (_blank, _self, _parent, and _top) as well any target windows you may have created using the New Target button in the Navigation Bar Properties panel. The default target values produce the same results as described previously for the Navigation Bar Properties panel.

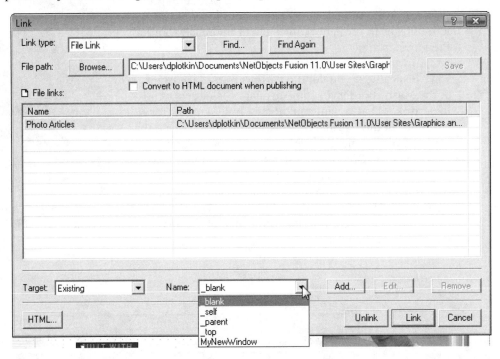

You can create and edit new target windows from the Link dialog box, and you have more control than you do with the Navigation Bar Properties panel. You can

- **Add a new target**   Click Add to open the dialog box where you can type in the name of the new target window.
- **Edit a target**   If you select a target you built from the Name drop-down list, the Edit button becomes available. Click it to reopen the dialog box where you can change the name.
- **Remove a target**   If you select a target you built from the Name drop-down list, the Remove button becomes available. Click Remove to delete the target. There is no confirmation, and the target is deleted even if you click the Cancel button in the Link dialog box.

Creating a Target using a Pop-Up Window (the third option in the Link dialog box Target drop-down list) is discussed later in this chapter, in the section "Create a Pop-Up Window for a Link."

Establish a Link Target Using MasterBorder Frames

As discussed in Chapter 3 (under "Handle the Frame Aspects of MasterBorders"), you can split a MasterBorder into four specified frames—one for each of the margins (left, top, bottom, and right). As a reminder, you use the four buttons in the AutoFrames tab of the MasterBorder Properties panel.

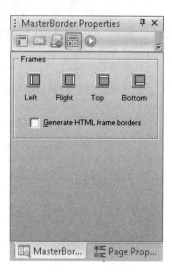

And why would you want to establish frames this way? Basically, if you do, the various frames (margins of the MasterBorder) become available as targets of hyperlinks. That is, you can direct a link to open (for example) in the left margin, enabling you to replace the contents of that margin, perhaps with a new Navigation Bar or picture. One handy use for this technique is to create a set of buttons (or images) in the top margin with links to various major sections (or sub-sites) of your web site. Clicking one of these links could then replace the left margin with a page containing the Navigation Bar and explanatory text for that section of the site. See Figure 9-6 for an example.

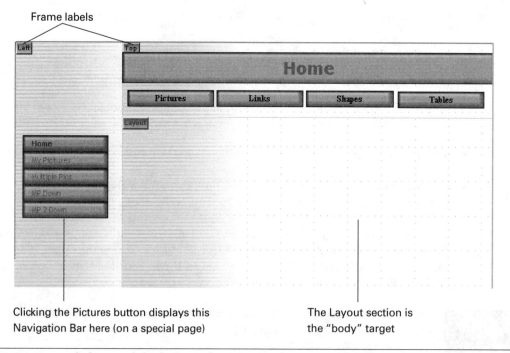

Frame labels

Clicking the Pictures button displays this
Navigation Bar here (on a special page)

The Layout section is
the "body" target

FIGURE 9-6 Click one of the links in the top margin to open a different page in the left margin.

When you direct a page (link) to open in the left margin (or any other margin), you'll only see as much of the page as fits in that margin. Thus, if you build a page with a Navigation Bar on it that is designed to open in the left margin, make sure to place all the items you want visible against the left edge of the page.

Another useful consequence of establishing frames is that another new target becomes available—called "body" (which is available for all links, including custom Navigation Bars). This target refers to the central Layout region of the page. Thus, clicking a link in the left margin could open the new page in the Layout section, leaving the left frame (with its links and Navigation Bars) still visible and available for use. This is useful for external links, since you can still click a Navigation Bar button to jump to another page in the site (or outside of it, for that matter). Figure 9-7 shows an example of displaying an external link in the "body" target.

 By the way, the frame targets are not available for a custom Navigation Bar. This is because the Name drop-down list in the Custom Navigation Bar Structure dialog box (which becomes visible after you pick Existing in the Target drop-down list) does not include the frames as targets.

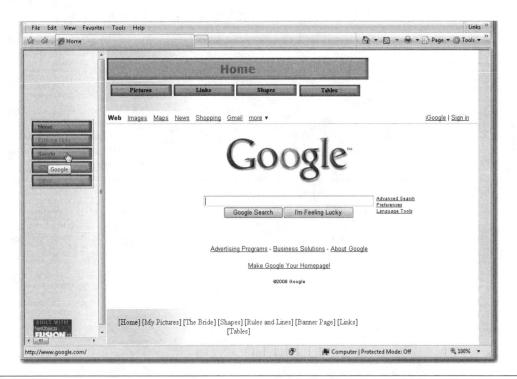

FIGURE 9-7   The left margin is still there, but the center area shows another page.

External links in a site-based Navigation Bar are only available if you added them by clicking the More Pages button (in the Navigation Bar Properties panel) and specifying the external links using the More Pages dialog box. You must establish the targets for More Pages by selecting each one in the right panel of the More Pages dialog box and then picking the target from the Target drop-down list (and associated Name drop-down list).

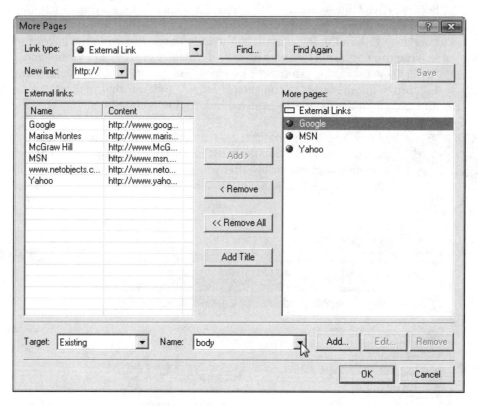

Realistically, the "body" target is only useful for external links. This is because if you open an internal page in the Layout area ("body" target), you get the MasterBorders/frames as well as the content, giving you an embedded set of frames (see Figure 9-8).

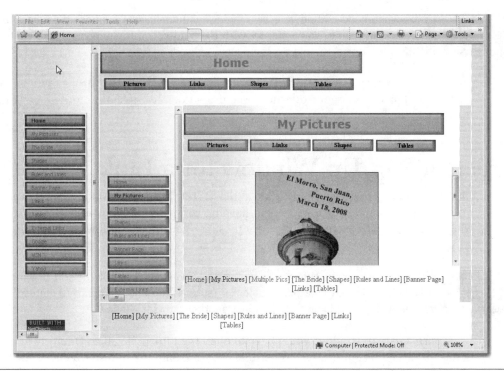

FIGURE 9-8 An internal web site page embedded in the Layout area ("body" target)

To pick a target for a site-based Navigation Bar, you select it from the Target drop-down list in the Navigation Bar Properties panel, just as before. But now you have the frames and the body targets as choices you can pick.

Note Unlike when hand-coding your own frames, you don't get to choose the names for the frames in Fusion. You are stuck with the hard-coded frame names: LeftFrame, RightFrame, TopFrame, and BottomFrame. Oh well.

To choose a target from the Link dialog box, change the Target drop-down list to Existing and pick the target from the Name drop-down list, just as before. But again, the list now includes the frames and body.

Create a Pop-Up Window for a Link

As you've already seen, you can create a new target that is a separate window, and even name that window. However, you have no control over the window size, or where it opens on the screen. To specify these for your new window, you need to define a "pop-up" window.

 Note Although Fusion calls this window a "pop-up" window, it is not the sort of window that will be blocked by a pop-up blocker (such as the one built into the latest version of Internet Explorer). It is just another browser window.

To use a pop-up window, you'll have to open the Link dialog box. One way to do that is to select a text or graphic hyperlink and click the Link button (in either the Properties panel or the Standard Tools toolbar) or choose Link from the shortcut menu. Once the dialog box is open, simply choose Pop-Up Window from the Target drop-down list and select the name of the pop-up window in the Name drop-down list. To create a pop-up window, click Add to open the Pop-Up Window: Properties Editor dialog box.

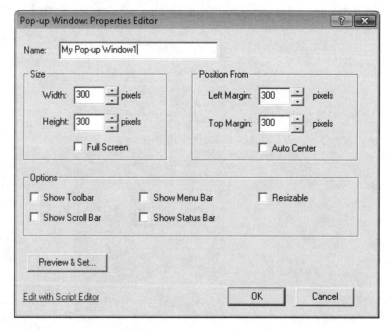

Use the following steps to define the window:

1. Type the name of the window into the Name field. This name is displayed in the browser title bar, so choose carefully.
2. Set the size of the window by entering a value in pixels into the Width and Height fields. A good value to use is 768 (height) and 1024 (width), as pretty much all computers can display this size window. Alternatively, select the Full Screen check box to size the window to full screen on the site visitor's computer.
3. Set the offset from the upper-left corner by entering values into the Left Margin and Top Margin fields. Increasing the left margin moves the window further to the right, increasing the top margin moves the window further down. You cannot use negative numbers. Alternatively, you can select the Auto Center check box to center the new window on the site visitor's computer.
4. Choose the options you want displayed in the window by making selections from the Options section of the dialog box. The choices are
   - **Show Toolbar** Shows all the visitor's standard toolbars, including Links, Google, Yahoo, and so on.
   - **Show Scroll Bar** Displays a vertical scroll bar, whether one is needed or not. Note that if the page is larger than the window, the scroll bar will be displayed whether you select this check box or not.
   - **Show Menu Bar** Shows the standard Windows menus.
   - **Show Status Bar** Shows the Browser status bar, typically located at the bottom of the Browser window. This is the bar that shows the magnification, error messages, and other information.
   - **Resizable** Enables the site visitor to click and drag the window borders to resize the window.
5. As you adjust the Window parameters, click the Preview & Set button to preview your window (see Figure 9-9). As long as you didn't choose the Full Screen option, this preview window is resizable—just click and drag the borders as you

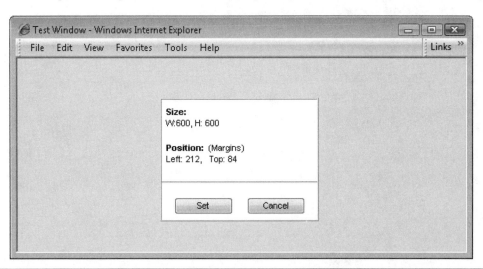

FIGURE 9-9 Preview your pop-up window to see if it works for you.

normally would. You can also relocate the window by clicking and dragging the title bar (just like any other window). Once you have the window at the size and position you want, click the Set button in the preview to transfer the settings into the Pop-Up Window Properties Editor.

I seriously (really) suggest that you make your pop-up window resizable, especially if you are going to use it to display pages in your web site. If the window is too small, the first things shown in the window are the margins, and whatever is left is used to display the Layout in a scrolling internal section. By allowing the window to be resizable, you enable the site visitor to change that and see the page content easily.

10

Create a Photo Gallery

HOW TO...

- Create a Standard Photo Gallery
- Pick images and customize a Standard Photo Gallery
- Create a flashy photo gallery using Flash
- Pick images and lay out the pages
- Set up the animation effects for your Flash Photo Gallery

One of the very neatest things you can do with your web site is to post your pictures on it to share them. Fusion enables you to build two different types of photo galleries: standard galleries based on HTML, and Flash galleries, with the ability to add custom animations that jazz up your gallery. Both of these tools are available in the Custom Components panel in the Advanced Tools section.

Build a Standard Photo Gallery

The Standard Photo Gallery does not have all the pizzazz of Flash, but it is very serviceable, with attractive templates for both the thumbnails and the "detail" (full image) pages. It is easy and quick to build and will work with any browser. It also avoids the security issues that you can have with Flash.

Create the Photo Gallery and Pick the Images

To create a photo gallery, choose the component, then click and drag on the page to define the extent of the gallery. This opens the Add Photo Gallery dialog box, where you can name the photo gallery and pick a profile for your initial configuration.

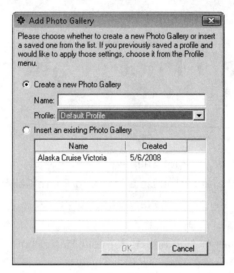

You can create and save profiles as you build your photo gallery, as described later in this chapter. Also, once you have created a photo gallery, you have the option to add an existing gallery from the Add Photo Gallery dialog box. To do so, select the Insert An Existing Photo Gallery radio box and pick the gallery from the list.

The next step is to add the images you want in the photo gallery. The Open dialog box is displayed automatically when you build the gallery initially.

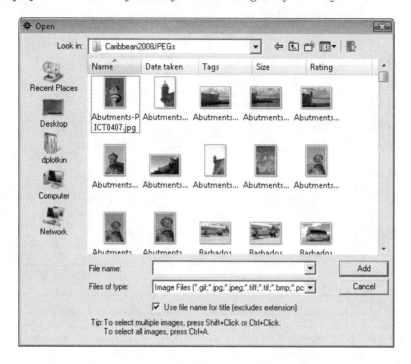

 You can go back and add additional photos later by clicking the Configure button in the Photo Gallery Properties panel, and then clicking the Add button in the Images tab of the Photo Gallery Properties Editor dialog box (see Figure 10-1 for a look at this dialog box).

To select the photos you want, select them from the Open dialog box. To select multiple images, click the first image, and then CTRL-click any additional photos. If you change your mind about including the photo, CTRL-click it again to remove it from the list. Alternatively, you can click the first image and then SHIFT-click on another image to select all images in between. If you want to use the filename as the Title of the image, select the Use File Name For Title (Excludes Extension) check box. Once you are done selecting images, click Add to close the Open dialog box and display the Images tab of the Photo Gallery Properties Editor (see Figure 10-1).

Configure the Included Images and Thumbnails

Once you have picked the images to include, you can provide titles and captions, as well as reorder and specify the size and quality of the thumbnails and the photo images. All of this work is done from the Images tab of the Photo Gallery Properties Editor, seen in Figure 10-1.

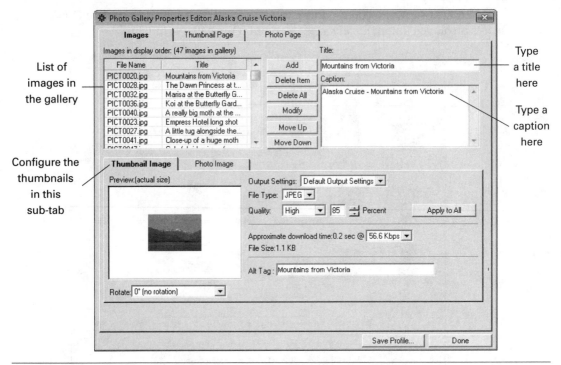

FIGURE 10-1 The Properties dialog is where you configure everything about the photo gallery.

Title and Order the Images

To add or adjust the title and caption, select the image from the list in the upper-left corner of the dialog box, type the title into the Title field, and add a caption in the Caption field. The buttons alongside the list of images enable you to do the following:

- **Add**   Reopens the Open dialog box, so you can choose and add more pictures.
- **Delete Item**   Deletes the selected picture.
- **Delete All**   Deletes all the pictures, leaving you with an empty gallery.
- **Modify**   This button also reopens the Open dialog box, but the image you choose replaces the image selected in the file list in the Photo Gallery Properties Editor dialog box.
- **Move Up**   Moves the selected image up one in the list. You can also click and drag an image up or down in the list. A thin red line appears in the list to show where the image will be positioned when you release the mouse button.
- **Move Down**   Moves the selected image down one in the list.

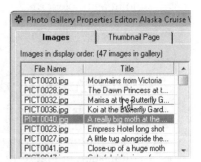

Specify the Thumbnail and Photo Image Quality

The Thumbnail sub-tab is where you configure the thumbnails that will be generated. Each thumbnail is a separate file (albeit a small one), and you can pick whether it is a JPEG or GIF file from the File Type drop-down list. You can also pick the quality by picking a value from the Quality drop-down list (Low, Medium, High, or Maximum), or by adjusting the value in the Percent field.

Remember, the higher the quality, the bigger the file. For thumbnails, quality doesn't matter too much, since the files are so small anyway. But it can make a big difference when it comes time to specify the Photo Image quality.

You can choose the assumed download speed from the Approximate Download Time drop-down list to predict how long it will take to download each image. You can also apply the settings for a single thumbnail to all the thumbnails by clicking Apply To All. This is a handy time-saver, as you rarely need to have different quality for each image. You can specify the Alt tag in the Alt Tag field. The Alt tag is the text used while the image loads, or instead of the image if a site visitor has turned off images in the browser (which makes for a pretty boring photo gallery!). It also appears as a Screen Tip when the site visitor hovers the mouse over the picture.

The Output Settings drop-down list enables you to save a specific set of quality settings to be reused later. Initially, the Output Settings drop-down list contains the value "Default Output Settings." If you change either the file type or the quality, the value switches to "User Settings." To save the settings, choose Save Settings from the drop-down list to open the Save Gallery Output Settings dialog box. Type a name into the Name field and click OK to save the settings.

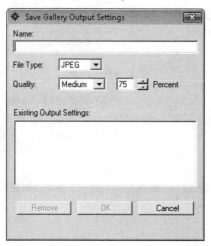

As you can see, you can change the settings in the Save Gallery Output Settings dialog box before naming and saving the settings. It's a bit tricky to change the Quality settings, though. You can't select the existing number with the mouse and then type over it, because nothing happens. Instead, click in the field and backspace over the existing numbers, and then type in the new value.

Once you have saved some settings, you can choose the setting name from the Output Settings drop-down list.

 You can delete a setting if you don't need it any more by selecting it in the Existing Output Settings list in the Save Gallery Output Settings dialog box and clicking Remove.

The last piece of functionality is to rotate the thumbnail. If the image is lying on its side or is upside down, make a choice from the Rotate drop-down list to correct the situation. You can rotate the image 90° left or right, or flip it over.

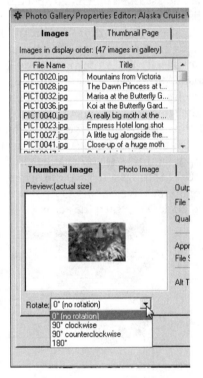

 If you rotate a thumbnail, the photo image is also rotated (which is, after all, what you'd want).

The Photo Image tab is where you configure the photo image settings. It looks exactly like the Thumbnail Image tab. However, because these photos are considerably larger, you need to be more careful about balance between image quality and size.

Set Up the Thumbnail Page

The Thumbnail Page tab is where you pick the design of the thumbnails that will be displayed on the photo gallery main page.

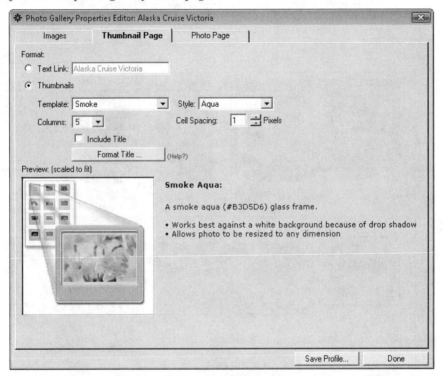

From this page you can choose the following options:

- **Text Link**   You can use a text link for each image instead of thumbnails by picking the Text Link radio button and filling in the field with the text you want to use. However, I don't recommend this option, because the site visitor is faced with a page of identical text links and won't have any idea what the pictures behind the text links look like.

- **Thumbnails** Pick the Thumbnails radio button to specify how the thumbnail page will look (see Figure 10-2 for a sample of a thumbnail page). You have a wide variety of options to choose from:
  - **Template** You can pick from a wide variety of templates in the Template drop-down list. Each one has a description, which tells you what works best (such as that it should be used against a white background).
  - **Template configuration options** Some templates have additional options you can pick from. For example, the Simple border template enables you to choose the Border width and Color. Other templates have variable styles you can apply by making a selection from the Style drop-down list. Finally, the Film style

FIGURE 10-2 Thumbnails give you an idea of what the image will look like when you click it.

enables you to pick from fixed width (all images have the same thumbnail width) or variable width (landscape images are wider than portrait images).

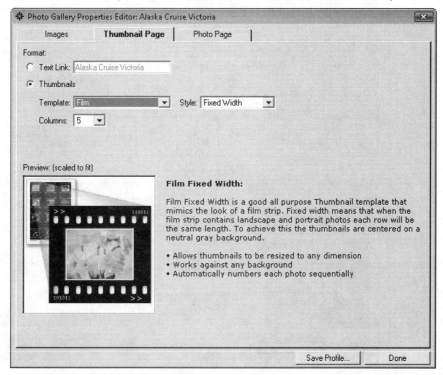

- **Cell Spacing** Some templates enable you to set the spacing between the thumbnails in pixels by entering a value in the Cell Spacing field.
- **Columns** You can pick the number of columns of thumbnails to display on the page. The more columns you add, the smaller the thumbnails are displayed. If all the thumbnails won't fit on a single page, Fusion extends the page to hold them all. If this is not what you want, you'll have to create multiple pages with links between them.
- **Include Title** Some templates enable you to include the image title alongside the thumbnail by selecting the Include Title check box. If you do include the title, you can click Format Title to open the Object Format dialog box, where you can set all the character, paragraph, border, and background parameters.

Once you finish configuring the photo gallery and click Done, it can take a significant amount of time to build the gallery on the page. Note also that there is no Cancel button. If you change your mind and don't want to change anything, click the red "x" button in the upper-right corner to exit the dialog box without changing anything. It's a *lot* quicker than clicking Done!

Set Up the Photo Page

The Photo Page tab is where you configure the layout of the page where the large images open when you click a thumbnail.

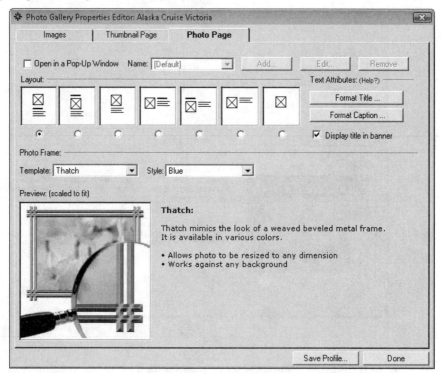

Your first choice is whether to show the image in a pop-up window. If you select the Open In A Pop-Up Window check box, you'll have the opportunity to either pick a previously defined window from the Name drop-down list, or create or edit one, using the same techniques discussed for the link targets.

Choose one of the seven boxes at the top of the Layout section to specify the layout of the image (represented by the x rectangle), the title (represented by the bold line) and the caption (represented by the stack of three lighter lines). Note that some of the layouts don't show the title, and one (at the right end) doesn't show either the title or the caption. If you choose a layout that includes the title or caption, you can click Format Title or Format Caption to open the Object Format dialog box, where you can set the character, paragraph, border, and background formatting, just as described for text boxes (Chapter 4).

 I do not recommend selecting the Display Title In Banner check box unless you have been careful to keep your titles short. Long titles can overflow the banner area, making for a messy page.

The fun part about configuring the page is to choose a Template and a Style from the drop-down lists. The Preview area gives you an idea of what the template looks like. The text alongside of the preview describes the template and any limitations. For example, some templates do not allow the image on the page to be resized, which limits your options.

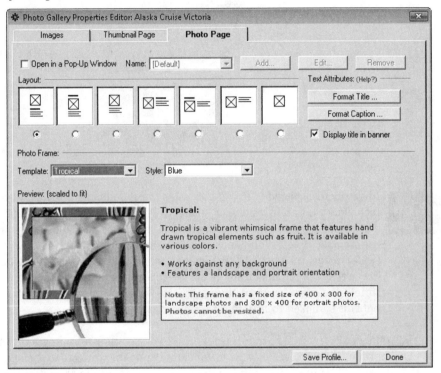

View the Thumbnail Result Page

Once you're done configuring the thumbnails and photos, click Done to see the thumbnail page, as shown previously in Figure 10-2. However, you aren't stuck with this arrangement. While you can't resize the Photo Gallery object (outlined with the green line), you can click inside it and drag it to a new location on the page. You can also click the Configure button in the Photo Gallery Properties panel to reopen the Photo Gallery Properties Editor.

You can configure the individual thumbnails as well. To do so, click the image to show a sizing handle in the lower-right corner.

To resize the thumbnails, click a thumbnail and either click and drag the sizing handle, or adjust the Width field in the Thumbnail Properties panel.

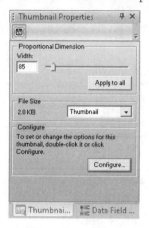

 I heartily recommend that you *not* resize the thumbnails this way. Although the technique works fine if all your images are either portrait or landscape, things get messed up if you have a combination of portrait and landscape thumbnails. For example, if you slightly enlarge the image width by working on a landscape (wide) image, the portrait (tall) images are shrunken considerably. What it looks like is that the tall dimension is made equal to the slightly enlarged width—which shrinks the overall portrait thumbnail size because the "width" (distance left to right) is shrunken to maintain the aspect ratio.

You can also rearrange the thumbnails. To do so, click and drag a thumbnail elsewhere on the page. As you do, a red arrow appears pointing to the spot where the thumbnail will be inserted. Simply release the mouse button to relocate the thumbnail.

When you have a mixture of landscape and portrait pictures, dragging and dropping a portrait picture can lead to some odd results—landscape images left behind in the row where the portrait image was located may suddenly be displayed in a tall (portrait) frame—which looks funny because of all the white space at the top and bottom of the thumbnail. The easiest way to fix this is to switch to a different page, and then back to the Photo page—which rebuilds the thumbnails correctly.

To adjust anything else about the thumbnail, click the Configuration button in the Thumbnail Properties panel to reopen the Photo Galleries Properties Editor dialog box.

View the Photo Result Page

When you create a photo gallery, Fusion automatically creates the pages needed to view the larger images. In a browser, you can see these pages by clicking a thumbnail (or a text hyperlink for the image, if you chose that option). This page can be seen in the Site view (see Figure 10-3) as well as any Navigation Bars based on the site structure.

 You may want to remove the larger photo page from the navigation structure so that the site visitor can't jump directly to it (but can only access it through the thumbnails). To do so, switch to Site view and select the Exclude From Navigation check box.

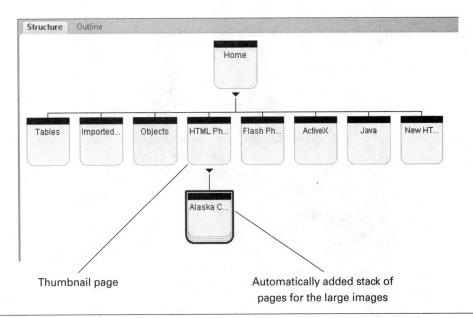

FIGURE 10-3 A photo gallery automatically adds a page for each large photo.

One thing you may have noticed in Figure 10-3 is that the icon for the large image page looks a little different—it looks like stacked pages. There is a reason for this—there are multiple pages in this stack—one for each image. The pages are connected with SmartLinks that enable you to navigate between the pages or return to the thumbnail page.

To configure the photo page, open it (see Figure 10-4) in Page view. Although you can only see a single page, any configuration changes you make to the page are also made automatically on the other pages in the gallery (stack). This even applies to changing the page size and margins, as well as page properties such as background color and image.

The options you can adjust on the photo page include

- **Size of the image** For templates that allow resizing (some do not), you can click and drag the sizing handle to change the size of just the current photo. Alternatively, you adjust the value in the Width field of the Photo Properties panel. If you do use the Width field, click Apply to apply the width change to the current photo, or the Apply All button to apply the change to all the photos. The border graphic resizes automatically when you resize the image.

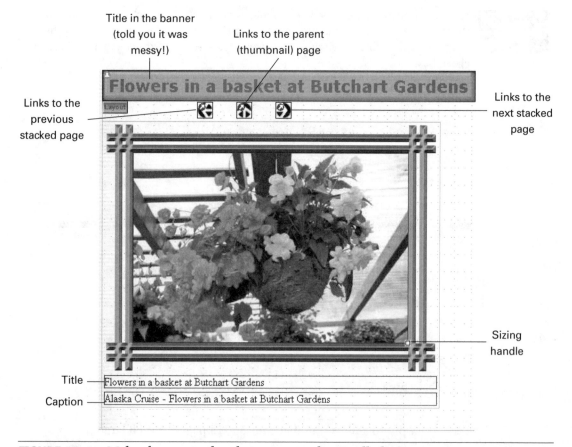

FIGURE 10-4 Make changes to the photo page to change all photos at once.

You Can Save a Profile with All Your Photo Gallery Settings

You can save settings associated with a photo gallery so that you can reuse them for another gallery. The profile stores the photo image output, thumbnail image output, thumbnail page settings (including format, template, style, and columns), and photo page settings (including layout, text attributes, title in banner, template, and style). To save the profile, go to Page view, and display the thumbnail page or photo page in the gallery. Open the Photo Gallery Properties Editor by clicking the Configure button in the Photo Gallery Properties panel. Click Save Profile, type a name for the profile, and click OK.

Note Keep in mind that for the large photos, the Width is applied to both the landscape photos and the portrait photos. If you increase the width of a portrait photo, it can get quite tall on the page to maintain the aspect ratio.

- **Configure the Title and Caption** Click either the title or caption to display the Format tab of a standard text properties panel (called either Title Properties or Caption Properties), where you can adjust the text properties such as font, size, style, color, paragraph, bullets—and even add a hyperlink. These options were discussed previously in Chapter 4.
- **Adjust the image navigation hyperlinks** As mentioned earlier, each page has a set of hyperlinks that navigate to the next or previous stacked page, or back up to the thumbnail page. Click one of these images to activate the Picture Properties panel, where you can pick a different image as well as make all the adjustments to the images discussed earlier in the book (see Chapter 5).

Build a Flash Photo Gallery

There are certain limitations to the HTML-based photo gallery. For one thing, you have to build individual pages of thumbnails that can scroll on forever if there are a lot of thumbnails. And although there are some very nice templates to choose from, there are no animation effects. Flash photo galleries enable you to build multiple albums, and each album can spill over multiple pages with links between the pages. But Flash galleries aren't perfect. In addition to the security issues, building a Flash gallery is *slow*—there are places where you can actually out-type the computer when you are entering titles and captions. Plus, there are so many tabs and sub-tabs for a multitude of options that you can get carried away and lost. And, of course, it's easy to overdo the animation effects and overwhelm the photos with flashing and sparkling!

Create the Flash Photo Gallery and Pick the Pictures

To create the Flash Photo Gallery, select the Flash Photo Gallery tool from the Advanced Tools section of the Custom Components panel. Then click and drag on the page to define the boundaries of the gallery and open the Photos dialog box (see Figure 10-5).

To choose the images, use the Folders pane to navigate to the location of the images. Clicking a folder displays the filenames or thumbnails for those images in the adjacent panel. Select the images by using click, SHIFT-click, and CTRL-click as described earlier in the chapter. When you have all the photos in a folder selected, click Add To Photo Gallery to add them to the currently active album. These images show up in the

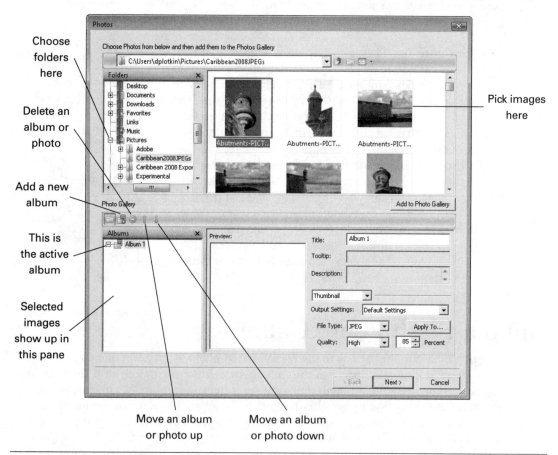

FIGURE 10-5 Pick the pictures you want to include and configure them in the Photos dialog box.

Albums panel. Clicking one of the images in the Albums panel displays a preview in the adjacent Preview panel.

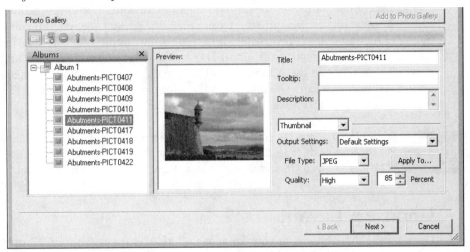

 Make sure to click the name of the album you want to add images to before selecting images and clicking Add To Photo Gallery. Images are added to the selected album.

You can use the text fields to the right of the Preview panel to specify the title, tooltip, and description. Much as with the photo gallery described earlier in this chapter, you can specify the File Type and Quality for both thumbnails (pick Thumbnail from the drop-down list) or the larger images (pick Detail from the drop-down list). And, you can save the output settings for reuse later. However, you cannot rotate images here; you'll have to wait until later to do that.

 Use CTRL-A or choose Edit | Select All to select all the images in the folder.

You can re-order the images in an album by clicking the image and using the green Up and Down arrows to move them up and down in the list. Unlike when working in a Standard Photo Gallery, you can't click and drag the images to change

Did You Know?

You Can Apply Your Image Settings to Everything

You can apply the file type and quality settings to either all the images in the current album or all the images in all the albums. To apply the settings to all the images in the current album, click Apply To and pick This Album from the fly-out menu. To apply the settings to all the images in all the albums, click Apply To and pick All Albums from the fly-out menu.

their order. To delete an image, select the image and click the Delete The Selected Albums Or Photos button (the red circle icon above the Albums panel).

As mentioned earlier, a Flash Photo Gallery can contain multiple albums. There is only a single album present when you create the gallery, which you can rename by selecting it in the Albums panel and typing a new name into the Title field. Alternatively, you can click the album, click it again to make it editable, and then type the new name in the Albums panel. To create a new album, click the New Album button (second icon from the left above the Albums panel) and type the album name into the Albums panel (replacing the default name).

 To delete an album, select the album and click the Delete Selected Albums Or Photos icon (red circle). You can re-order the albums by selecting an album and clicking the green Up and Down arrow buttons above the Albums panel.

Choose a Layout

Once you're done choosing your images and associating them with albums, click Next to proceed. This displays the Design dialog box with the Layout tab highlighted (see Figure 10-6). Choose one of the predefined layouts in the scrolling

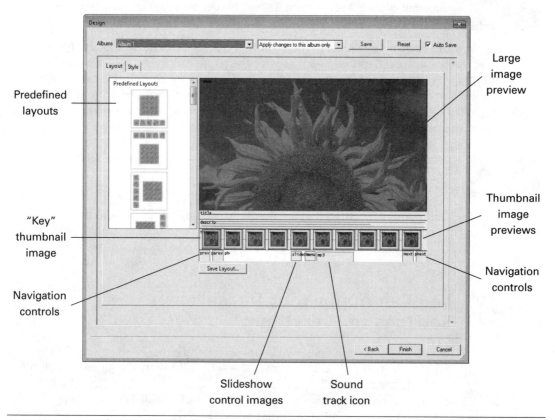

FIGURE 10-6 Choose your layout for each album.

list on the left to see a preview of the layout in the Image section alongside of the layouts.

 Expand the dialog box as much as you can to see the preview of the layout. If the dialog box is too small, you'll have to use the scroll bars to see various parts of the preview.

Customize a Layout

Once you've picked a base layout, you can customize the size and offset for the large image, detail (area behind the image), title field, description field, thumbnails, sound track icon, and navigation controls.

Customize Everything Except the Thumbnails

To change the size and location of pretty much everything except the thumbnails (which have their own special controls), select the item you want to change, which then shows red tabs in the upper-left and lower-right corners. Selecting an item shows the Width, Height, X offset, and Y offset in the Selected Object section of the dialog box. Make the changes you want and remember to click Apply. If you move to another object *without* clicking Apply, the changes will be lost.

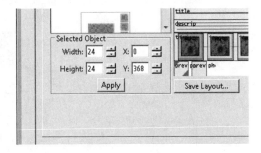

 If you change your mind and want to start over, simply click one of the Predefined Layouts to reapply that layout (you will be asked to confirm).

Another way to adjust the size and position is to click the item, which then displays a red tab in the upper-left and lower-right corners. Click and drag this tab to resize the object, or click inside the selected item and drag to relocate it. Just be aware that there are limits on both size and location. For example, you can't drag the large image very far to the right, as other objects (such as the Title and Description fields) bump up against the page border. Of course, you can make these items (and the image and detail) smaller, which gives you far more leeway in relocating them.

Customize the Thumbnails

There is a *lot* you can do to customize thumbnails, including changing the size, adding title text, rearranging them, and removing them altogether.

When you first view the thumbnails in the Layout tab, you'll notice that one of them is green (see Figure 10-7). This thumbnail is the "key thumbnail." Changes you make to this thumbnail are reflected in all the other thumbnails. This is handy, as you don't have to adjust each of the potentially numerous other thumbnails.

Click in this outside rectangle to change the overall size of the thumbnail

Click in this inside rectangle to change the thumbnail image size

Click in the thumbnail container to customize the thumbnail locations

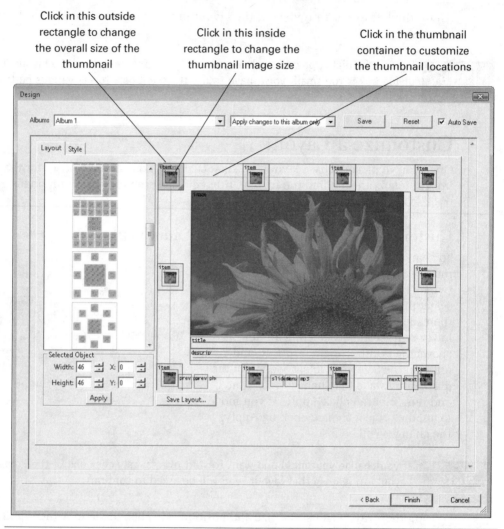

FIGURE 10-7 The key thumbnail controls all the properties for the other thumbnails displayed in the same Thumbnail container.

Note
When you make a change to the key thumbnail (such as resizing it or adding the title), you will not see these changes reflected in the other thumbnails in the dialog box. However, if you close the dialog box (click OK) and reopen it (choose Configure from the Photo Gallery Properties panel), you will see the changes reflected. You can also click in the Item container (the outer rectangle) and then drag the mouse slightly to see the changes applied to all the thumbnails.

Resize the Thumbnail   To adjust the overall size of the thumbnail, click the outside rectangle of the key thumbnail and adjust the size by either changing it in the Selected Object panel or clicking and dragging the red corner tabs.

Resize the Thumbnail Image   To adjust the size of the image contained within the thumbnail, click the inner rectangle (image) of the key thumbnail and change its size by either changing it in the Selected Object panel or clicking and dragging the red corner tabs.

Display a Text Title for a Thumbnail   To display the text title for each thumbnail, right-click the thumbnail (outside) rectangle of the key thumbnail and choose + Title from the shortcut menu.

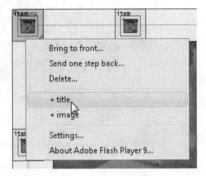

To resize the Title text box, select it and use the Selected Object panel or click and drag the red corner tabs. To move the Title text box, click and drag it—or use the X and Y fields in the Selected Object panel.

Delete a Thumbnail Image or Thumbnail   To remove the thumbnail image from the container, right-click the image container of the key thumbnail and choose Delete from the shortcut menu. If you want to add it back again, choose + image from the shortcut menu.

Although you can remove a thumbnail (click the outside rectangle and choose Delete from the shortcut menu), it is pointless to do so. That's because the moment you make any changes (such as resizing or relocating the thumbnails), the "deleted" thumbnail is added back again. This is also true for the key thumbnail, which will get added back again if you switch tabs (Photo/Design tabs).

Rearrange the Thumbnails   All the thumbnails sit in an area called the "thumbnail container" (visible in Figure 10-7, shown previously). You can click the thumbnail container to display the Hollow Grid panel in the lower-left corner of the dialog box.

You'll also see the red sizing tabs in the upper-left and lower-right corners of the thumbnail container.

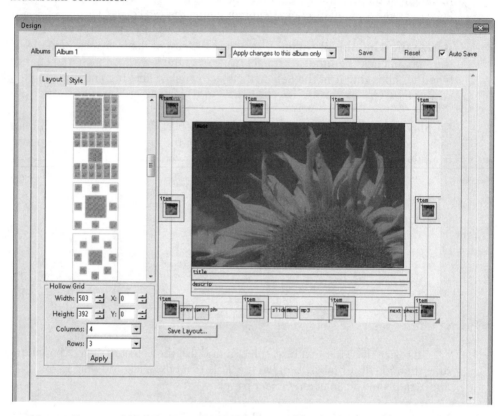

The Hollow Grid panel contains the standard Width, Height, X, and Y fields, which you can use to change the size and location of the thumbnail container (you can also click and drag the container or its red corner tabs). In addition, you can change the two drop-down lists to configure the layout of the thumbnails within the container:

- **Columns** Set the Columns drop-down to either Variable or the number of columns of thumbnails that you want. If you specify a number, that number of columns of thumbnails is displayed, evenly spaced across the thumbnail container. The thumbnails will be automatically shrunken if they won't fit in the container. Setting the value to Variable displays the current number of thumbnails bunched against the left side.
- **Rows** Set the Rows drop-down to either Variable or the number of rows of thumbnails that you want. If you specify a number, that number of rows of thumbnails is displayed, evenly spaced across the height of the thumbnail container. The thumbnails will be automatically shrunken if they won't fit in the container. Setting the value to Variable displays the current number of thumbnails bunched against the top.

But what if you want to just click and drag individual thumbnails to locate them wherever you want (within the thumbnail container)? To do that, right-click in the thumbnail container and choose Transform To Custom Type from the shortcut menu. You can now click and drag any thumbnail to any position in the thumbnail container. However, realize that once you perform this action, there is no longer a key thumbnail. That is, all the thumbnails are independent, so you'll have to deal with each one individually.

Tip   Perform all your thumbnail configurations (such as sizing and adding titles) *before* you transform to custom type!

Save Your Changes to the Albums

Once you've made your changes, you have lots of choices about how to apply them:

- **Save and Reset**   Click Save to keep a temporary copy of the settings. If you change your mind about your customizations, click Reset to return to the settings as they appeared the last time you clicked Save.
- **Save the Layout**   To save a custom layout, click Save Layout, fill in the layout name, and click OK. The layout then appears at the bottom of the scrolling list of Layouts (in the Saved Layouts section).

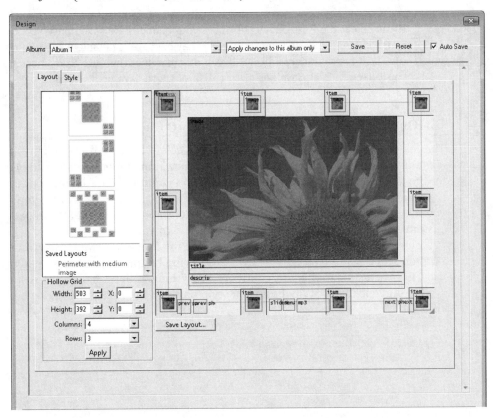

The saved layout includes only the changes you've made to the layout (such as the location and size of the image, title, thumbnails, etc.). It does not include the changes you make to the style from the Style tab (discussed later in this chapter).

- **Apply changes to this album only**   To apply the changes you've made just to the album currently selected in the Albums drop-down list, set the adjacent drop-down list to Apply Changes To This Album Only. The changes include both the changes to the layout and the changes to the style.
- **Apply layout to all albums**   Choose this option from the drop-down list if you want the current layout to be applied for all the other albums. If you change the layout for one album, that layout will be applied to all the other albums as well, overriding any changes you may have made. This change does not include the style.
- **Apply settings to all albums**   This option in the drop-down list refers to the changes you make in the Style tab (discussed later in this chapter). These changes include animations, effects, and much more. To cascade the style settings you make to all the albums without affecting the layouts of the other albums, select this option.
- **Apply changes to all albums**   To apply the changes you've made to all the albums in the Albums list, set the adjacent drop-down list to Apply Changes To All Albums. With this option, your changes (both layout and style) will be applied to all the albums as you make the changes.

 If you select the Auto Save check box, your changes are saved once you click the Finish button (and also the OK button that becomes available when you reopen the Flash Photo Gallery Editor). If you do *not* select the Auto Save check box, then you'll need to click Save and then Finish or OK to save your changes.

Choose and Configure a Style

The Style tab (in the Design tab) of the Photo Gallery dialog box (see Figure 10-8) contains all the options for specifying the frames, animations, sounds, and backgrounds for the album, thumbnail, photo, and navigation controls. The vast number of tabs and controls in each tab can make for an overwhelming experience—just remember that you don't have to change anything—the defaults actually work pretty well, and you can customize little by little to get everything exactly to your liking.

The first step is to pick either a style from the Predefined Styles list (on the left side) or a style you saved previously (listed at the bottom of the Predefined Styles list). To save a style to this list, configure everything as described in the rest of this section and click Save Style. Provide a style name in the Save Style dialog box, and click OK.

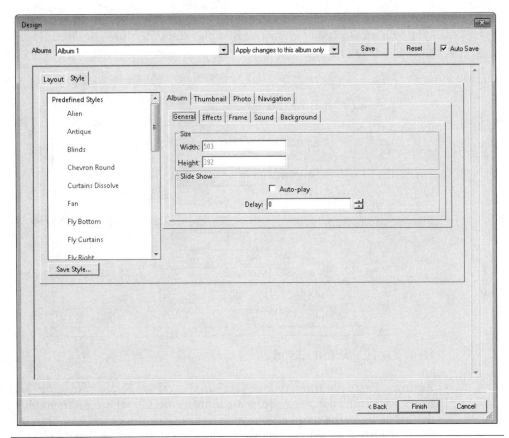

FIGURE 10-8 Start from a predefined style and build from there . . .

Configure the Album

The Album tab has no less than five sub-tabs: General, Effects, Frame, Sound, and Background.

Use the General Tab   The General sub-tab enables you to see (but not change) the size of the album container on the page. You can also select the Auto-play check box so that the slide show will begin automatically after the delay (in seconds) given by the Delay field.

Use the Effects Tab   The Effects sub-tab enables you to specify special effects that take place either On Load (when you first play the slide show) or On Unload (when the slide show ends).

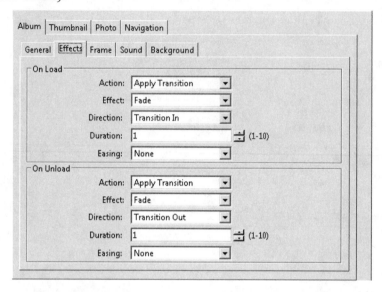

Here is what you can specify:

- **Action**   There are three types of actions: No effect, Apply Transition, and Apply Filter. Both transitions and filters are animations, but where filters modify how the image looks (by doing things such as changing the contrast or blurring the image), transitions actually hide or show parts of the image itself (with effects such as dissolves, fans, and blinds).
- **Effect**   Both filters and transitions have "effects," which specify the overall animation that takes place. For example, filters include effects such as Adjust Contrast, Gradient Bevel, Edge Enhance, and Blur. Transitions include effects such as Bitmap Pixel Dissolve, Fold, Iris, and Squeeze).
- **Filter and Transition Parameters**   Most (though not all) effects have a set of parameters that control how they perform. For example, the Bitmap Pixel Dissolve transition has a Direction (such as Transition In), a Duration (number of seconds for the transition), and an "Easing" (a modification to the overall effect, such as Elastic In or Bounce Out).

Use the Frame Tab   The Frame sub-tab enables you to specify how the frame around the entire album looks and behaves. Once you pick a frame from the Frame drop-down list, you'll see a preview of the frame. You can pick an animation from the Animation drop-down list (for those that support animation), and a color from the Color bar. The color you pick is used for the animated portion of the shape.

For example, if you pick Chase from the Animation drop-down list, the little lights that chase each other around the frame are drawn in the color selected in the Color bar.

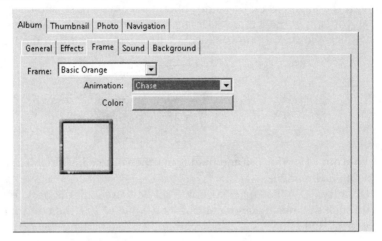

The Simple Border and Line Border frames do not support animation, but they allow setting opacity, colors, and margins (Simple Border) as well as thickness (Line Border).

Use the Sound Tab   The Sound sub-tab enables you to specify a music file that plays along with the slide show.

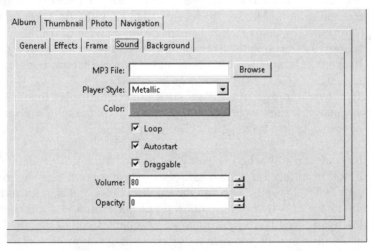

In addition to picking the MP3 (music) file, you can pick the following options:

- **Choose the Player Style**   There are two player styles available—Metallic and City. Pick the one you want from the Player Style drop-down list. You can click the Color bar and choose the color of the player from the ColorPicker.

- **Set the Play parameters** The three check boxes just below the Color bar enable you to select to continually play the song while the slide show is playing (Loop), start the music when the slide show starts (Autostart), and click and drag the player icon in the window (Draggable). If you don't use Autostart, the site visitor will have to start the music by clicking the play button in the Player, shown here.

- **Volume** Use the Volume field to set the volume between 0 and 100. At zero, the sound is inaudible.
- **Opacity** Use the Opacity field to set how much of the background shows through the music player control. At a value of 100, the control is fully visible, at 0 it is invisible.

It is a bit tricky to set the Opacity. If you simply select the current value, type in a new one, and click OK, the change is ignored. To get the change to "take," type in a value close to the one you want, and then use the up/down arrow buttons on the right side of the field to adjust the value to the target value. Alternatively, type in the new value and then click in another editable field *before* clicking OK.

Use the Background Tab The Background sub-tab enables you to set the background color and image. To set the color, click the Background Color bar and pick the color from the Color Picker. Alternatively, you can make the album background transparent by selecting the Transparent check box, enabling you to see the page color and background through the portions of the album that are not displaying pictures, frames, etc.

To choose a background image, click Browse to display the Open dialog box and pick an image. If the image is not big enough to fill the whole album background, you can choose to repeat it using the following options:

- **Repeat** Specify whether you want to repeat the image or not (choose No Repeat if not) from this drop-down list. The "Repeat" option tiles the image in both the X (left and right) and Y (up and down) directions. You also have the option to tile the image only in the X direction (Repeat-x) or in the Y direction (Repeat-y).
- **Position** The Position drop-down list enables you to specify which of the nine quadrants (top left, top center, top right, etc.) you want to place the image in. If you repeat the image, the specified position is where the first image is placed, and the tiling is done outward from that first image.

Configure the Thumbnails

The Thumbnail tab has three sub-tabs: Item, Image, and Title.

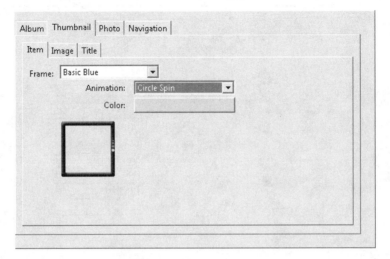

Use the Item Tab   The Item sub-tab enables you to choose a frame, animation, and animation color for the overall thumbnail (which corresponds to the outside rectangle in the Layout tab). The options are identical to those available for setting frames for the album, described earlier in this chapter.

Use the Image Tab   The Image sub-tab has two sub-tabs of its own: Effects (see Figure 10-9) and Frame. The options in the Frame sub-tab are identical to the options in the Album Frame sub-tab and the Thumbnail Item sub-tab. However, this frame is around the image within the overall thumbnail (which corresponds to the inner rectangle for the thumbnail in the Layout tab).

 I recommend using a frame for either the Item (outside thumbnail rectangle) *or* the Image, but not both. Each frame reduces the size of the image, so having two frames can make the image so small it is impossible to see what the image looks like. In addition, having two animated frames in such a tiny space makes the thumbnails *very* busy and unattractive. You have been warned!

Use the Effects Tab   The Effects sub-tab provides still more effects that you can set up for the thumbnails. They are

- **On Preload**   This section enables you to choose an action (show a Progress bar or not) and the style of the Progress bar displayed as the thumbnails are loaded by picking an option from the two drop-down lists. For any reasonable connection speed, these effects go by so fast they probably aren't worth bothering with.
- **On Load**   This section enables you to pick an action (No Effect, Apply Filter, or Apply Transition) and specify all the parameters that go with the action. The action is applied as each thumbnail is displayed on the screen.

Choose the
Style tab

Choose the
Thumbnail tab

Choose the
Image tab

Choose the
Effects tab

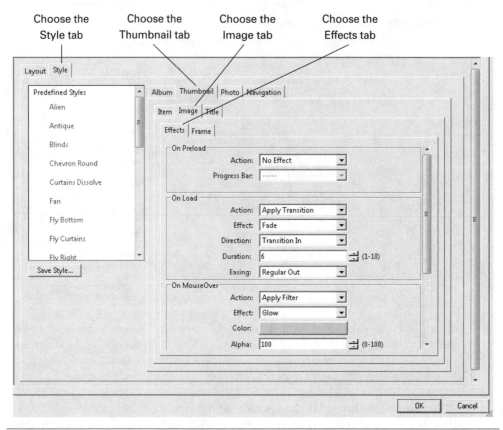

FIGURE 10-9 The Effects sub-tab of the Image sub-tab of the Thumbnail tab of
the Style tab (whew!)

 I don't typically bother with setting an On Load Action. It increases the load time for
the thumbnail images, and makes your site visitor wait longer for essentially what
amounts to "eye candy". Watching and waiting for these effects quickly gets tiresome.

- **On Mouse Over**   This section enables you to pick an action that takes place
  when the site visitor moves the mouse over a thumbnail. In addition to No Effect,
  Apply Filter, and Apply Transition (with their appropriate parameters), you have
  the option to Reset To Original Photo. Reset To Original Photo is especially useful
  if you applied an On Load action that left the thumbnail image in a state where
  it would be hard to recognize the image. For example, if you specify an On Load
  Action of Apply Filter and an Effect of Negative, all your thumbnails will end up
  looking like photographic negatives. If you specify Reset To Original as the action
  for On MouseOver, simply moving the mouse over each image returns it to its
  original form.

Here is a simple tip—don't use Apply Filter for the On Load action!

- **On Mouse Out** This section enables you to pick an action that takes place when the site visitor moves the mouse away from the thumbnail after it was over the thumbnail. The Action and Effect options are identical to On MouseOver.

Use the Title Tab The Title sub-tab enables you to set the font, size, color, style (Bold, Italic, Underline), and paragraph alignment.

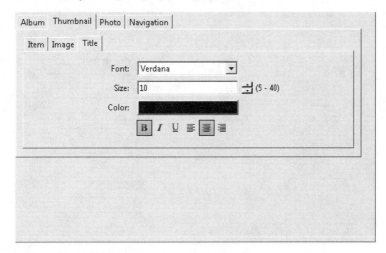

Configure the Photos

The Photo tab controls the behavior of the large image on the page. It has three sub-tabs: Image, Title, and Description. The Title and Description sub-tabs enable you to specify the font, size, color, style, and alignment for the title and description text fields. They work identically to the Thumbnail Title sub-tab.

The Image sub-tab has two sub-tabs of its own: Effects (see Figure 10-10) and Frame. The Frame sub-tab establishes the look and behavior for the frame around the large image, and the options are identical to the options in the Frame sub-tabs for the Album, Thumbnail Image, and Thumbnail Item.

The Effects sub-tab enables you to specify what the site visitor sees as the large image is displayed. The options are

- **On Preload** This section enables you to choose an action (show a Progress bar or not) and the style of the Progress bar displayed as the image is loaded. Simply pick an option from the two drop-down lists. Unlike thumbnails, the large image can take an appreciable amount of time to load, so you may want to use this option.

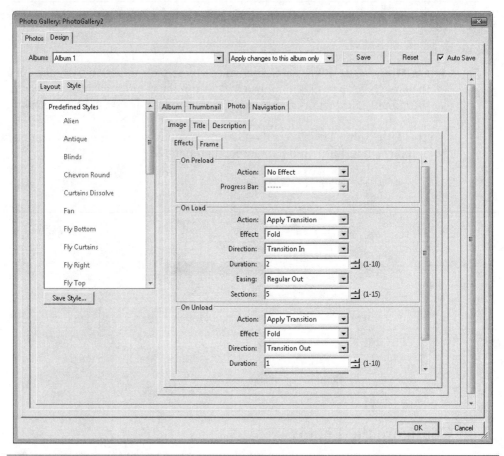

FIGURE 10-10 Specify how the image fades in and out.

- **On Load** This section enables you to pick an action (No Effect, Apply Filter, or Apply Transition) and specify all the parameters that go with the action. The action is applied as each image is displayed on the screen.
- **On Unload** This section enables you to pick an action that is applied as the image is unloaded just prior to displaying the next image. For example, if you use the Fade transition, the image fades out just before the next image is displayed.

Configure the Navigation Controls

The Flash Photo Gallery displays a set of controls for changing photos, changing pages, controlling a slide show, and showing menus (see Figure 10-11).

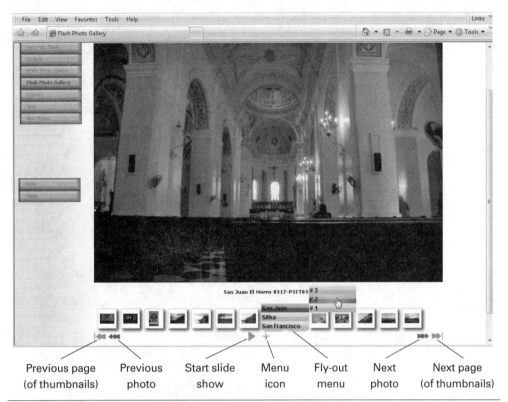

FIGURE 10-11   Control the photos and play a slide show with the navigation controls.

You Can Make a Real Mess with Photo Actions

You should really apply both the On Load and On Unload actions with care and restraint. This is especially true with the On Load filters. Remember that the filters (like Negative, Black and White, Blur, etc.) modify how the image looks, and when the filter is done, the site visitor sees only the result of applying the filter. Thus, for example, if you apply the Negative filter, the site visitor will see the large image as a negative—hardly a good situation. The On Unload action also delays displaying the next image—the site visitor has to sit through the transition. This gets old pretty fast. So, like I said, exercise restraint!

The Navigation tab has sub-tabs for each of the controls, which you can use to configure the controls. The first tab is the Menu tab, where you configure the menu that enables you to jump right to a particular album or page in the gallery.

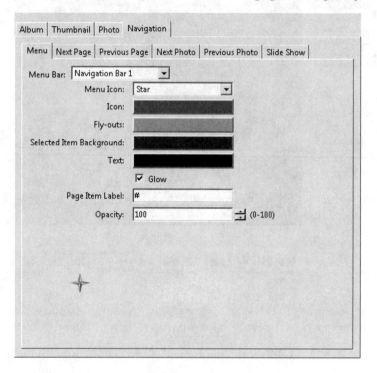

Use the Menu Tab   The Menu sub-tab options are

- **Menu Bar**   Use the options in the Menu Bar drop-down list to pick the style of the fly-out menus that appear when you move the mouse over the Menu icon. The styles vary in shape and text font. To get an idea of what the menu bar looks like, move the mouse over the Menu icon near the bottom of the Menu tab to see sample fly-outs (see Figure 10-12).
- **Menu Icon**   Pick the menu icon from the Menu Icon drop-down list. The list includes a variety of shapes—you can see a preview near the bottom of the Menu tab, as shown in Figure 10-12. The Menu icon appears in the Flash photo gallery. When the site visitor moves the mouse over the icon, a menu appears that enables the visitor to pick a different page of thumbnails.
- **Icon color**   Pick the color of the Menu icon by clicking the Icon color bar and picking the color from the ColorPicker.
- **Fly-outs color**   Pick the background color of the items in the fly-out menu by clicking the Fly-outs color bar and picking the color from the ColorPicker. This color is used for the non-current entry—that is, the page or album that you are not currently viewing (as shown in Figure 10-12).

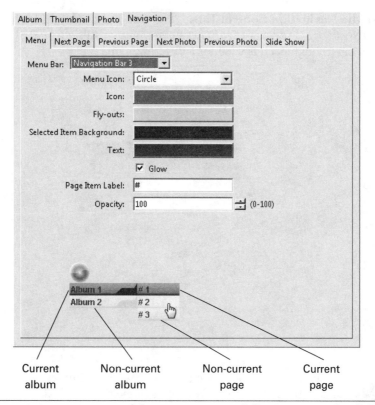

Current   Non-current   Non-current   Current
album   album   page   page

FIGURE 10-12   See a preview of the Menu icon and fly-out menus from the icon
in the dialog box.

- **Selected Item Background color**   As noted in the previous bullet, the "fly-outs"
  color is used for the background of the non-current entry. The Selected Item
  Background color is used for the current entry in the fly-out menu. For example,
  if you are currently viewing Page 1, and there are three pages in the album, Page 1
  will be shown in the "Selected Item Background" color, whereas Pages 2 and 3 will
  be shown in the "Fly-outs" color.
- **Text color**   Pick the color of the menu text by clicking the Text color bar and
  picking the color from the ColorPicker. If you want the text to show a glow effect
  within the menu, select the Glow check box.

 Make sure that the Text color has a very different contrast from both the Fly-outs
color and the Selected Item Background color. Otherwise, it will be very hard to
read the menus.

- **Page Item Label**   Choose the symbol and text to display in the fly-out menus for
  the pages. This text is followed by a sequence number for the page.
- **Opacity**   The opacity of the Menu icon. A value of 100 represents "fully solid,"
  and 0 is invisible (and not very useful unless you have only a single album with a
  single page).

Use the Navigation Control Tabs   The rest of the sub-tabs in the Navigation tab (Next Page, Previous Page, Next Photo, Previous Photo, and Slide Show) are all identical, though each is used for a different icon.

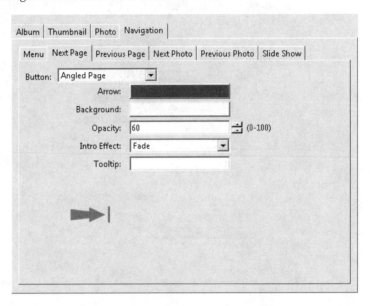

Note   Although the Slide Show tab looks exactly like the other tabs, the selection of icons in the Button drop-down list is different.

The options you can pick are

- **Button**   Pick the icon/image you want to use for the control from the Button drop-down list. There are quite a few different icons you can use—just make sure to use a different one for each control.
- **Arrow color**   Choose the color to use for the control from the Arrow color bar by clicking the bar and selecting a color from the ColorPicker.
- **Background color**   Choose the color to use for the background of the control by clicking the Background color bar and picking the color from the ColorPicker.
- **Opacity**   Specify the opacity of the control from the Opacity field. 100 is a "fully solid" control, while 0 is invisible.
- **Intro Effect**   If you want the control to appear using a Flash effect, pick the effect you want from the Intro Effect drop-down list. The icon at the bottom of the tab displays a preview of the effect when you pick it from this list.
- **Tooltip**   Type the symbol or text you want to use for the tooltip into this field. A tooltip is text that appears when you hover the mouse over the icon. It can be really helpful if the site visitor isn't sure what the various controls do.

   Type in explanatory text, such as "Previous page." Just using the default symbols isn't all that helpful!

How to... View and Make Changes from the Flash Photo Gallery Page

You can go back and reconfigure the Flash Photo Gallery at any time by selecting the Photo Gallery object and clicking the Configure button in the Photo Gallery Properties panel. This opens the Photo Gallery dialog box, which contains both the Photos tab (where you add and remove photos and albums and set quality) and the Design tab (where you configure the look and feel of the Flash photo gallery).

You can also make changes to the Flash Photo Gallery from the Photo Gallery Properties panel.

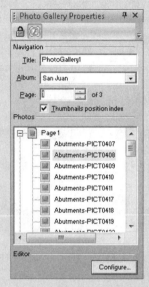

> **Tip** To get back to the Photo Gallery Properties panel to choose a different album or page, click in the photo gallery but not on a thumbnail image or the large image.

To view a different album, select the album from the Album drop-down list. You can also view a different page within an album by choosing the page from the Page field. If you want to see index numbers on the thumbnails, select the Thumbnails Position Index check box.

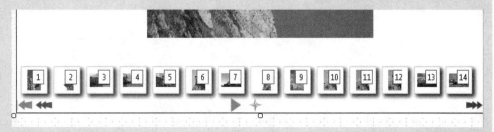

(continued)

The bottom portion of the Photo Gallery Properties panel displays the pages and the images that appear on each page in a tree structure. You can collapse a page to hide the list of images by clicking the – symbol alongside the page name. To re-expand the list, click the + symbol alongside the page name.

The most important adjustment you have to make from the Flash Photo Gallery page is to rotate the thumbnails and images. To make these adjustments, use the following steps:

1. Pick the album and page you want to work on.
2. Click each thumbnail in turn. The image corresponding to that thumbnail appears in the large picture section of the page, and the Picture Properties panel appears for the thumbnail. Make sure the General tab is visible and use the Rotate drop-down list to ensure that the thumbnail is displayed correctly (not lying on its side or upside down!).

 Make sure to click the image in the thumbnail, and not the outside rectangle. Only if you click the image in the thumbnail will the Picture Properties panel display and the large image change.

3. Click the large image corresponding to the thumbnail. The Picture Properties panel that is active now applies to the large image.
4. Use the Rotate drop-down list to rotate the image, or the Horizontal or Vertical buttons to flip the image.
5. If necessary, use the Crop tool to chop out pieces of the image and have it fit the frame better. This will be especially useful if a portrait (tall and narrow) format image needs to fit into a landscape (short and wide) format frame.

If need be, you can use the Adjustment tab or the Remove Red Eye tab to make additional adjustments to the image in the frame.

 Technically, you can also make these changes to the thumbnail. However, they are so small that it usually isn't worth the effort, except perhaps to crop the thumbnail to match the large image.

11

Add Behavior with Custom Controls

HOW TO...

- Create a dynamic advertisement banner
- Create your own menus
- Hunt things down with Google
- Create an interactive site map
- Change pictures on your site automatically

You can give your site pizzazz by juicing it up with controls that don't just sit there but instead respond to your visitors and catch their attention. Of course, it's possible to overdo this sort of thing, but judicious use of these components can make your site easier to use and more memorable. Fusion includes a variety of controls that add these features.

Advertise with an Ad Banner

An *Ad Banner* displays multiple different images with transitions between them. A changing banner like this is much more likely to catch the site visitor's attention than a static (non-changing) banner.

 Note To preview the rotating ad banner, you'll need to publish your site locally, as explained in the upcoming How To box.

To create an Ad Banner, choose Ad Banner from the NOF Standard Components section of the Custom Components panel. Then click and drag on the page to create the banner. All of the configuration for an Ad Banner is done from the Rotating Ad Banner Properties panel.

Choose from the following options to set up the rotating Ad Banner:

- **Banner Type** There are three types of banners: Image Size, Standard Banner, and Custom.
  - Image Size automatically sets the banner to the size of the first image. If that image is smaller than any of the other images, you'll only see part of the larger images unless Automatic Resizing is set to Enabled. If you *do* set Automatic Resizing to Enabled, any larger images are resized to the size of the first image. You'll also get a warning that the browser must be more recent than version 4 of Internet Explorer and Netscape (does anyone use old browsers any more?).
  - Standard Banner Size enables you to pick the Banner Size from a drop-down list, which appears when you make this selection. Options include Full Banner (468 × 60), Half Banner (234 × 60), a vertical banner, and various-sized buttons.
  - Custom enables you to specify the Width and Height in the fields, which appear in the Properties panel when you make this selection.
- **Pause Time (seconds)** The amount of time to show each banner before moving to the next one.
- **Number of Images** The number of images, which make up your rotating ad banner. Each of the images has three lines in the Rotating Ad Banner Properties panel: Image, URL for Image, and Transition.
- **Image** This field is repeated for each image (Image 1, Image 2, etc.). Click in the field and then click the... button to browse and pick the image you want to use from the Picture File Open dialog box.
- **URL for Image** This field is repeated for each image. Click the field and specify a URL for the image you want to use.

Pick either an Image or a URL for an Image—not both. One or the other serves as the source for the image to use.

- **Transition**   This field is repeated for each image. It specifies the transition that occurs between each of the banner images. Values include Column, Fade, Rotate, and Smash.

How to...   ## Publish Your Web Site Locally

Many of the components discussed in this chapter cannot be previewed unless you publish your site and open it in a browser. Components that require publishing often (but not always) show up on the page as a gray rectangle when you switch to Preview mode (click the Preview button near the lower-left corner of the workspace).

While publishing your web site remotely (to a web presence provider) is fairly involved (and is covered in Chapter 16), publishing your web site locally is relatively straightforward and enables you to preview many of the components. To publish your web site locally, click the Publish Site button in the Views bar to open the Publish Site dialog box.

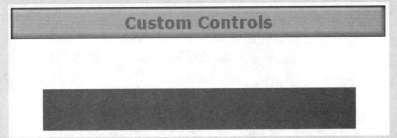

(continued)

Make sure the Publish Files To drop-down list is set to Local Publish. Make a choice from the Pages To Publish drop-down list:

- **Entire Site** Publishes everything, including pages that haven't changed since the last time you published the site.
- **Current Page only** Publishes just the page you are viewing, which is displayed in the field just below the drop-down list. If you wish, you can select the check box to publish just the changed Assets (images, text boxes, components, and so on). To publish locally, however, this is rarely worth it, since the publish is very fast (it's just written to your hard drive).
- **Selected Pages** Publishes just the pages you select. Making this selection opens the Site Structure – Select Page(s) dialog box, where you can select check boxes alongside each page you want to publish. The current page is selected by default.

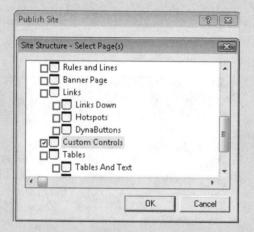

 To reopen the Site Structure – Select Page(s) dialog box, click Change Pages.

To finish up, click Publish to publish the site to your hard drive and open the site in your default browser.

Go Anywhere with the Go Menu

If you'd like to build a set of custom pull-down menus with destination hyperlinks, you can use the Go menu (located in the NOF Standard Components section of the Custom Components panel) to do so. You can place internal, external, and Smart links in the menu, and specify whether the site visitor has to push a button to navigate to the link. Here is a sample of a Go menu in operation.

To preview the Go menu, you'll need to publish your site locally.

To build a Go menu, select the tool and then drag a rectangle on the page to specify the location. This opens the Go Menu dialog box.

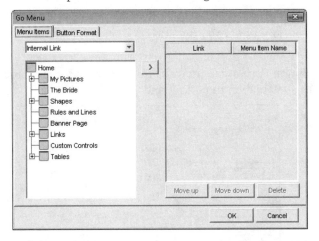

The Go Menu dialog box has two tabs: one to specify the Menu Items, and the other to specify the Button Format. You have the following options for adding menu items:

- **Internal Link**   Pick Internal Link from the drop-down list; then choose which pages to include and click the > button to add the link to the menu. You can double-click the Menu Item Name (which is what is shown in the menu) and change it.
- **External Link**   Choose External Link from the drop-down list to add an external link. Choose the type of link from the left drop-down list and type the rest of the URL into the adjacent field. Type the Asset Name into that field (what is shown on the menu) and press ENTER to create the URL. Click the > button to add the external link to the list of menu items. You can edit the Menu Item Name (which came from the Asset Name) by double-clicking it and editing the text.

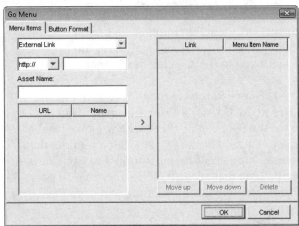

- **Smart Link**   Select Smart Link from the drop-down list to add a Smart link. You are given the opportunity to add links for Home, Up, Next Page, Previous Page, and First Child Page (unless the page has no child pages). Select one of these items and click the > button to add it to the menu item list. You can double-click the Menu Item Name (which defaults to the Smart link name) and change it.

Note   You can rearrange the order of the menu items by selecting one and clicking Move Up or Move Down. You can also click Delete to discard an item.

The Button Format tab provides three choices for the button push to execute the jump to the destination hyperlink and previews what each looks like.

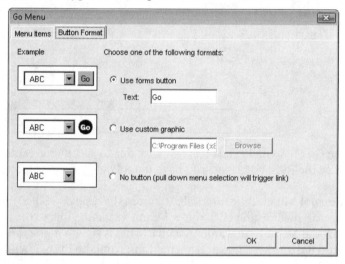

The three options are

- **Use forms button**   This is a text button—just specify the text in the Text field.
- **Use custom graphic**   Uses a custom graphic for the button. To select the graphic, click Browse and pick the image file. The default is a round "Go" button.
- **No button**   As the name implies, no button is provided—just selecting the hyperlink in the Go menu sends you to the selected destination.

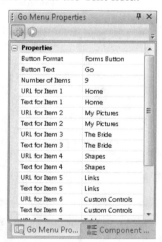

Once you've created the Go menu, you can adjust the properties in the Go Menu Properties panel. Simply click in any of the fields and either make a choice from a drop-down list (Button Format), type a value into the field (Text for Item x, Number of Items, Button Text), or select a link from the Link dialog box (URL for Item x). To get to the Link dialog box, select the URL field and click the ... button.

Hunt Things Down with Google Search

You can add Google to your web site with the Google Search component, located in the NOF Standard Components section of the Custom Components panel. You can choose from several different types of search services, and even customize the look. Here is a sample.

   To preview the Google Search, you'll need to publish your site locally.

To create the Google Search component, choose Google Search and then click and drag on the page to establish the location. This opens the Google Search dialog box.

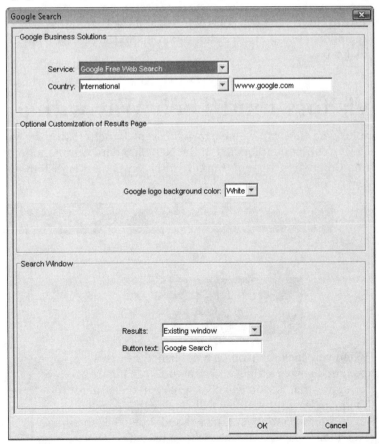

Here are the options you can specify:

- **Service**   Choose the service you want to use from this drop-down list. These include Google Free Web Search (the one most people are familiar with), as well as SafeSearch and Web Search with site search.
- **Country**   Google offers search in many different languages and locales, each with its own search site. For example, the German site is www.google.de. To choose one of these sites to use, specify it in the Country drop-down list, or type a web site into the adjacent field. The "International" option is the one most Americans are familiar with: www.google.com.
- **Google logo background color**   You can specify the background color for the logo from this drop-down list, though the options are limited to white, gray, and black.
- **Results**   The Results drop-down list in the Search Window section enables you to specify where the search results are presented: in the existing window or in a new window. If you use the Existing window, the search results replace the entire window, so the site visitor is no longer on your web site.
- **Button text**   You can specify the text of the button that executes the search by typing that text into the Button Text field in the Search Window portion of the dialog box.

Help Visitors Find Their Way with a Site Map

Complex web sites can be easy to get lost in! To help with that, Fusion provides a Site Map component located in the NOF Standard Components section of the Custom Components panel. Initially, this component is just an image on the page, as shown here.

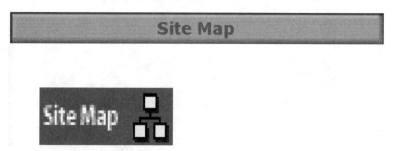

When you click the icon on a published site, this component displays a "live" site structure (see Figure 11-1) in a window—that is, you can click a page in the structure and the main browser window will display that page.

To create the component, pick it and then click and drag to locate it on a page. This establishes a button that the site visitor clicks to open the Site Map. If you want to change the image used, click the Image field in the Site Mapper Properties panel.

Show the site as
an outline with
text page names

Search for a
page in the site

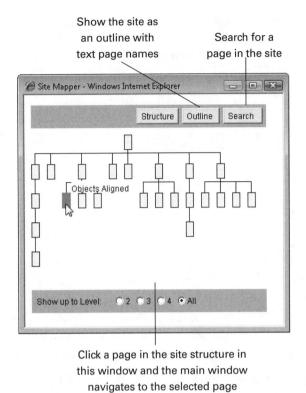

Click a page in the site structure in
this window and the main window
navigates to the selected page

FIGURE 11-1   Use the Site Structure to navigate to a page in the site.

 Place the Site Map button in a MasterBorder to ensure that it is always available on every page.

When a site visitor clicks the Site Map button, the map opens in a separate window, seen in Figure 11-1. The visitor can hover their mouse button over one of the pages (represented by the yellow rectangles) and see the name of the page (the page also turns red). Clicking the page navigates to that page in the main window. The visitor can also choose how many levels of the structure to see in the window by choosing one of the radio buttons in the Show Up To Level toolbar at the bottom of the window.

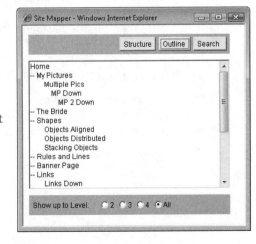

The three buttons at the top of the window provide three different views of the site structure. Choosing Outline provides the structure as an indented outline (with the page names visible), as shown here.

As with the Structure version, the site visitor can click one of the pages to navigate the main window to that page. You can also search for a page by its name. To do so, click the Search button in the top toolbar, type a search term into the field at the bottom of the window, and click the Search button in the bottom toolbar. The window returns a list of any page names that contains the text string.

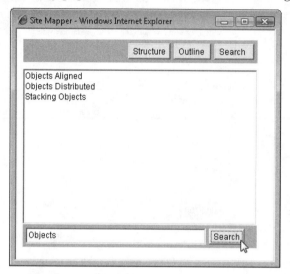

Simply click one of the listed pages to navigate to that page in the main window.

 If the list is blank, Fusion failed to find a match to the search string. That is, the site has no page name containing the string.

Automate Pictures on Your Site

Fusion provides two components that enable you to change pictures on a web page automatically. The first is a rotating picture, which displays a list of pictures, changing them at the intervals you specify. The other component is the time-based picture, which displays a picture based on the time of day.

Insert a Rotating Picture into a Web Page

To create a rotating picture on a web page, choose Rotating Picture from the NOF Standard Components section of the Custom Components panel. Click and drag on the page to specify the location, which opens the Rotating Picture dialog box.

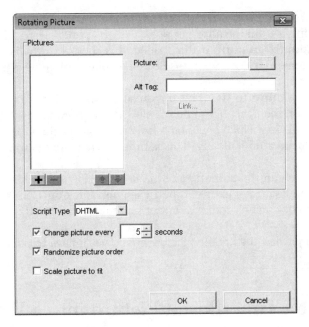

To add a picture, use the following steps:

1. Click the + sign to add a picture, which shows the default name in the Pictures list.
2. Click the ... button alongside the Picture field and choose a picture from Picture File Open dialog box. This changes the name of the picture in the Pictures list to the filename.
3. Type an Alt tag into the Alt Tag field to specify the text the site visitor will see if they haven't enabled images in their browser. The name of the picture in the Pictures list changes to the Alt Tag.

4. If you want to attach a hyperlink to the image, click the Link button to open the Link Target dialog box. Pick either the Site Page radio button (and choose a page from the drop-down list) or the URL radio button (and type in a URL).

You can rearrange the order of the pictures using the Up and Down arrow buttons below the list of images. You can also remove an image from the list by selecting it in the list and clicking the – button. Your other configuration options are

- **Script Type**   The rotation of the images can be driven by dynamic HTML (DHTML) or by Java (Applet). Early browsers didn't support DHTML, but this option doesn't trigger the security warning in Internet Explorer, so it is a good choice. But Java works, too.

- **Change picture every**   Set how frequently the picture changes (in seconds) by picking it from the adjacent field.
- **Randomize picture order**   Select this check box to display the images in random order; leaving it unselected displays the images in the order in which they appear in the list.
- **Scale picture to fit**   This option scales the picture to fit into the rectangle you drew on the page. If you don't select this option, the picture is displayed at its original size, which could be *considerably* bigger than the page—causing the page to expand automatically. This is probably *not* what you want.

You can edit the properties of the Rotating Picture by clicking the rectangle to display the Rotating Picture Properties panel. Click once in the "Click to edit" field, and then click again on the ... button to reopen the Rotating Picture dialog box.

 Note   To preview the Rotating Picture effect, you'll have to publish the site locally.

Insert a Time-Based Picture into a Web Page

To create a time-based picture on the page, choose Time-Based Picture from the NOF Standard Components section of the Custom Components panel. Click and drag on the page to specify the location, which places the component rectangle on the page and opens the Time Based Picture Properties panel.

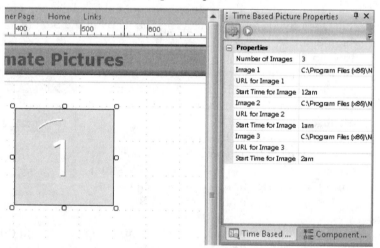

To configure the time-based pictures, first specify the Number Of Images in the first field in the panel. Each image has three fields: the location of the image file

Each Picture Opens at Full Size

One of the more painful aspects of using a time-based picture is that each image you pick opens at full size on the page. Not only does this expand the page to a potentially huge size (to fit the image), but it forces you to resize the image by clicking and dragging the sizing handles. Make sure to hold down the CTRL key while doing so to preserve the aspect ratio of the image. Better yet, resize the images to the size you want using a photo program before inserting them into the web page.

(Image 1), the URL for the image (URL for Image 1), and the Start Time for Image 1 (and so on for each image). Specify either a file location or a file URL, but not both. To specify an image file, click the Number Of Images field, and then click the ... button to open the Picture File Open dialog box so that you can choose a picture.

To specify the start time for the image, click the field and pick a value from the drop-down list.

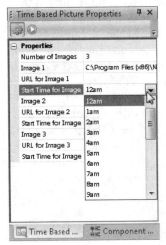

You can't rearrange the images in the Time Based Picture Properties panel. However, you can rearrange the *order* in which the pictures show by picking the appropriate time from the Start Time For Image field.

You can make some other modifications to the time-based picture by clicking the Component Properties < img > tab at the bottom of the panel to switch to the Component's HTML Grid Inspector.

You can adjust the height and width (in the HTML – General section) easily by clicking and dragging the component—but you can also type new quantities into these fields. You cannot directly type in values for the X and Y fields in the Positioning section, but you can click and drag the component on the page to change its position. You can change the Alt tag by typing the tag into the Alt field (in the HTML – General section). Finally, you can change the images used to represent the component on the page by selecting a new value for the Src field. To do so, click the field, and then click either the ... button or the Insert A Data Source button. Clicking the ... button displays the Picture File Open dialog box, where you can select a different image—but just for the first picture. If you click Insert A Data Source, the Data Sources dialog box opens, from which you can pick a defined data source—but that data source must contain a list of all the pictures.

PART III

Advanced
Web Tools

12

Customize Your Web Site with Flash, Java, and ActiveX

HOW TO...

- Execute animations using Flash
- Add Java applets and ActiveX controls to your web site
- Create and configure actions that enable objects to respond to events

If all you need to do with your web site is deliver information, much of what is discussed in this chapter won't apply to you. But if you want a lively, interactive web site, Fusion provides a host of tools to achieve that. You can animate with Flash components, add Java applets and ActiveX controls, and even build pages with objects that respond to your actions.

Add Pizzazz with Flash Components

"Flash" provides a way to add animations to your page. You've already seen some examples of Flash-based objects, such as banners and Navigation Bars. However, there are many Flash components available in Fusion. Just check the Flash Components panel for a list of Flash component categories, such as 3D Letters, Numbers, and Symbols; Shapes (arrows, lines, rectangles, triangles); text effects; and time measurement controls.

Understand Flash and Flash Components

"Flash" is actually a combination of a special file format and a player. The file is built with a purchased tool in which you create the animated objects and specify what parameters (such as color, animation effect, speed, and so on) can be adjusted by the person using the file. You've seen some of these properties in the Properties panel for Flash-based Navigation Bars and Banners. However, in order to see the item and enjoy

291

the animated effects, you must have a Flash Player, which is a free download from Adobe. If you go to a web site that contains Flash-based objects and you don't have the player, you'll be prompted to download and install it.

The Flash components available from the Flash Components panel provide a large number of prebuilt Flash files so that you can use them (and configure them) when building your web site in Fusion.

 Some of the Flash components (such as the 3D Letters) don't show their animation until you execute an action, such as moving the mouse over the component. This sensitivity is built right into the file.

Add Flash Components to a Web Page

Adding Flash components is easy: simply open the Flash Components panel, click the category of Flash component you want (like 3D Letters), and pick the component. Then just click and drag on the page to establish the position and size of the component. The Flash component shows a static (non-animated) version of the object.

 To see the Flash component in action, switch to Preview mode by clicking the Preview button at the bottom of the screen. Note, however, that if you don't size the component large enough on the screen to contain the object, it will show as a white rectangle instead of previewing the static Flash object.

Configure the Flash Components

Once you've placed the Flash component on the screen, the Component Properties panel appears.

To configure how the Flash component works, change the values in the fields. The available fields depend on the design of the component. For example, the 3D Letters enable you to set a variety of colors (Background, Fill, Wireframe), set the initial rotation in all three axes (X, Y, and Z), establish the depth, and even set which axis to rotate around. On the other hand, the Animated Text component (in the Flash Text Effects section) enables you to specify the text itself as well as choose from a wide variety of animation effects.

Automate Your Web Site with Java

Java is a programming language that runs on all computer platforms. Although it is certainly possible to program large, comprehensive applications in Java, most items are smaller, relatively self-contained applications (applets) that provide a particular piece of functionality. There are a vast number of Java "applets" you can find and download, such as clocks, graphic effects, navigation controls (menus, image maps, banners, and buttons), games, calculators, and even applets for networking, e-mail, and chat.

 Note If you are running Windows Internet Explorer and find that Java is not supported (due to a disagreement between Microsoft and Sun), you can install the Java runtime you will need by navigating to http://www.java.com/en/index.jsp.

Add a Java Applet to a Page

To place a Java applet on a page, open the Plug-Ins section of the Custom Components panel and select Java Applet. Then click and drag on the page to define where the applet will go. This opens the Open dialog box, which should show you the folder containing the Java applet or Bean.

Locating a Java Bean

Fusion can be finicky about where it will load and run a Java Bean from. If you simply try to place the Bean from wherever you have it stored on your hard drive, you'll get an error.

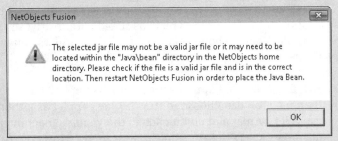

To avoid this, copy the applet to the NetObjects/NetObjects Fusion 11/Java/Beans subdirectory (for more on Java Beans, see the upcoming Did You Know? box). Then restart Fusion if it was running.

What Java Beans Are

Another option in the Plug-Ins section is "Java Beans." A Java Bean is a stand-alone implementation of an applet. Everything you need is included in the .jar file. On the other hand, Java applets may have other support files that must be present in order for the applet to function properly. A Java applet has a .class extension on the filename, but it may require other .class files, graphic files, HTML files, and so on. You'll have to read the documentation for the applet to know for sure—or just be safe and include all the files that come with the applet when you download it—most aren't very big.

Note NetObjects Fusion contains a simple digital clock applet and a shadow text Bean that you can experiment with.

Configure a Java Applet

Many (though not all) Java applets have parameters you can set from the Java Properties panel.

This Properties tab is the same for all Java applets. The File and Class fields indicate the location of the class file (which, as stated earlier, drives the applet) and the name of the class file. There is no reason to change these unless you want to break the applet, so don't. The rest of the parameters are

- **Alt Tag** Text that appears if the site visitor's machine can't run Java.
- **Run as** You can choose to run the Java applet as either an "applet" or a "servelet." An applet downloads to the visitor's machine and runs from that machine. A servelet runs on the web server. However, the server host must have allowed the server to run Java—and not all of them do.

- **Additional Files**   Applets may need additional .class files to run properly (check the documentation). To specify those additional files (which will then be uploaded to your web site when you publish the site), click the Additional Files field and then click the ... button. This opens the Java Applet Files dialog box. From there, click Add, choose the additional files from the Add Java Applets dialog box (which is just a standard Open dialog box), and click OK to add them to the site.

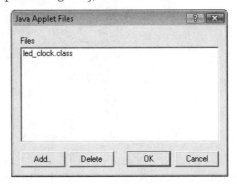

- **HTML**   On occasion, a Java applet will require specific HTML in the web page. A good example is when the initial parameters need to be specified (check the documentation). If you need to place HTML in the code for the page, click the HTML field, and then click the ... button to open the Object HTML dialog box. Edit the HTML and click OK to save the changes to the page.

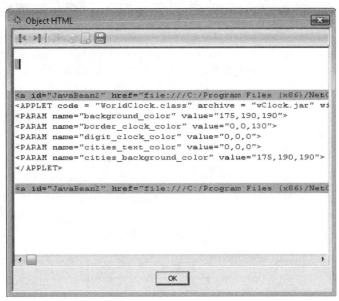

Java Beans have the same General Properties as applets. In addition, they may have specific "Bean Properties" as well, depending on the Bean. Some of the properties can be changed; others are fixed and are simply displayed in the panel.

For example the Bean with these properties enables you to change the background color by clicking the background color block, clicking the . . . button, and choosing the color from the ColorPicker. Other properties (like enabled) have a drop-down list (containing True and False in this example).

 Some properties are grouped together, such as Font. These are shown with a + sign to the left of the property name. Click the + sign to expand the list of properties to change any allowed values (such as picking a font face and size).

The Parameters tab enables you to specify parameter/ value pairs that specify how the applet or Bean looks or operates. Depending on how the applet or Bean is built, the Parameters tab may be prepopulated with parameter names, and all you need to do is fill in the values. Of course, you may need to check the documentation on what values are expected, unless (as in this example), the programmer left you a clue in the Parameter info section at the bottom of the panel.

To fill in a value for a parameter, double-click it to open the Enter Value dialog box. The name of the parameter is already present in the Name field, so enter the value and click OK.

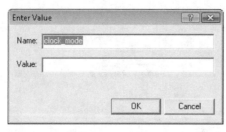

If the parameters are not filled in (and the Bean or applet accepts them), you can create a parameter/value pair by clicking the + sign at the bottom of the panel. This simply opens the Enter Value dialog box (seen previously), where you can enter the parameter name and value, again, taken from the documentation. To remove a parameter, simply click the – symbol. You can rearrange the order by clicking a parameter and using the up and down buttons.

Add an ActiveX Component to a Page

ActiveX components are available both as items included with Windows and controls that you can download and/or purchase. They add functionality to a web page that wouldn't be there otherwise. Entire applications (such as photo editors, download controllers, complete contact lists, and more) are built in ActiveX, so you can add considerable power to your web site with them.

The downside to ActiveX components is that they are only supported by Internet Explorer—no other browser will recognize or use them. And even Internet Explorer will (unless you change the default security configuration) force you to allow the ActiveX control to run, an extra step necessitated by the existence of some malicious components that can do very bad things to your computer.

Add an ActiveX Control to a Page

To add an ActiveX component to a page, open the Plug-Ins section of the Custom Components panel and select ActiveX Control. Then click and drag on the page to define where the control will go. This opens the Insert ActiveX Control dialog box, with a list of the ActiveX controls installed on your computer. Select the control and click OK.

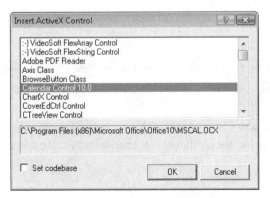

 For most ActiveX controls, you can click and drag the sizing handles to resize the control.

Configure an ActiveX Control

You can configure an ActiveX control using the ActiveX Control Properties panel. The General Properties section, which is the same for all ActiveX controls, enables you to specify an Alt tag, the Code Base, and whether to include the source code with your web site. The Control Properties section enables you to pick values for the parameters associated with the control. These vary by controls. For example, you can change the background color by picking it from a list.

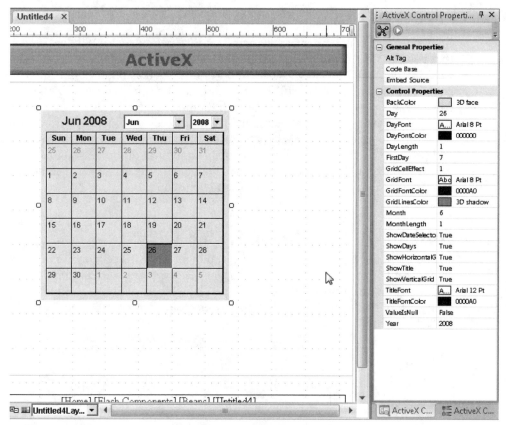

 Unlike when working with Java, you can actually see the ActiveX control on the page—and the configuration changes you make are visible right away.

Build Dynamic Pages

Dynamic pages enable you to attach "actions" to objects on the page. Most objects permit access to the Actions tab (white right-arrow on a red circle background), where you can specify the actions. You can move objects on and off the page, hide or show them, click and drag them, and cause all this to happen based on various events (mouse over, page open, etc.).

Understand Actions

You can add any number of actions to an item. For example, you could display an image of the highlighted button when the mouse rolls over it (on mouse over), and return the image to the default (non-highlighted) button when the mouse is no longer over the button (on mouse out).

An action consists of three parts: the trigger, the message, and the target. The trigger event causes the action to begin. A typical trigger event can be a mouse click or mouse over, entering or exiting a page, and so on.

The second part is the "message" and its various parameters, which specifies what the action does. An action message might be to show or hide an object, make an object fly off the page, make an object stick to the pointer so that the site visitor can drag it around the page, display a dialog or alert, or even display a custom message, which could then trigger another action (which is watching for that message) to occur. The parameters modify the message. For example, if the message is to make the object fly off the screen, the parameters might specify in which direction the object should fly.

The third component is the target, which is the item that actually performs the action. The target can be one or more objects on the page, the page itself, or a MasterBorder.

You add an action to the object that triggers it and specify the target, which performs the action. For example, if you want to have Picture A fly off the page when the visitor clicks a button, you add the action to the button with the trigger event "when clicked," plus the action message "fly off the page" and Picture A as the target. To sequence actions, you can trigger one action with another. To then have Picture B fly onto the screen, you add an action to Picture A with the trigger event "motion ended," the action message "fly onto the page," and Picture B as the target.

Add Actions to Objects and Pages

To add an action to an object (including a MasterBorder or a Layout) or a page, select the object and click the Actions tab. If you don't want the object to be visible when the page is first displayed, clear the Object Initially Visible In Browser check box. Then, use the following steps:

1. Click the + button to display the Set Action dialog box and start defining the action.

2. Type a descriptive name for the action into the Name field.
3. Specify the action's trigger by clicking the right-arrowhead button alongside the When field. This displays a list of trigger categories (such as Motion); passing the mouse over a category causes the fly-out menu to display the triggers themselves.

The list of trigger categories depends on the type of object you are adding the action to. For more information on triggers, see "Understand Triggers and Messages," later in this chapter.

Trigger categories

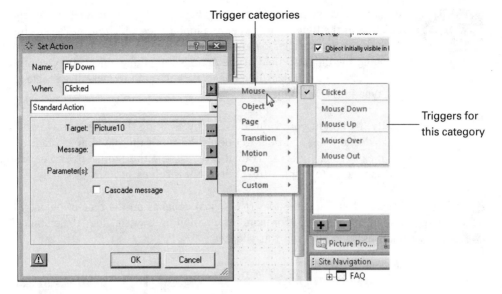

Triggers for
this category

4. Make sure Standard Action is displayed in the action type drop-down list, unless you want to script your own JavaScript actions or use an animation you created in Timeline mode. See "Considerations for Scripted and Timeline Actions," later in this chapter.

5. Place the target in the Target field. The default is the selected object; to change that, click the ... button to display a resizable Object Tree window. Simply select the object you want to use as the target.

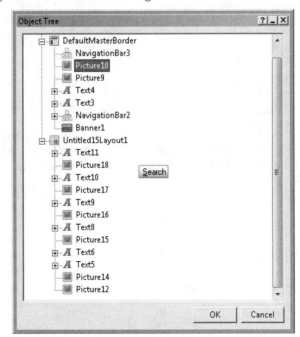

Not sure which picture is which (they have names like Picture18)? Simply click a picture in the Object Tree panel and look to see which image is selected (it shows the sizing handles). You can also rename an object (including pictures) by changing the ObjectID field in the Actions tab of any object. Or, you can click the object name in the Object Tree panel, click it again to make it editable, and then just type in the new ObjectID.

6. Specify the action you want to occur by clicking the right arrowhead button alongside the Message field to open the fly-out menu. This displays a list of action categories (such as Transition); passing the mouse over a category causes a fly-out menu to display the actions themselves.

The list of action categories (Messages) depends on the type of object you are adding the action to. For more information on triggers, see "Understand Triggers and Messages," later in this chapter.

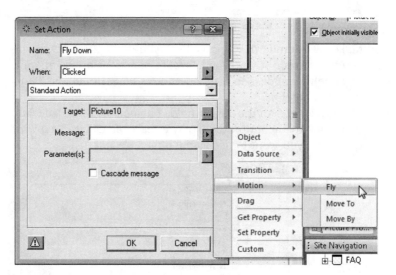

7. If appropriate, specify the Parameters from the Parameter(s) field by clicking the right arrowhead button to open the fly-out menu. The list of available parameters depends on the Message. For example, the Fly message has the list of parameters shown here.

8. Some message parameters also include a set of values that enable you to further customize the action. To open the list of values (shown in the Parameter Values dialog box), select Values from the Parameter(s) fly-out menu. The available parameters depend on the Message; here is the Parameter Values dialog box for the Fly message.

If you do open the Parameters Values dialog box and then click OK (whether you change any values or not), the Parameter(s) field displays "Values" instead of the original choice. If you instead click Cancel, the field will display the original choice.

9. Some message parameters also include the ability to view and modify the script that drives the action. To view the script, select Expression from the Parameter(s) fly-out menu. You can then modify the expression yourself (if you know JavaScript).

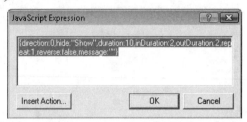

If you do open the JavaScript Expression dialog box (whether you modify the script or not) and click OK, the Parameter(s) field displays "Expression" instead of the original choice. If you instead click Cancel, the field will display the original choice.

Considerations for Scripted and Timeline Actions

In Step 4, if you choose a Scripted Action, enter the script in the resulting text box. You will, of course, have to know how to write a JavaScript.

If you select Timeline Actions, you'll see a new version of the Set Action dialog box.

Either choose an existing animation from the Animation drop-down list (which you must have previously built using Timeline mode) or select New Animation and type in a name for the animation. If you do pick a new animation, you'll go to Timeline mode to build the animation once you click OK. Also note that the list of messages (in the Message drop-down list) is unique for animations and includes such choices as Stop, Pause, Play, Go To, and Cancel Animation. It also includes parameters to control the animation, such as whether to loop the animation (Loop Animation check box), delay a certain number of seconds, or even play the animation backward.

 Timeline mode (and animations built using the Timeline mode) are not covered in this book.

Modify Action Execution

You can modify an action once you have built it using the Actions tab of the Properties panel.

You Can Insert Another Action into the JavaScript Expression Dialog Box

Simply click Insert Action to display a list of actions defined for this object. What this means is that you can cascade actions (cause another action to take place immediately after the current action) without using custom messages (for more on Custom Messages, see "How To Chain Actions Together with Custom Messages," later in this chapter).

From there, you can

- **Change any of the fields**   To reopen the action, simply double-click it to reopen the Set Action dialog box. From there, you can change the values in the fields or select new values from the fly-out menus. Then click OK to save the changes to the action definition.
- **Change the order of the actions**   Two actions that respond to the same trigger execute in the order they are shown in the Actions tab. To change that order, select an action and click the up or down arrow to rearrange the actions.
- **Delete an action**   If you don't need an action any longer; click the – button to delete it.
- **Suppress execution**   If you don't want to publish (and execute) an action now but might want to use it later, deselect the check box alongside the action. You should also do this if you just want the action to be available in a scripted action that you write yourself.

Understand Triggers and Messages

The trigger categories available in the When fly-out menu depend on the object you're adding the action to. The categories are

- **Mouse**   Mouse triggers are used to detect mouse actions, such as clicking an object, mouse down or up, or passing the mouse over or away from object. Mouse actions cannot be used for text objects, layouts, or frames.

 Although you cannot use a mouse action attached to some items (such as layout), those objects can be the target of a mouse action. For example, the target of a When Clicked trigger can be the Layout.

- **Object**   Triggers response to an object being hidden or shown by another action that targets the object.
- **Page**   Triggers the action when the page finishes loading or when the page is exited—that is, when the visitor moves to another page.

- **Transition, Motion, Drag**   Each of these categories has a "started" action and an "ended" action. The start or end of one of these actions triggers an action in the target. For example, when you finish dragging an object (Drag Ended), this could trigger an action to put the object back to its original position (Object | Restore Position).
- **Custom**   This is where you create custom messages, which other actions can watch for, thus enabling you to "pass" a message from one object to another. The other object can then respond to the message with its own action. For more information on custom messages and chains of actions, see "How To Chain Actions Together with Custom Messages," later in this chapter.

The choice of Message categories (available from the Message fly-out menu) depends on the type of object you are targeting. The categories are

- **Object**   This includes options for hiding and showing an object, arranging the stacking order of an object in relation to other objects, saving or restoring the position of the object, adding a delay between the trigger and the action, setting the object to an image (specifying the filename) or using an image (from the Style settings). These last two are handy for specifying a highlighted button image or a depressed button image when (for example) the site visitor passes the mouse over the image or clicks it. Note that these options are only available for an image target.
- **Data Source**   For text and image targets, this option is available to manipulate data in data sources. This includes moving through pages of data, as well as adding, editing, deleting, and updating data records. For more information on publishing data, see Chapter 15.
- **Transition**   Causes the object to be drawn using one of the available transitions, such as Wipe, Peek, and Iris.
- **Motion**   Causes the object to move across the page, or onto or off the page.
- **Drag**   This option causes the target to stick to the mouse pointer so that the site visitor can drag the object across the page. For example, you can set the object to Start Drag with a parameter of Until Mouse Up, which would release the object. In addition, you have options to constrain the drag to the containing object and set up collision detection—which could then trigger another action.
- **Get Property, Set Property**   This option either gets or sets properties (such as the position) of the targets. The results are usually used in scripted actions or as parameter values.

The Location, Dialog, and Window options appear only if the target is a MasterBorder or a Layout, or if it is linked text (as described in the section "Add Actions to Linked Text," later in this chapter). They also do not function when you Preview; you must publish locally to see the effect of these Messages.

- **Location**   This option enables the site visitor to jump to a new URL if the action is triggered.

- **Dialog**   This option displays one of three types of dialog boxes: Alert, Confirm, or Prompt. In all cases, you can enter just the message to display. In the case of the Prompt, you can also enter a Default Value.

- **Window**   This option sets the size, position, and scroll position, and it retrieves or sets some Window properties (such as the name). In addition, these actions can move the focus to the window, blur it, send a message to the window, and even open a new window. As with Get Property and Set Property, window properties are usually used in scripted actions.

Only actions for linked text seem to be able to respond to the Window Focus or Window Blur message—that is, these are options in the Linked Text "When" field, as described in the next section.

- **Browser**   This option retrieves the type of browser, perhaps so that you can set up different actions depending on the browser type.
- **Custom**   This is where you specify a custom message, which can then be used in the When field to trigger another action. For more information on custom messages and chains of actions, see "How To Chain Actions Together with Custom Messages," later in this chapter.

Retrieve and Use Properties with Scripted Actions

You can retrieve a property (such as the Window name) within a scripted action so that you can use its value in the script. To do so, use the following steps:

1. Create a Standard Action that retrieves the property. For example, you could add a picture to the page, and attach an action that returns the Window name (in the Set Action dialog box, choose Message | Window | Get Name) when the picture is clicked (set the When condition to "Clicked"). Don't forget that the Target must be the MasterBorder or the Layout!
2. Create a Scripted Action that uses the same trigger (When Clicked in this example).
3. In the Set Action dialog box, click Insert Action to display a list of actions you've already defined.

4. Pick the action that retrieves the property. This places the name of the action in the script as $(ActionName), where "ActionName" is the name you gave the action that retrieves the property. What is actually returned when the script is run is the value of the property. Thus, you can check for (and act on) these values.

 Want to see the property value returned so that you know what to look for in your script? Put the following in your script: alert($(ActionName)). This will cause an Alert box to pop up containing the value. Of course, you'll want to remove this from the script before publishing your web site.

Add Actions to Linked Text

In addition to adding actions to a text object, you can add a Smart Link to text within the text object, and then add actions to the linked text. However, while the linked text can initiate an action, it cannot be a target. To create an action for linked text, use the following steps:

1. In Page view, select the text to which you want to add a link.
2. Select the text and choose Link from the Object or shortcut menu, or click Link in the Standard Tools toolbar. This opens the Link dialog box.

3. Choose Smart Link from the Link Type drop-down list and Blank from the list of Smart links.

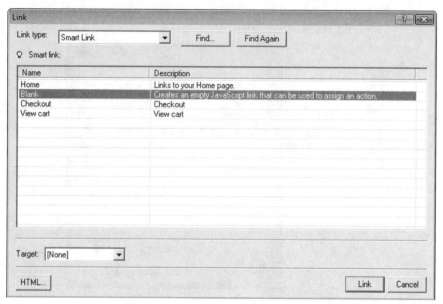

4. Then click Link to create the link.
5. Click the link you selected earlier. The Text Properties panel now contains a Link tab, indicating that a link has been defined for the text. Click the Link tab.

6. Click Actions to display the Actions dialog box. It works identically to the Actions tab in the Properties panel, described earlier in this chapter.
7. Define the actions you want for the linked text.

Note The When fly-out menu has an extra option (Window) for linked text. The items in the Window fly-out menu enable the linked text to respond to a Focus or Blur message.

Chain Actions Together with Custom Messages

You can create specialized action sequences by using custom messages. After you create a custom message, it becomes available in the When fly-out menu as a trigger and in the Messages fly-out menu as an action. You can then send it from one object (the action is to send the message) to another (which responds to the received message as a trigger). The use of custom messages makes it easier to change object responses by buffering the trigger from the action.

For example, let's say you had a bunch of small pictures on a page, along with a button that says "Fly away," and that you want each picture to fly off the page in a different direction when you click the button. You could certainly build a set of actions for the button, each action targeting a different picture, with the appropriate action (Fly) and parameter (direction). However, another way to approach this would be to simply create a custom message that is sent by the button to each object (or to the containing object—see "Cascade Messages to Lower Levels," later in this chapter). Each image could then have an action that is triggered by receiving the message. This approach localizes the behavior (response) to the picture itself. Thus, if you later want to change the picture behavior—such as having it *not* respond to the message or fly off in a different direction—you would just go to the actions attached to that picture and make the adjustment. This is far easier than hunting through the actions attached to other objects to try to find the action that triggers the picture to fly away (believe me, *I know*). In addition, you can attach actions to other objects on the page to send the same custom message (causing the images to respond the same way). And, it is easy to add more objects to the page (such as additional pictures) that also respond to the message.

Custom messages also make it possible to propagate a chain of actions in a specified order. To do that, you create the action that you want for the first object in the chain—for example, a button shows a different image when clicked. In addition, you have the object respond to the trigger by sending a custom message. The second object in the chain "watches" for the message and responds to it (for example, a picture flies off the screen). However, it *also* responds to the message by sending a custom message of its own. The third object in the chain watches for that message, and so on. In other words, each object in the chain performs an action and also passes a custom message to the next object.

To create a custom message, use the following steps:

1. Select the first object in the chain (or the one that you want to isolate from the responses of other objects). Switch to the Actions tab in the Properties panel and click the + button to open the Set Action dialog box.
2. Click the When or Message fly-out menu and click Custom | Edit to display the Custom Messages dialog box.

(continued)

3. Click the + button to display the Add Message dialog box.

4. Type the custom message into the Add Message dialog box and click OK to create the message and add it to the list of available custom messages.

The custom message is used in a script, so it is best not to use spaces or special characters (!@#$ and so on) in the custom message. Limit yourself to alphabetic characters.

To actually use the custom message, you must do two things: create an action that sends the message, and create an action that responds to the message. To create an action that sends the message from the Set Action dialog box for the triggering object, click the Message fly-out menu and pick Custom, and then pick the message you want to send from the list of available messages.

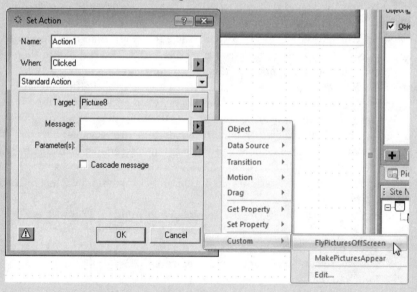

To create an action that responds to the message from the Set Action dialog box for the target object, click the When fly-out menu and pick Custom, and then pick the message that you want the target object to respond to, as shown here.

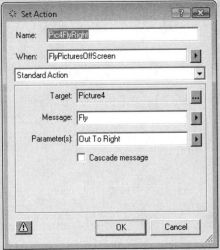

Cascade Messages to Lower Levels

As you have seen, you can use any object (except linked text) as a target for an action. If you check the Cascade Message check box in the Set Action dialog box, the message is sent not only to the target, but to every object that the target contains. For example, if you send the message to a Layout, everything the Layout contains receives the message as well. Even if the Layout doesn't know how to respond to the message (for example, a custom message for which there is no matching trigger for the Layout), the items within the Layout will respond if *they* have a trigger that knows what to do with the message.

The implication to this feature is that you should plan your page layout with actions in mind. For example, if are going to want three different objects to respond to a specific message, enclose those objects in a Layout, Layout Region, Text Box, or some other containing object. Keep in mind that the containing object will respond to the trigger if it knows how, as well as pass along the message to the contained objects (assuming you selected the Cascade Message check box) so they have a chance to respond as well.

Note   Actions sent to a Layout or a MasterBorder apply to the entire page, not just the Layout or MasterBorder. Also, the Object | Hide action directed at a container (such as a Layout or Layout Region) hides the contents of the container without the use of cascading messages. Thus, if you hide a Layout, the entire page goes blank.

13

Collect Data with Forms

HOW TO...

- Create a form and fields using the built-in Forms Handler
- Manage your data with the Forms Handler Manager
- Set up error handling and e-mail notifications
- Configure the database for your data
- Build and configure a form from scratch

Up until now, the flow of information has been one way—from the web site you are building to the site visitor. Site visitors can view the information you provide, but not respond. You have no way to collect information from them—for example, registration information or feedback about the site. Fusion enables you to create "forms" to remedy this situation. With forms, you can collect information in fields, ensure that a human being (and not a spamming robot) is typing in the information, enforce error checking, and more. Before Fusion, you had to be pretty competent at programming to create a form and route the gathered information into a database—but not any more. Nothing discussed in this chapter requires you to write even a single line of code.

Build Forms Using the Forms Handler

The Forms Handler component automates a great deal of the tediousness of building a form. However, you trade flexibility for this convenience—you have very little control over how the form is laid out, and other options (such as error handling) are more limited than with a regular form. Still, for simple forms, the Forms Handler works well.

 You cannot see the Forms Handler in Fusion at all—not even when you publish locally or Preview. You *must* publish your site to the web (or to a local web server if you have one) in order to see the form. All you can see in Fusion is a graphic indicating that a Forms Handler component exists on the page.

Create the Forms Handler Area

To start out creating the form, choose the Forms Handler component from the NOF Forms Handler section of the Custom Components panel. Then click and drag on the page to define the area where the form will be located. This opens the NOF Forms Handler dialog box.

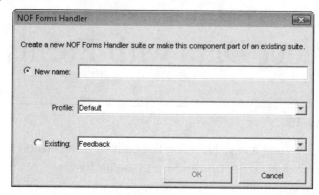

When you use the NOF Forms Handler, you are actually creating what is called an "NOF Forms Handler suite." This suite typically includes the Forms Handler component, used to collect information from your site visitor, and the Forms Handler Manager component, which enables you to view and modify that information using a page on your web site (see "Create a Forms Handler Manager," later in this chapter). Both of these components use the same database (see sidebar "How To: Configure a Database for a Form," later in this chapter). Since you can only place one of these components on a page, the implication is that you'll need two pages—one for the Forms Handler component, and one for the Forms Handler Manager component. Fusion uses the name of the suite (entered in the NOF Forms Handler dialog box) to associate the two components that form part of a suite. Thus, when you create the Forms Handler component, enter a new suite name in the New Name field. When you create the Forms Handler Manager component, choose the same suite name from the Existing Name drop-down list.

 You can add more than one Forms Handler component (form) to each suite; however, the Forms Handler component writes to the same database as the other Forms Handler components in the suite, so you have to ensure that the form fields are exactly the same for all Forms Handler components in the suite.

Add and Arrange Fields

Once you create the form area (associated with a Forms Handler suite), the Forms Handler dialog box opens (see Figure 13-1). This is where you specify everything about the form, including the fields, field format, error events, database, and e-mail settings.

The Fields tab displays a list of the default fields included in the Forms Handler component, including first and last name, address, city, state, zip, phone, e-mail,

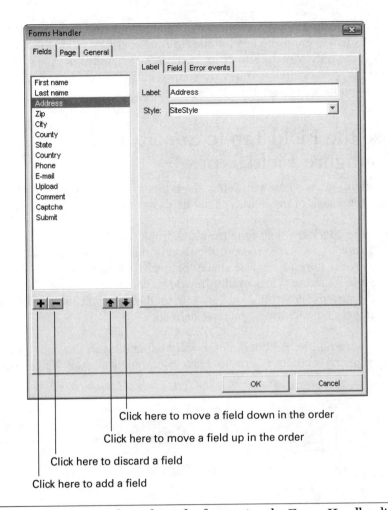

FIGURE 13-1 Set up everything about the form using the Forms Handler dialog box.

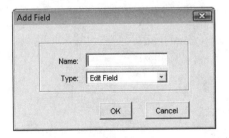

and others. To remove one of these default fields, click the – button. To rearrange the fields, select the field and click the up or down arrow buttons. To add a new field, click the + button and choose Standard Controls from the pop-up list. This opens Add Field dialog box.

Type a name into the Name field and pick the field type from the Type drop-down list. Then click OK to add the new field to the list.

The specifics of each field type are discussed later in this chapter, in the section "Add Fields to the Form."

The Fields tab has three sub-tabs: Label, Field, and Error Events. The Label tab enables you to enter the label name (in the Label field) that will appear on the form. This is the only way the site visitor will know what data is expected in that field, so word the label carefully. You can also pick either the current SiteStyle or any CSS styles you have defined from the Style drop-down list.

Use the Field Tab to Specify and Configure Field Types

The Fields tab is where you select the type of field you want to use for each piece of data. Regardless of the field type, all fields have the following options available:

- **Type**   Pick the field type from the drop-down list.
- **Name**   This is the name of the field in the database. To avoid issues, it is best to use only normal text—no spaces or special characters.
- **Style**   Use the values in this drop-down list to set the style of the field (the default is the current SiteStyle). Again, as with the Labels, you can pick the current SiteStyle or any custom CSS styles you have defined.

The rest of the field parameters vary depending on the field type, as detailed in the following sections. Figure 13-2 shows examples of each field type.

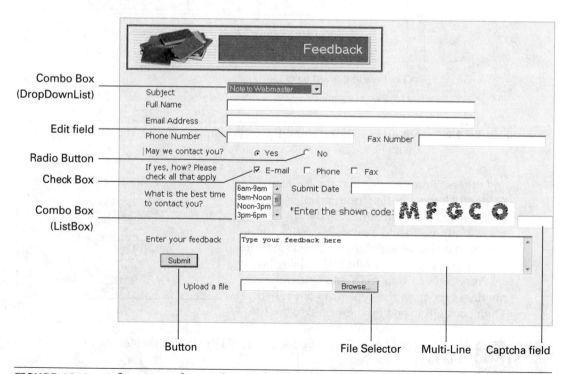

FIGURE 13-2   A form is made up of many fields, each with its own field type.

Understand an Edit Field

An Edit Field is a single line of text, usually used for such things as names, addresses, and other data of this nature. If you select the Password Field check box, the text typed into the field will be shown as asterisks, rather than the typed text. You can specify an initial value for the field by typing it into the Text field. You can also set the visible length (which establishes how long the field is on the form) as well as the maximum length (the longest allowable string allowed) for the field.

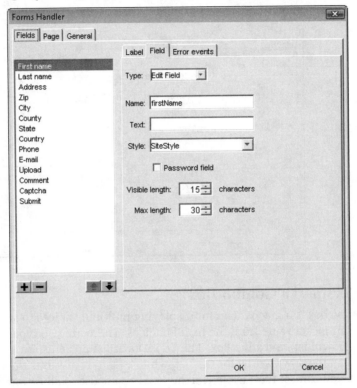

Understand a Multi-Line

A Multi-Line field is one that contains multiple lines of text. You can specify an initial value for the field by typing it into the Text field. You can also set the visible length (which establishes how long the field is on the form) as well as the visible height (in lines), as shown in the following illustration.

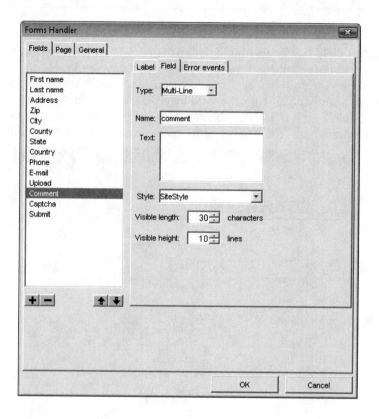

Understand a Combo Box

A combo box is a mechanism for displaying multiple choices to site visitors so that they can pick a value from the list of choices. There are two types of combo boxes—a "DropDownList" and a ListBox. The DropDownList presents the list of choices when you click the down arrow for the list, while a ListBox presents the options in a box for which you can set the Visible Height. You can choose to allow multiple selections by selecting the Allow Multiple Selections check box (for the ListBox only).

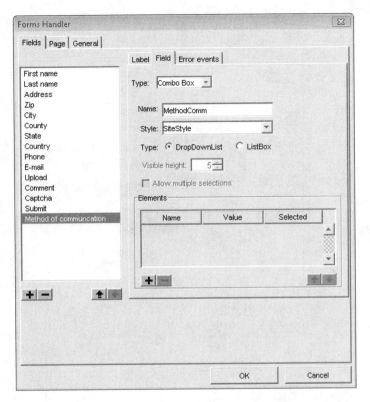

To create the list of values, click the + button to make a line editable in the Elements area. Type the name you want to see in the list into the Name column. If you want a different value to be written to the database when the item is selected, type it into the Value column. To specify the default value, select the check box in the Selected column for the appropriate line, as shown in the following illustration.

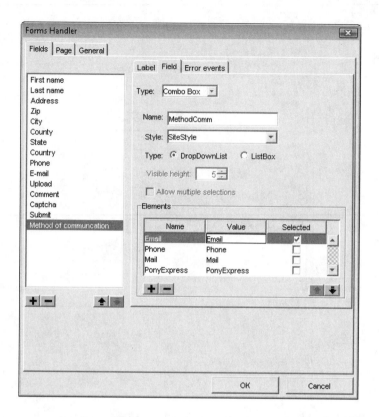

   You can remove a value by clicking the – button, and rearrange the order of the items by selecting an item and clicking the up or down arrows.

Understand a Radio Button

A "radio button" is one button that is part of a set of buttons. If you select one button in the set, any other selected button becomes unselected. As a result, all the radio buttons in a set must be associated to one another so that Fusion "knows" when you've selected one button in a set—and can clear any other selected button. To associate a set of radio buttons into a group, make sure the Name field (in the Field tab) is the same for each button. To specify what value gets written to the database when the radio button is selected, type that quantity into the Value field. To set one of the radio buttons to be initially selected on the form, choose the Checked radio button in the Default section of the dialog box. Remember that only one of the radio buttons in a set can be set to Checked.

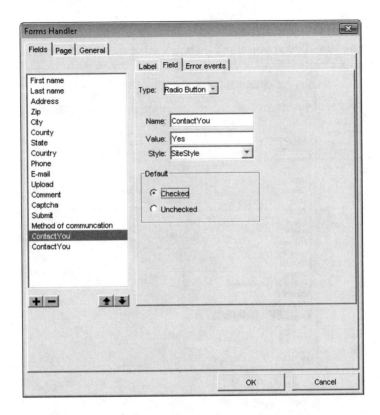

 This type of control is named for the old car radio buttons—when you pushed one button in, the currently depressed button would pop out. Anyone remember those?

Understand a Check Box

A check box (not too surprisingly) is a box that the site visitor can click in to place a check mark in it. The Field tab looks exactly like the Field tab for the radio button (discussed previously). However, although check boxes tend to be grouped (such as a set of check boxes to indicate how you'd like to be contacted), they work differently than radio buttons. Each check box must have its own name because the results are stored in a separate field in the database. To specify what value gets written to the database when the check box is selected, type that quantity into the Value field. To set the check box to be initially selected on the form, choose the Checked radio button in the Default section of the dialog box.

Understand Buttons

A button is just what you think—a button that the site visitor can click to execute a command.

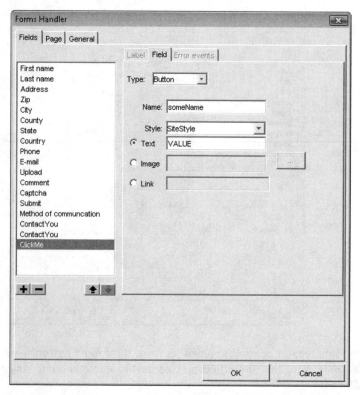

There are three types of buttons: Text, Image, and Link. All three use the Name field as the value sent to the Forms Handler when the button is pressed by the site visitor.

- **Text** To specify the text that appears on the button, type it into the Text field.

> **Note** There *must* be one Submit button (used for submitting the form results) on the form. This button is part of the list of default fields, and you can neither delete it (the − button is unavailable) nor change the Name.

- **Image** Uses an image to represent the button. This is handy if you've built your own graphic buttons. To specify the image, select the Image radio button and click the...button to choose the image from the Picture File Open dialog box. Clicking the image button executes a Submit.
- **Link** Uses link text to represent the button. That is, the submit button will take on the "form" of a link. To specify the link text, select the Link radio button and type the text that will be displayed as a link into the Link field. Clicking the Link button executes a Submit.

Understand File Selectors

The File Selector field enables site visitors to upload files directly to your web site.

The control includes a Browse button to enable site visitors to either type in a path and filename, or navigate to and pick the file they want to send, which is then uploaded to your web site when the Submit button is clicked. The field is labeled using the entry from the Label field in the Label tab. You can place a value in the Text field if you wish; however, neither this field nor the Name field are actually visible on the form, so there is little point in doing so. You can also choose the visible length of the Text field in the form.

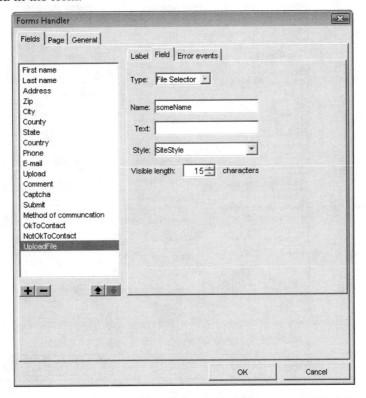

 You choose the destination directory on your web site in the General tab, discussed later in this chapter.

Understand a Captcha Field

If you've ever built a web site that gathers user input (such as with a Guest Book or feedback form), and then been flooded with spam advertising all kinds of nasty stuff, you've probably been the victim of a program that scans the web looking for these types of forms and sends you a flood of unwanted responses.

To combat these programs, "Captcha" was invented. In essence, Captcha pretty much requires human interaction by displaying a graphic image containing letters and numbers. To the human eye, the image looks like text, and you must type that text into a special field before submitting the form. To a machine, though, it's just a graphic image, and most of these programs can't read the text (there are starting to be a few that can—< sigh >).

Fusion includes Captcha capabilities—just pick the Captcha Field type to add it to your form.

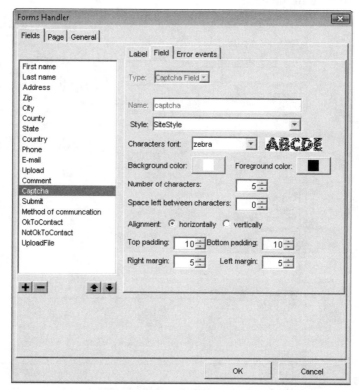

Once you do, you can configure the Captcha field in the following ways:

- **Characters font**   Choose one of the several graphic styles to use for the imaged letters from the drop-down box.
- **Background color/Foreground color**   Click these buttons to set the background color of the text and the foreground (text) color from the ColorPicker.
- **Number of characters**   Use this field to set the number of characters in the Captcha string.

- **Space left between characters**   Use this field to space the characters out more than the default distance (indicated by a 0 in this field).
- **Alignment**   Choose one of the radio buttons to align the letters horizontally (left to right) or vertically (stacked up and down).
- **Padding**   Use the Top Padding and Bottom Padding fields to establish the space above and below the Captcha string.
- **Margins**   Use the Right Margin and Left Margin fields to establish the amount of space to the left and right of the Captcha string.

Set Up Field Error Handling

The Forms Handler enables you to specify errors that you want handled. That is, if (for example) the site visitor skipped a field that you always want populated, you can present an error message and refuse to accept the submitted form until that error is corrected. To configure the error handling for a field, select the field in the list and click the Error Events sub-tab of the Fields tab.

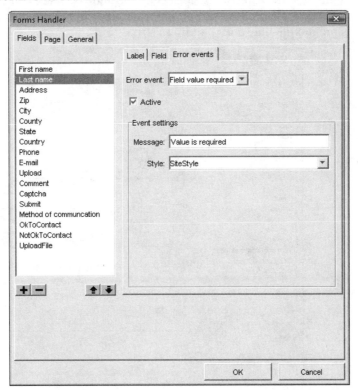

The general technique for setting up an error message is pretty straightforward—pick the error event you want from the Error Event drop-down list and enter the values for the Event Settings. All of the event settings have a message field for the error message. The error events are listed in Table 13-1, along with the type of fields they apply to and event settings you can use (in addition to the error message).

TABLE 13-1 Error Events and Their Settings

Error Event	Event Settings	Field Types
Field value is required		All field types except buttons
Field value too short	Min length field	Edit Field, Multi-Line
Field value too long	Max length field	Edit Field, Multi-Line
Invalid code		Captcha field
Invalid file name		File Selector
Attached file is too big	Max size field	File Selector
Invalid extension	File Extensions list	File Selector

As noted in the table, you can limit the types of files the site visitor can upload by specifying valid file extensions. To specify the allowed extensions, click the + button to create a new line in the Allowed Extensions section of the dialog box. Type the extension into the line, and then press ENTER.

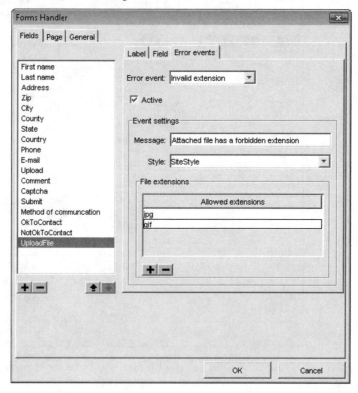

To activate a particular error, select the Active check box. The check box is selected and unavailable for Captcha fields, as there is no point in *having* a Captcha field unless you enforce error handling.

Set Up Page Error and Success Handling

You can set up overall error handling and specify a page to show to the site visitor when the form has been successfully submitted from the Page tab of the Forms Handler dialog box.

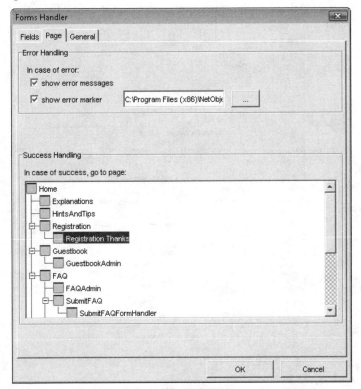

To activate overall error handling, select the Show Error Messages check box. You can highlight errors in the form using an "error marker." To turn on the error marker, select the Show Error Marker check box. You can specify the graphic to use for the error marker by clicking the...button alongside the adjacent field and picking the image from the Picture File Open dialog box.

To display a page after the site visitor has successfully submitted the form, pick the page from the Success Handling section at the bottom of the dialog box.

Create a page that thanks the visitor for submitting the information. This page should not be in the site navigation, as the visitor should be able to reach it only through submitting a form. Just remember to provide a way for the site visitor to navigate to another page (a Navigation Bar works well for that).

Set Up Scripts and E-Mail Settings

The last tab in the Forms Handler dialog box is the General tab. This is where you set up scripting preferences (Fusion generates scripts to drive the Forms Handler) and e-mail settings so that an e-mail can be sent every time someone submits a form with data.

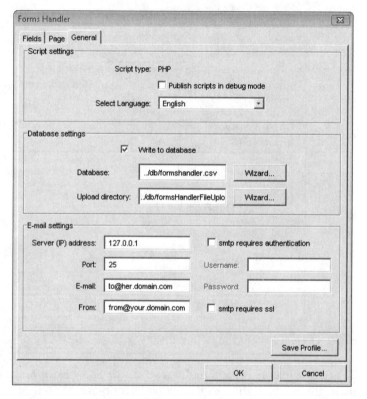

You specify the Script Type in the Current Site Options dialog box (Tools | Options | Current Site). Pick the script type from the Site Generation section in the middle of the dialog box. You have two options—PHP and ASP. Check with the site provider to see which one they support. Note that they may support both.

Set Up the Script Settings

The scripting preferences include whether to publish scripts in debug mode and the publishing language (English or German). Publishing the scripts in debug mode makes them considerably larger (and slower to execute) but provides more useful error messages so that you can figure out what is going wrong. Once you are sure the scripts are executing properly, you can deselect this check box to use the smaller, more nimble scripts.

Set Up the E-Mail Settings

If you want an e-mail to be sent each time someone submits a form, fill in the E-Mail settings. The settings are

- **Server (IP) address**   The address of the mail server that sends the e-mail. You'll have to obtain this from your site provider.
- **Port**   The port number on the mail server. Although port 25 is the "standard" port, you'll have to make sure this is the right port by checking with your site provider.
- **E-mail**   The e-mail address to which you want the e-mail sent.
- **From**   The e-mail address you want shown as the source of the e-mail. This doesn't have to be a real e-mail address, but using a specific e-mail address for each form will help you sort the e-mails you receive.
- **SMTP authentication and SSI**   These are specific protocols meant to enhance e-mail security. If the SMTP require authentication, you'll need to fill in the Username and Password. Again, you'll need to find out the protocols from your site provider.

Did You Know?

You Can Save and Reuse Your Form Settings

Once you've specified all the form settings (including the fields, error handling, label names, and database configuration), you can save all that information as a "profile." To save the profile, click the Save Profile button in the General tab of the Forms Handler dialog box. This opens the Save Profile dialog box, where you simply fill in the Profile name and click Save. When you want to create another Forms Handler component that is very similar to the saved profile, choose the profile from the Profile drop-down list in the NOF Forms Handler dialog box. You can then proceed to customize the form to add in any changes, using the techniques detailed in the next few sections.

How to... Configure a Database for a Form

There is obviously no point in collecting information unless you put it somewhere—specifically, a database. From there, you can view and edit the information using the Forms Handler Manager (discussed later in this chapter) or download the database file to your computer and work with it there.

The "database" you can use for collecting form data is the simplest kind—just a file with each database record on a separate line, otherwise known as a "flat-file database." The data elements in each record are typically separated by a delimiter (such as a comma).

Note The Forms Handler has some pretty significant limits on the database format it can use: it must contain comma-separated values (CSV). On the other hand, a CSV file can be opened and edited in any spreadsheet program. And in case you're wondering: yes, site visitors can use commas in their entry—the data is encased in quotes in the database.

The first step in setting up a database is to create the path to the database in the Database field. The directory should be one that site visitors have write access to (because they are writing values to the database) but not browse access (so they can't find and edit the database). The suggested database folder is one called "db" off the root directory of your web site, which is denoted this way (along with a file called FormResults.csv): ../db/ FormResults.csv. You will need to use the tools supplied by your site provider to create and configure the permissions for this folder. This folder is also a good place to create a folder to store any files uploaded using the form (if you need that). Use the Upload Directory field for that.

Once you've specified the path and filename, you can use the wizard to create the folder and the database filename. Click the Wizard button alongside the database field to open the DB Creation Wizard dialog box. The Path To Database and Name (of the database file) are already populated.

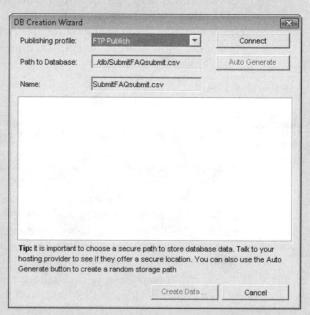

To create the folder and the database file, use the following steps:

1. Pick the remote publishing profile from the Publishing Profile drop-down list. You must have set up this publishing profile prior to using the wizard by following the steps detailed in Chapter 16.
2. Click Connect and wait while the connection is established. Once the connection is established, the button reads "Disconnect" and the structure of your web site is displayed in the lower section of the dialog box.

3. Select the folder that will hold your database folder (probably the root folder, denoted by a /). Right-click the folder and choose New Folder. Enter the name of the folder in the New Folder dialog box and click OK to create the folder.
4. Select the folder and click Create Data to create the new file inside the specified folder.

You can build the file upload directory pretty much the same way: create the directory that will hold the file upload directory (if it doesn't already exist), and then click Create Data to create the file upload directory. Also, once you've created the folder to hold your databases (typically named DB), you can just select it to create the new database file inside that folder.

Edit the Forms Handler

Once you've created and configured the Forms Handler component, it is represented by a graphic on the page.

Simply double-click the graphic to re-open the Forms Handler dialog box. You can also use the NOF Forms Handler Property panel to edit the component.

To edit the component, click in the Click To Edit field, which reveals a...button. Click that button to re-open the Forms Handler dialog box.

Create a Forms Handler Manager

The Forms Handler Manager component is an amazing convenience. While you can certainly download the database file and work with it on your local machine (and then re-upload it), it is much more convenient to simply navigate to the page containing the Forms Handler Manager component from which you can view the records, and add, edit, or delete them. Figure 13-3 shows a sample of the Forms Handler page.

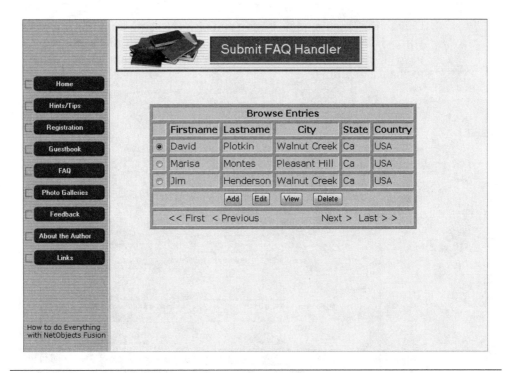

FIGURE 13-3   Manage your database records right from a web page with the
Forms Handler Manager.

To add a Forms Handler Manager component to a page, use the following steps:

1. Select the component from the NOF Forms Handler section of the Custom
   Components panel.
2. Click and drag on the page to create the component. This opens the NOF Forms
   Handler dialog box.

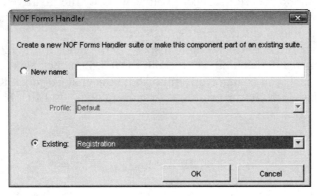

3. Choose the Existing radio button and pick the same item that you used for the Forms Handler component. This opens the Manager dialog box, which should have all the same values filled in as for the Forms Handler. You shouldn't need to change anything.

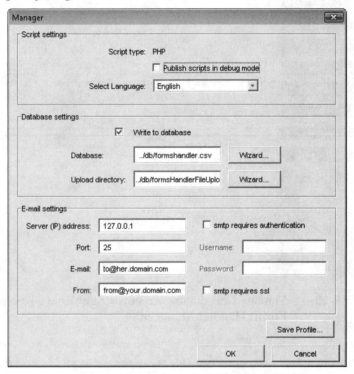

Once you've built the Forms Handler Manager component and published it to the web (as discussed in Chapter 16), you can use it to manage your records as follows:

- **Pick the record you want to work with**   Click the radio button in the far left column to choose the record you want. Only the first five fields are shown in this view (as shown previously in Figure 13-3), so make sure these fields are specific enough to locate the record you want.

- **Edit a record**   Click Edit to display all the fields in the record (see Figure 13-4). Click in any field and edit the values, and then click Save Entry to save the new values. If you change your mind about the changes, click Reset to put the record back the way it was prior to your current changes. Click Back to return to the list of entries.

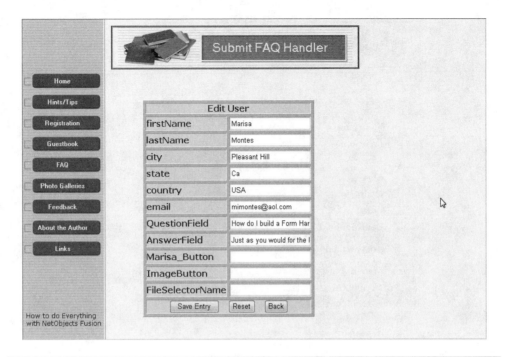

FIGURE 13-4 Edit an existing record by changing the fields.

Note Unlike when you enter information using the Form, no validation is done when you edit data in the Forms Handler Manager. The new values are just sent to the database, and they may make no sense when analyzed later—so exercise care when editing the values.

- **Add a new record** This presents a very similar screen to the one shown in Figure 13-4. Now, however, the fields are all empty, and you can browse for a File Selector field by clicking Browse. Simply type in the values you want and click Add Entry.

- **View a record** Displays the record in a non-editable form on a screen very similar to the one shown in Figure 13-4. However, you can see all the text in a field, as shown in the following image, unlike the single short line of text visible for Add and Edit. Click Back when you are done viewing the record.

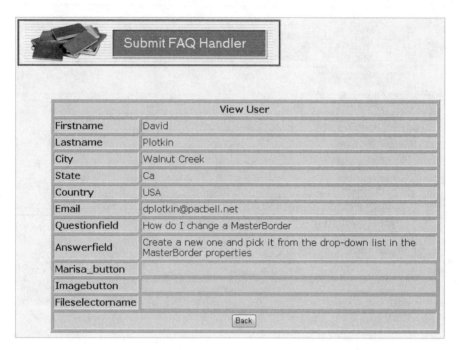

View User	
Firstname	David
Lastname	Plotkin
City	Walnut Creek
State	Ca
Country	USA
Email	dplotkin@pacbell.net
Questionfield	How do I change a MasterBorder
Answerfield	Create a new one and pick it from the drop-down list in the MasterBorder properties
Marisa_button	
Imagebutton	
Fileselectorname	

Back

- **Delete a record**   Deletes the selected record with no confirmation.

As with the Forms Handler, the Forms Handler Manager is simply represented on the page by a graphic—you can't see the component itself until you publish to a web server. To edit the Forms Handler Manager component, double-click the graphic, or click the graphic and then use the Click To Edit field in the NOF Forms Handler Property panel.

Build Forms "From Scratch"

As we saw earlier in this chapter, there are significant limitations with using the Forms Handler component. Fortunately, you don't have to use it—you can build and configure your own form, though it's quite a bit more work. And, you have quite a number of ways you can create the form area, into which you add form fields, buttons, and so on.

Create a Form with the Form Area Tool

To create a form with the Form Area tool, select the tool from the Form Tools toolbar. Click and drag with the tool on the page to establish the form area. Fusion displays the Create Form dialog box.

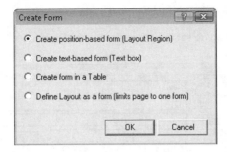

From this dialog box, you can select how you want to create the form:

- **Create position-based form (Layout Region)**   As you might guess, this option creates a Layout Region and embeds the form in the Layout Region. Since you can position the Layout Region and set its parameters, this is a very flexible option.
- **Create text-based form (Text Box)**   This option creates a text box and embeds the form in it. Your options for locating the fields are limited by the text box—the location must align to a character and line boundary; you can't just click and drag the field to any location, as you can with a Layout Region form or a Layout form. Further, the location is impacted by which wrapping option you pick (how text wraps around the embedded fields). You set the wrapping using the Align tab of the Form Field Properties panel (see Figure 13-5).
- **Create form in a Table**   This option creates a table and embeds the form in the table. As with a text box–based table, your layout options are limited—you must place your fields in the table cells, and arrange them using the Align tab to set position and wrapping.
- **Define Layout as a form (limits page to one form)**   This option converts the Layout on the current page into a form. Since the Layout takes up the whole page, you can have only one form on the page.

FIGURE 13-5   Use the Align tab to set how the text wraps around the field and where the field sits in the text box.

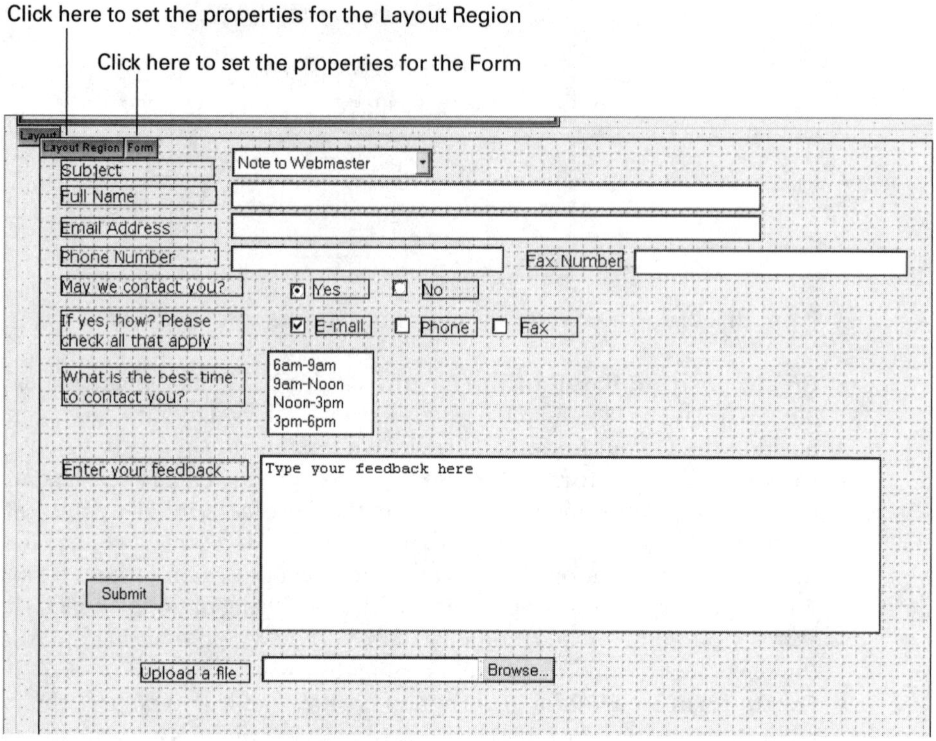

Click here to set the properties for the Layout Region

Click here to set the properties for the Form

FIGURE 13-6   The form is embedded in an area—and you can see the labels for both the area and the form.

After you choose your form option (we'll use a position-based form for the rest of the chapter), the area has two labels: a label for the type of the area (such as Layout Region) and the Form label (see Figure 13-6). To set the properties for the area in which the form is embedded (Layout Region, Layout, Table, etc.), click the label for that area. To set the properties for the form, click the Form label.

Turn an Area into a Form

You can take an existing Layout, Layout Region, Text Box, or Table and turn it into a form by simply selecting a check box. Select the following:

- **Table**   Table Is A Form check box
- **Text Box**   Text Box Is A Form check box
- **Layout Region**   Form check box
- **Layout**   Layout Is A Form check box

Once you do that, the Form label appears next to the area label, as described earlier.

Configure the Form Properties

Once you have created the form, you can configure its operation. To do so, click the Form label to display the Form Properties panel.

The General tab displays the following fields:

- **Name**   The name of the form. This is how to reference the form using a script.
- **Action**   Use this field to pick how you want to "drive" the form. Forms Handler (PHP) or (ASP) is the only value in the drop-down list. This option uses the built-in forms handler, which is very convenient and is suitable for most uses, as you don't have to fill in the Method (Post or Get) or Encoding fields. If you want to write your own script (using a CGI file), select the . . . button and pick the CGI file from the Open dialog box. You *will* have to fill in the Method and Encoding fields for yourself.

- **Parameters** The area at the bottom of the General tab is where you specify name/value pairs that are passed to the form script. If you are writing your own script, you'll have to fill in the name/value pairs you need by clicking the + button and filling in the name and value in the Enter Value dialog box. If you choose to use the built-in Forms Handler (PHP) or (ASP), the list of names is pre-populated for you, showing you the parameters that the Forms Handler requires. This list should look familiar—these are exactly the same parameters that were needed by the Forms Handler component, described earlier in this chapter. There is one additional field—the e-mail subject field (Subject). This is what shows in the Subject line in the e-mail sent when a form is successfully submitted.

 To change the values (which you'll need to do, as the defaults are worthless), double-click a line in the parameter list to open the Enter Value dialog box. Note also that you cannot add new values, as any additional values will cause an error in the script.

The Form Hidden Fields Properties tab enables you to pass fields (and the value to pass) to the form database without the user's seeing the fields.

Don't forget to provide fields in the database to hold these values!

To create the hidden field and provide a value, click the + button and enter the name and value in the Enter Value dialog box.

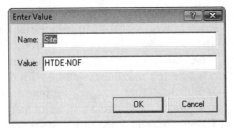

To rearrange the fields, click a field and use the up or down arrow buttons. To delete a field, select the field and click the – button.

Add Fields to the Form

Unlike when using the Forms Handler component, you have complete control over where you place the various fields in a form you build yourself. Using the form field controls located in the Form Tools toolbar, you can pick a control, click and drag on the form to establish its location, and configure the form field using the Properties panel. You can also click and drag the field to relocate it, and click and drag the sizing handles to resize the field (in most cases). These fields should look familiar too—they are virtually the same types of fields as are available for the Forms Handler component, discussed earlier in this chapter. Each has various configuration options that you can set from the left-most tab in the Properties panel (which has different names, depending on the type of field). These are pretty much the same as the options discussed for this type of field when used in the Forms Handler component. For the Edit Field (for example), you can choose the type (Single-Line, Multi-Line, and Password), Text (default text), Character width and maximum characters, and the Style.

There are a few differences for forms you build for yourself. They are

- **Multi-line Wrap field** The Wrap field for Multi-Line fields enables you to establish how multiple lines of text will wrap when the data won't all fit on one line. The choices are
  - **Off** No wrapping. Everything is one line, which makes it pretty hard to edit long strings. The data is stored in the database all in one field.
  - **Virtual** The text wraps in the Multi-Line field, but the wrapping information is not sent to the database—everything is stored in one string.
  - **Physical** The text wraps in the Multi-Line field, and the line end/return information is sent to the database along with the text. Thus, when viewing the data in an application (such as a word processor or spreadsheet program) that recognizes the wrapping, the text will wrap just as it did in the form.
- **Forms Field Label** This is a text box that you can type in and format just like any other text box. It is designed to be used to label form fields—you can associate it with a form field by selecting the field from the drop-down list in the Form Label Inspector tab. Associating the label with a field enables you to use the error style for the label as well as for the field when a site visitor enters invalid data into the field (see "Set Validation Rules for Form Objects," later in this chapter).

- **Dynamic Check** This check box is available for Check Box and Radio Button fields. Select the Dynamic Check check box and click the...button to pick a data source. The data source is used to determine whether the check box field should be selected or not, or which radio button in a group should be selected.
- **Enable Data Context** This check box is available for Combo Boxes. Once you select it, you can click Config to open the Data Source Config dialog box. This dialog box enables you to pick a Recordset and a name and value to specify the values that appear in the Combo Box.

- **Dynamic Condition**   This check box is available for Combo Boxes. Once you select it, you can click Config to open the Dynamic Select dialog box. This dialog box enables you to compare the values in the combo box with either a data source (click the DS radio button) or a constant (click the Compare With Constant radio button).

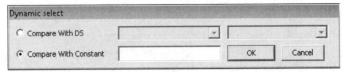

 Setting up databases, recordsets, and connectors is beyond the scope of this book, but you'll need to set them up in order to use the data-driven features such as Dynamic Conditions. The User Guide has a complete explanation starting on page 940.

- **Button types**   You have different options for the types of buttons you can create when you build your own form. For one thing, you cannot create a Link button. The types of buttons you can create are
  - **Submit**   Clicking this button executes a "submit" action to the server. You can, if you wish, type a different text string into the Value field, which would leave you with the confusing situation that the Submit button was labeled with something else.
  - **Reset**   Clicking this button clears the form of all the entered data, enabling the site visitor to start over. You can specify the button text by entering it into the Value field.
  - **Close Window**   Clicking this button closes the form window without submitting the form information. You can specify the button text by entering it into the Value field.
  - **Button**   A "Button" button is just a button with text on it. You can specify the text by entering it in the Value field. In order to make the button useful, select it and then select the Actions tab, where you can specify the actions that the button will initiate.

 The Close Window button works this way—there is an action in the Actions tab that specifies the When field as "Clicked," the target as the area (such as a Layout) that contains the form, and the Message as "Close" (for the window).

- **Image**   This type of button enables you to pick a graphic to use as a button. As with the Button button, you must use the Actions tab to attach actions to the Image button.

 Pick an image that contains text to tell the site visitor what the button is for. You can't add text to an image button within Fusion.

Set Validation Rules for Form Objects

You can set many more validation rules for fields on forms you build yourself than you can for fields on forms based on the Forms Handler component. To set validation rules, click the Form Fields Inspector tab to display a list of fields.

Establish the Validation Rules

To establish validation rules for a field, click the Validate button to open the Validate Form dialog box (see Figure 13-7), displaying the Field tab.

Use the following steps to establish validation for a field:

1. Pick the field from the Field drop-down list. The Validation options appear in the Validation options pane on the left side of the dialog box.
2. Select the validation options you want (one at a time) from the Validation options pane and click the > button to add the option to the field. It will then appear in the Validate field as pane.

 You can adjust the order of the validations by selecting a validation and clicking the tiny up or down arrowhead buttons below the Validate Field As pane.

3. Adjust the Parameters in the Parameters pane, as discussed later in this section. The available parameters depend on the validation type. For example, the LengthInRange validation has a minvalue and a maxvalue—double-click either number and enter a value in the Value column. On the other hand, a phone number has several valid formats you can pick from the Value drop-down list.

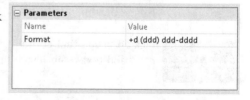

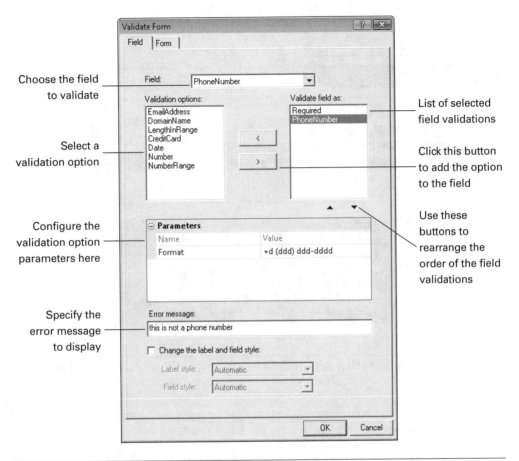

Choose the field to validate

Select a validation option

Configure the validation option parameters here

Specify the error message to display

List of selected field validations

Click this button to add the option to the field

Use these buttons to rearrange the order of the field validations

FIGURE 13-7   Choose field validations from the Field tab in the Validate Form dialog box.

Be Smart About Error Messages

The generic error messages supplied (such as "the number of chars is not in the interval" for LengthInRange) are not helpful and you should *not* use them. The error message should tell the site visitor how to correct the problem. For example, the LengthInRange error message should state the valid range. Thus, you might use something like "You must type in more than 3 characters and less than 50 characters." This is especially true when you are validating formats (such as e-mail, phone number, credit card, and date). There are so many ways to type these quantities into a field that you *must* tell the site visitor what they did wrong. Even better: put the expected format into the label for the field! And one more thing—the error messages are listed all together in a dialog box (see Figure 13-8), so it can be hard to figure out which field the error message applies to. As a result, you should build the name/label for the field into the error message, such as "The Name field must contain between 3 and 50 characters."

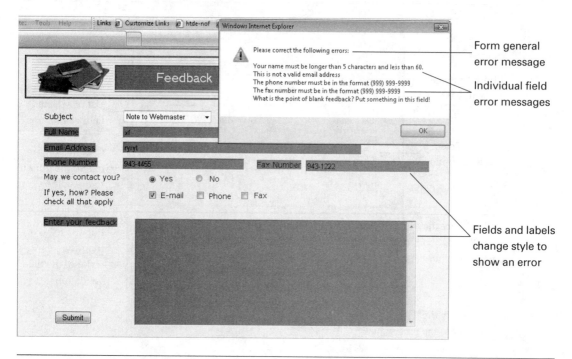

Form general error message

Individual field error messages

Fields and labels change style to show an error

FIGURE 13-8 The fields that failed validation are displayed on the form and in a dialog box.

4. Enter the error message that should be displayed if the field fails the validation.
5. If you wish, you can specify the label and field styles that will result if the information supplied by the site visitor fails the validation. For example, if the site visitor types in a string that is too long for a LengthInRange validated field, you can display a different style for the Label and/or Field. Choose the style you want from the Label Style and Field Style drop-down lists. Figure 13-8 shows a sample of a form with field validations that failed.

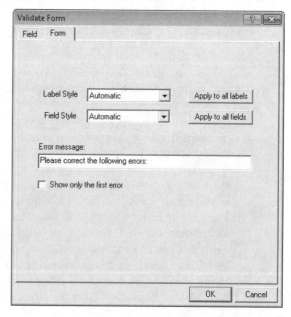

The Form tab of the Validate Form dialog box provides additional configuration options for validations.

The handiest option in the Form tab is the ability to choose a Label Style and a Field Style (from those drop-down lists) and then click the Apply To All Labels or Apply To All Fields button. That way, you don't have to specify the styles individually. You can also customize the error message displayed on the form above the list of individual field errors. To do so, type the message into the Error Message field. Finally, you can limit the list of displayed errors to just the first error by selecting the Show Only The First Error check box. I'm not sure why you'd want to, though—in my opinion, it's best to let the site visitor know everything that needs to be corrected.

Understand the Validation Parameters

There are basically three types of validations you can use:

- Validations that establish a range, such as LengthInRange (for the number of characters in a string) and NumberRange (for the value of the number that is supplied). These validations need both a minimum value (minvalue) and a maximum value (maxvalue).

- Validations that establish an input requirement, such as Required (something must be filled in) and Number (the item supplied must be numerical). These validations do not have any parameters.

- Validations that establish a pattern for the input. Some of these validations (such as E-mail and domain name) do not require you to specify a parameter, as the format is built into Fusion. The others (Credit Card, Phone Number, and Date) provide a list of possible formats to check against in the Value column. Realize that you can pick only one validation format, and you really should give site visitors a clue as to what format will work (see the preceding sidebar). Here is the Value parameter list for dates.

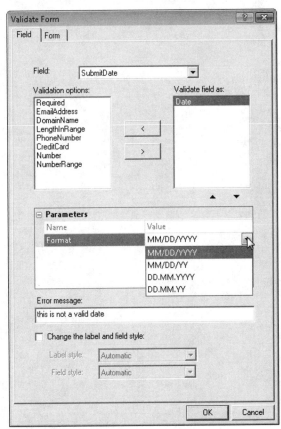

14

Create Advanced Functionality with Custom Components

HOW TO...

- Create Frequently Asked Questions (FAQs)
- Administer the FAQs to add, delete, and edit them
- Create and manage a Guestbook
- Set up a secure web site for visitors with a username and password
- Administer the site and make its pages secure

As with forms, it used to be that you need to be a pretty good programmer to implement functionality such as Frequently Asked Questions (FAQ), a Guestbook (where site visitors could provide comments and others could read those comments), and a secure web site, requiring a user ID and password in order to access the site. Fusion provides that functionality as a set of custom components, which simplifies the job of setting up these features.

Lay Out an FAQ

Frequently Asked Questions (FAQs) are an integral part of many web sites. This is especially true of sites set up to impart specialized information—such as how to use a software package. You *can* manually engineer such a site by using hyperlinked questions to "jump" to the text containing the answer, and with frames and bookmarks, it is possible to do a pretty good job of it. However, you must modify the page each time you want to add a new question or edit an existing one.

Fusion's FAQ component set makes it easier not only to build the FAQ functionality, but also to maintain the questions and answers using a web page on your site. The set consists of four distinct components:

- **FAQ Details**   This component displays the actual questions and the first part of the answer, along with the rating average, hits, and modification date (assuming you configured the component to show these). The question is a hyperlink; clicking the hyperlink expands the answer to show the entire answer.
- **FAQ TOC**   This component lists the FAQ categories as well as how many questions are in each category. Ideally, this component should be located on the same page as the FAQ Details, so that clicking a category displays the questions in that category without changing pages.
- **FAQ Search**   This component provides a search field so that site visitors can search the FAQs to find any that mention a term they are interested in. Ideally, this component should be located on the same page as the FAQ TOC and FAQ Details, so that the site visitors can see the answers to their search without changing pages.
- **FAQ Admin**   This component is where you actually maintain the FAQs, including defining categories, creating the questions and answers, and defining the rating/ranking criteria. The component includes a search tool to help you find the FAQs you want to edit. This component must be on its own page (with no navigation links) and must be published before you can define the FAQs—there is no way to define them locally on your machine prior to publishing the components. For information on how to use the tools in this component, see "Set Up the FAQ on the Web Site," later in this chapter.

Build the FAQ Page

As mentioned earlier in this chapter, it is best to co-locate the FAQ Search, FAQ TOC, and FAQ Details components on the same page. Doing so might lead to a Fusion page that looks like the one shown in Figure 14-1.

Note   You can't see a preview of the FAQ components on the page in Fusion—all you can see are the graphic images shown in Figure 14-1. To see how the FAQ page is going to look, you'll have to publish your web site to the Internet. Even publishing locally won't show you the preview.

Laying the components out this way leads to a published web page that looks like the one shown in Figure 14-2 (after FAQs have been defined using the FAQ Admin component). Clicking one of the questions expands the question and shows the full answer, as well as a drop-down list for the site visitor to rate the FAQ (see Figure 14-3).

Add the FAQ Details Component

To add the FAQ Details component to the page, select the component from the NOF FAQ Section of the Custom Components panel. Then click and drag on the page to establish

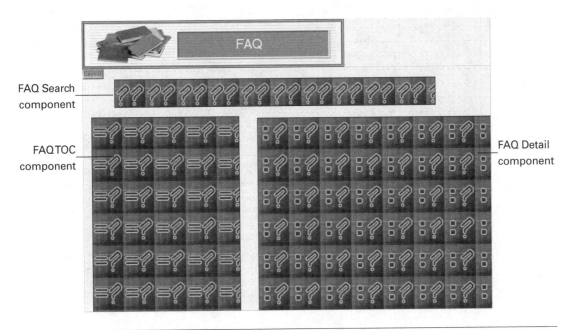

FAQ Search component

FAQ TOC component

FAQ Detail component

FIGURE 14-1 The three FAQ components are all on the same page.

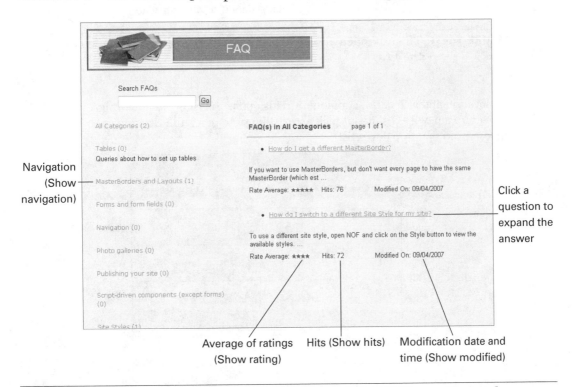

Navigation (Show navigation)

Click a question to expand the answer

Average of ratings (Show rating)

Hits (Show hits)

Modification date and time (Show modified)

FIGURE 14-2 The FAQ web page, showing categories (FAQ TOC), questions and answers (FAQ Details), and the search field (FAQ Search)

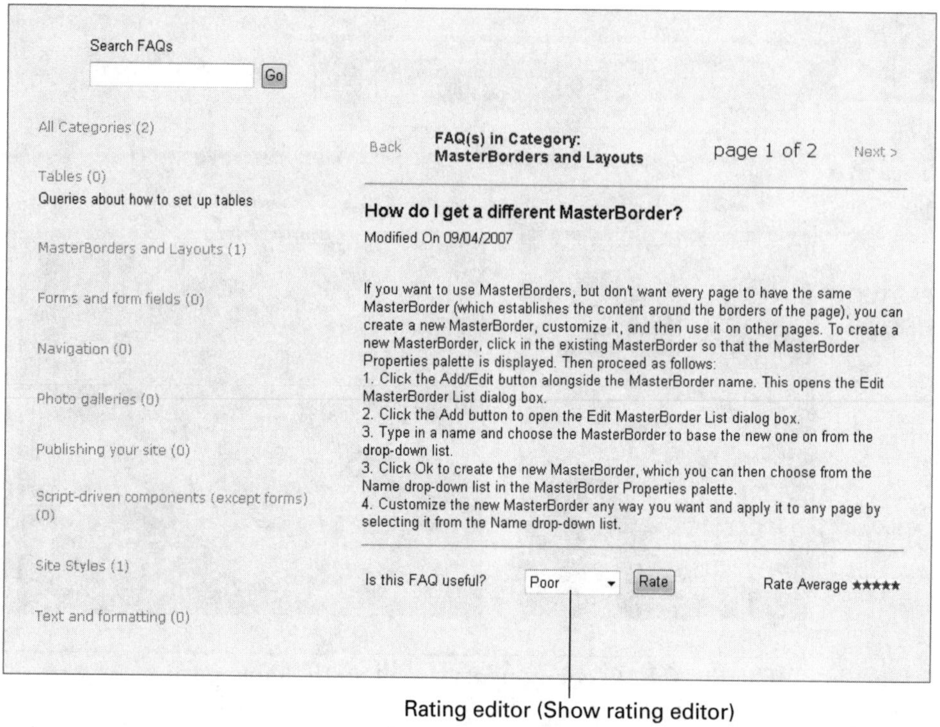

Rating editor (Show rating editor)

FIGURE 14-3 The expanded answer also gives the site visitor a chance to rate the FAQ.

the location and size of the component. This opens the NOF FAQ dialog box, where you can set up a new FAQ suite, or pick an existing suite (click the Existing radio button and choose from the drop-down list).

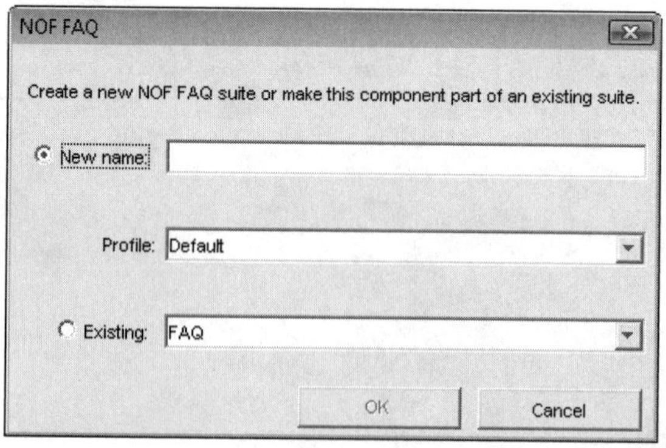

This opens the FAQ Details dialog box, where you can configure the component.

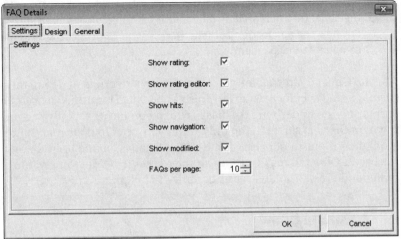

 You can move and resize the component graphics just like most other objects—just click and drag inside the component to move it, and click and drag a sizing handle to change the size.

The Settings tab enables you to specify what you want to see in the FAQ details section of the page as well as the number of FAQs to show on each page. Figures 14-2 and 14-3 (shown previously) display the page elements you get for each check box.

Use the Design tab to pick the Style for FAQ Details Component section of the page. You can pick from the current SiteStyle, or from two supplied styles ("black and white" or "comic with color"). The two supplied styles show a preview of the styles in the Preview section.

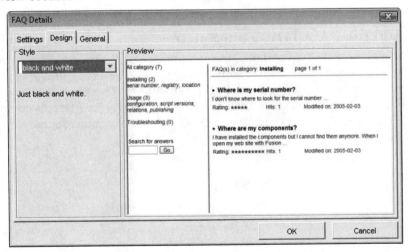

Note   The Preview section of the dialog box shows all three FAQ components on the same page. However, the sample layout does not reflect your layout, and if you change the style, that new style is reflected in all three previewed components. This is not how the application actually works—you can choose a different style for each component independently.

The General tab enables you to publish your scripts in debug mode, select a language, and specify a database prefix. The database prefix is used for the generated scripts and the underlying database (which you never actually see unless you hunt it down on the web server). The only thing you need to do is make sure that the prefix is unique—it must not be the same as the database name used for any other form databases. Oh—and make sure this prefix is set to be the same value for all the FAQ components, as Fusion uses this quantity to link them up.

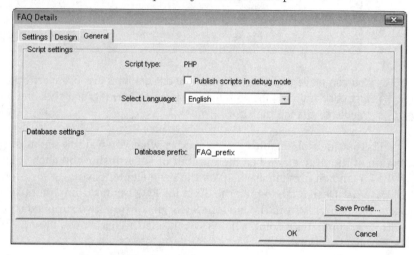

Add the FAQ TOC Component

To add the FAQ TOC component to the page, select the component from the NOF FAQ section of the Custom Components panel. Then click and drag on the page to establish the location and size of the component. This opens the NOF FAQ dialog box, where you must pick the Existing value for the FAQ Details component you just set up. Once you click OK, the FAQ TOC dialog box opens so that you can configure the component.

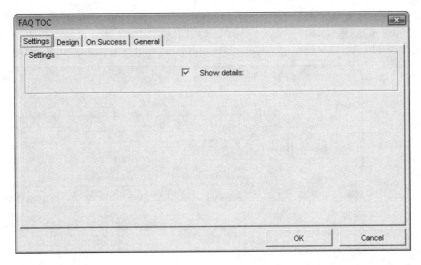

The Settings tab has only a single check box. Selecting the Show Details check box displays the number of questions in each category.

The Design tab is identical to the one for the FAQ Details component—you use this to set the style for the TOC section.

The On Success tab enables you to specify the page where the TOC will be displayed—which must be the same page that contains the FAQ Details component. Don't pick any other page—the results are unpredictable and you get some strange error messages.

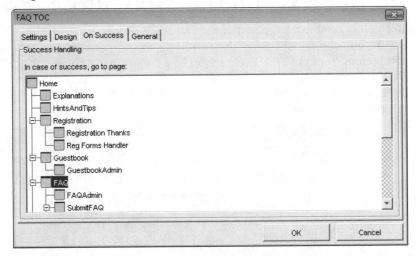

The General tab is identical to the one used for the FAQ Details component.

Add the FAQ Search Component

To add the FAQ Search component to the page, select the component from the NOF FAQ section of the Custom Components panel. Then click and drag on the page to establish the location and size of the component. This opens the NOF FAQ dialog box, where you must pick the Existing value for the FAQ Details component you just set up. Once you click OK, the FAQ Search dialog box opens so that you can configure the component.

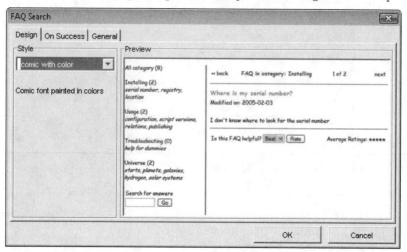

All three tabs are identical to those in other FAQ component dialog boxes. For the On Success page, again, you *must* designate the page containing the FAQ Details component.

Set Up the FAQ on the Web Site

To actually establish FAQs, you'll need to add a page to your web site containing the FAQ Admin component. As with the other FAQ components, you pick the FAQ Admin component from the NOF FAQ section of the Custom Components panel. After you click and drag on the page to establish the location and size of the component, choose the Existing FAQ selection from the NOF FAQ dialog box, and click OK, the FAQ Admin dialog box opens.

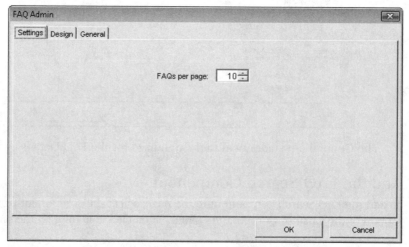

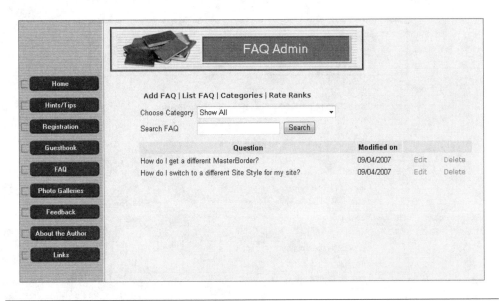

FIGURE 14-4   Maintain the FAQs using the FAQ Admin component published to your web site.

Other than the Settings tab (where you can establish how many FAQs you want on a page), the settings are identical to the tabs in the other FAQ component dialog boxes.

 You must place the FAQ Admin component on its own page. And since this is *not* a page you want anyone else to have access to, you should exclude it from Navigation, and even password-protect the page (see "Secure Your Web Site," later in this chapter).

In order to actually create the categories, questions, answers, and rating factors, you must use the *published* FAQ Admin component on your web site (see Figure 14-4). The default view shows a list of all the questions on the site, though you can narrow the categories by picking one from the Choose Category drop-down list and then clicking Search. You can also search for a set of questions by entering the search string in the Search FAQ field and clicking Search.

 To return to the page listing the FAQs, click the List FAQ link near the top of the page.

Create FAQ Categories

To create the FAQ categories—which appear in the Choose Category drop-down list— select the Categories link at the top of the screen. This displays the current list of categories (which will be empty when you access the page for the first time).

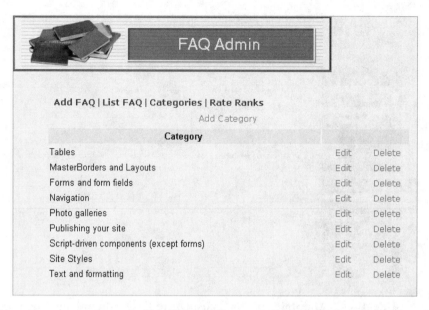

To create a new category, click the Add Category link at the top of the page. The resulting web page enables you to add a Category Name and a Category Description. Then click Save to create the new category.

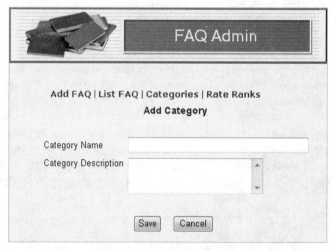

To return to the list of categories, click the Categories link again. From this page, you can edit a category by clicking the Edit link, which takes you to the same page as for a new category, except with the content filled in. Simply make the changes you want and click Save.

Note   Changing the name of the category does not disassociate the FAQ from the category. The FAQ remains attached to the category and displays the edited name of the category.

Create a New FAQ

To create a new FAQ, click the Add FAQ link at the top of the page. This opens the same page as editing an FAQ, except that there is no content. To create the FAQ, choose the category, fill in the question and answer in the appropriate fields, and click Save.

Edit an Existing FAQ

To edit an existing FAQ, click the Edit link alongside the question to display the Edit screen.

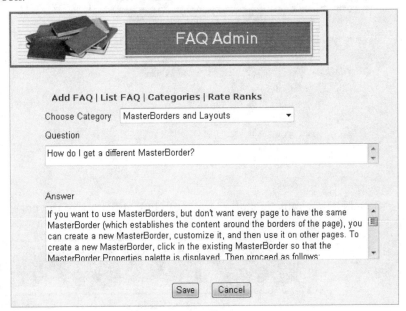

From this screen, you can

- **Change the category**   Pick a new category from the Choose Category drop-down list.
- **Edit the question**   Reword the question by changing it in the Question field.
- **Edit the answer**   Reword the answer by changing it in the Answer field.
- **Save your changes**   To save the changes, click Save. If you change your mind, click Cancel to abandon the changes.

To delete the question, click the Delete hyperlink alongside the question in the list of FAQs (alongside the Edit link).

Create FAQ Ratings

If you enable this feature (when configuring the FAQ Admin component), site visitors can rate the FAQ and the answer as to how useful it is. You can configure the values that appear in the Is This FAQ Useful drop-down list by clicking the Rate Ranks link at the top of the page. This provides a list of rank rates (the numeric value) and rank names (the description).

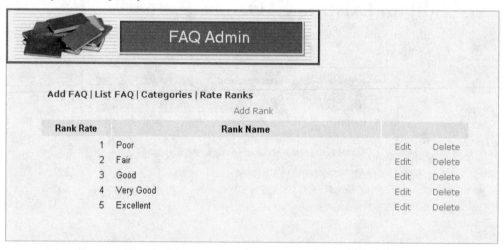

To add a new rank, click the Add Rank link at the top of the page to display the page where you can add the new rank.

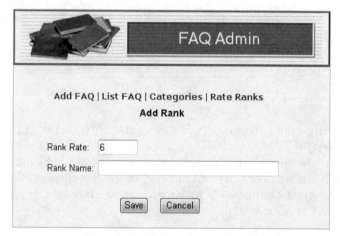

 Note You can't specify a Rank Rate that already exists, and the Rank Rate field accepts only single-digit integers between 1 and 9. Thus, you are limited to nine ratings—which really should be enough!

To edit an existing rank, click the Edit link for that rank, which takes you to the same page as for a new rank, except with the content filled in. Simply make the changes you want and click Save.

 Make sure to add a link back to the FAQ page in the FAQ Admin page.

Get Feedback with the Guestbook

A "guestbook" is a section of a web site in which visitors can say pretty much anything they want to and those comments are visible to other visitors. Unfortunately, Guestbook pages are also where spammers and other miscreants tend to pollute your site content with all kinds of nasty material. Fusion provides a Guestbook component, as well as a Guestbook Admin component that displays visitor comments but also helps you control the material that your visitors see. Figure 14-5 shows a Fusion Guestbook on my web site.

One of the nice things about this Guestbook is that the fields you need to enter the comments and the comments that have been entered are all displayed on the same page (these comments are not visible in the figure, but they are present on the page). In addition, the Guestbook doesn't have to take up the whole page, leaving room for text (like the warning to spammers) and other objects.

The Guestbook is actually composed of two components: the Guestbook component and the Guestbook Admin component. These must be on separate pages, and typically, the Guestbook Admin page does not show up in the Navigation.

![Guestbook page screenshot showing navigation links: Home, Hints/Tips, Registration, Guestbook, FAQ, Photo Galleries, Feedback, About the Author, Links. Main area reads "Please sign our guest book and let me know what you think of the book and the site!" with a note to spammers, a form with fields: *Name, E-mail, HomePage, City, State/Province, Country, *Comment, and a captcha code "EQWUB" with "*Enter the shown code:"]

FIGURE 14-5   Enter comments in a Guestbook on a web site.

Create the Guestbook Page

To create the Guestbook page, choose the Guestbook component from the NOF Guestbook section of the Custom Components panel. Click and drag on the page to establish the size and location of the Guestbook component. This opens the NOF Guestbook dialog box, where you can pick a new Guestbook suite (fill in the name in the New Name field) or choose an existing Guestbook suite.

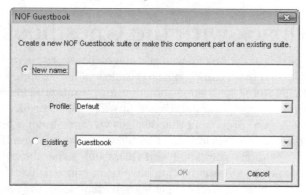

Once you've provided the name, the Guestbook dialog box opens, where you can configure the Guestbook settings.

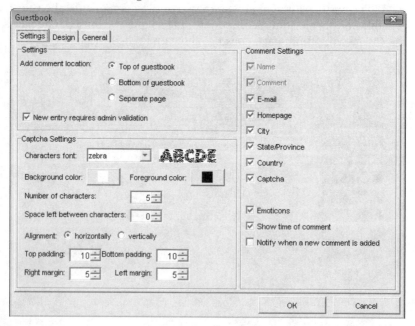

 As with most other objects, you can move and resize the component.

Configure the Guestbook Page

The three Add Comment Location radio buttons enable you to specify where you want the "comment" section—that is, the section into which the site visitor will enter comments. The default you normally see (as in Figure 14-5, seen previously) is to place the new comment section above the Guestbook (previously entered comments). But you can change that to place the new comments section below the Guestbook (by choosing Bottom Of Guestbook) or even on a separate page.

The New Entry Requires Admin Validation check box is very important. It determines whether the site administrator has to "validate" the comment before it is displayed in the Guestbook (see "Manage the Guestbook Entries with the Admin tool," later in this chapter). If you don't select this check box, the comments are posted immediately. Although you can certainly delete them later, until you do, your site visitors will see them. This has become more important as clever spammers have built scripts to circumvent the Captcha field (discussed next) and post garbage in your Guestbook.

The Captcha Settings section enables you to configure the Captcha field. As mentioned earlier in this book, the Captcha field displays an image that looks like letters, and the site visitor has to type the letters correctly in order to submit to the Guestbook. This defeats all but the most sophisticated web robots.

Finally, the Comment Settings section enables you to pick what fields to include in the Guestbook, whether to include Emoticons (those smiley faces), whether to show the comment time, and whether to send an e-mail when a new comment is added. This last is a very good idea when you require admin validation, as good comments should be displayed soon after they are submitted, and spam/garbage should be deleted periodically. The nice thing about the e-mail is that it includes the contents of the comments, so you know right away what you need to do.

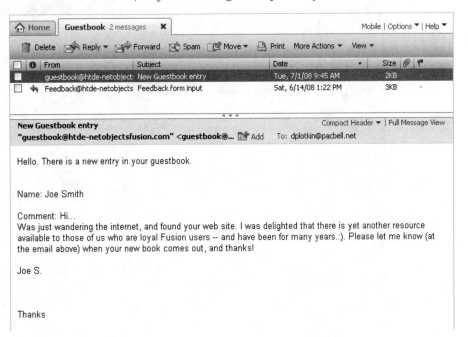

The Design tab works much like the Design tab for the FAQ Details component, though the style options are different (and there are more of them).

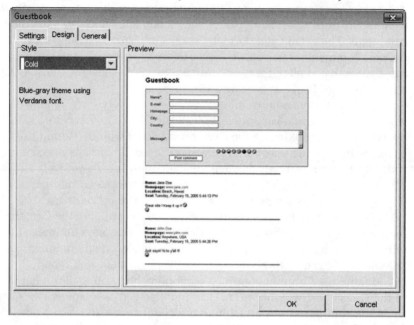

The General tab enables setting script settings, specifying the database, and setting up the e-mail options. It works identically to the Forms Handler component General tab.

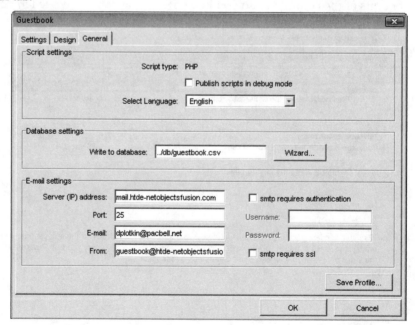

Create the Guestbook Admin Tool

To create the Guestbook Admin page, choose the Guestbook Admin component from the NOF Guestbook section of the Custom Components panel. Click and drag on the page to establish the size and location of the Guestbook Admin component. Choose the Existing radio button, pick the Guestbook suite name from the drop-down list, and click OK. This opens the Guestbook Admin dialog box.

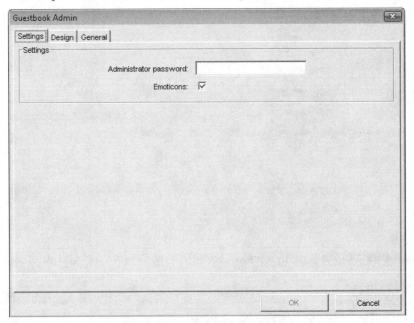

The Settings tab of the Guestbook Admin dialog box enables you to set an Administrator Password. This password appears on the Guestbook Admin page in the web site (see Figure 14-6). You must type in the correct password before you get access to the maintenance functions on that page.

 The Design and General tabs are identical to the Guestbook component.

Manage the Guestbook Entries with the Admin Tool

Once you type in the proper password and click Login, you gain access to the submitted comments and maintenance functions (see Figure 14-7). If there are multiple pages of comments, you can navigate between them by clicking the page number in the Pages section in the upper-right corner.

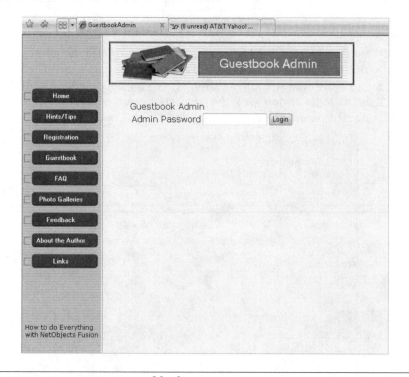

FIGURE 14-6 Type in a password before you can manage your Guestbook entries.

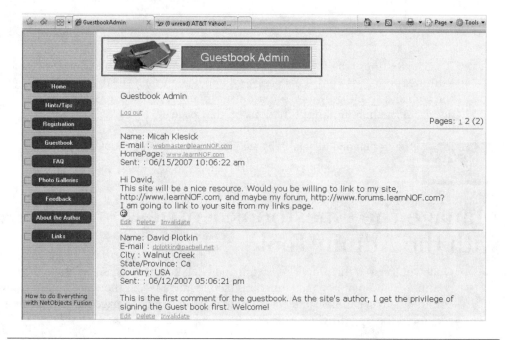

FIGURE 14-7 Review the list of submitted comments and decide which ones to keep.

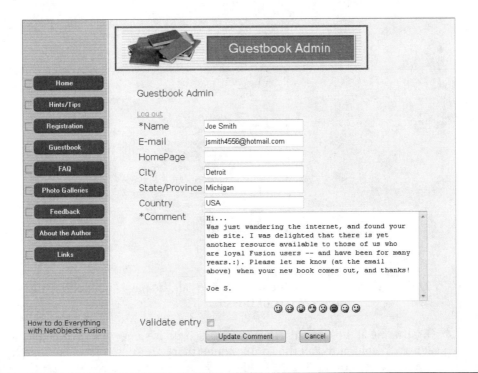

FIGURE 14-8   Edit a comment to make it more palatable for your web site.

There are three links for each submitted comment.

- **Edit**   This enables you to edit the comment before posting it. Clicking this link opens the comment on a page that mirrors the Guestbook page (see Figure 14-8). You can make any changes here and update the comment (click the Update Comment button, which returns you to the list of comments). If you selected the Validate Entry check box before clicking Update Comment, the comment is "validated," meaning that it will now show up in the Guestbook.
- **Delete**   If the comment is one you never want to post on your web site, click the Delete link to discard the comment (after confirming).
- **Validate**   To display the comment, click the Validate link. Only Validated comments are displayed in the Guestbook.
- **Invalidate**   This link is only available for comments that have been validated. If you change your mind, you can click the Invalidate link, and the comment will no longer be visible in the Guestbook.

Secure Your Web Site

Up until now, we've been assuming that anyone who wants can view your web site. But what if you want to limit the site to just people who have signed up (and perhaps paid)? Fusion supports building a "secure" web site (one that requires

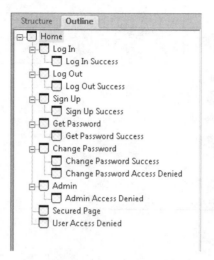

FIGURE 14-9 This site structure provides all the pages needed for the security requirements of the site.

a user name and password), though setting it up is somewhat involved. Once you've set up and configured all the components (there are six of them), anyone trying to access a page with the Secure Page component on it will have to enter that userid and password. This approach provides quite a bit of flexibility—you can decide whether a page should be available to just anyone or only to "members." And you can change your mind at any time by simply adding or removing the Secure Page component.

Because there are so many components, you should plan your site out ahead of time. This is especially true because some components require three pages—the page that holds the component, the "success" page (that site visitors see if they successfully complete the requirements of the component) and the "Access Denied" page that site visitors see if they don't. Figure 14-9 shows a sample site structure you might use. You could probably simplify this some—perhaps by combining some of the success pages or access denied pages—but for the purposes of this book, I've built single-use pages to help you understand what each page is for.

 The site is shown in Outline view so that you can see the full name of all the pages in the site.

The components needed are

- **Log In**   Enables site visitors to enter their user name and password to log in to the site.
- **Log Out**   Enables site visitors to log out of the site.
- **Sign Up**   Enables site visitors to submit the required information to obtain a user name and password. Depending on how the Admin component is configured, either the signup is automatically successful, or the site administrator has to review and validate the signup before the site visitor can use it.

- **Get Password** Enables site visitors to request their password via e-mail. They just enter the e-mail address for the account (which must be provided during signup) and it appears in their in box a few minutes later.
- **Change Password** Enables site visitors to change their password by inputting their old password and the new one (twice).
- **Admin** Provides the tools for the site administrator to review, edit, validate, and delete site users. To access this page, you must log in with the administrator ID and password, which you establish when you configure the component.

When you add one of the security components to a page, the first step is to choose to create a new NOF Security Site "suite" or to use an existing one in the NOF Secure Site dialog box (if you have previously created one). For the first component you create, you should specify a new name for the suite; otherwise, pick the Existing name for the suite. This is important, as it is the suite name that links the components together.

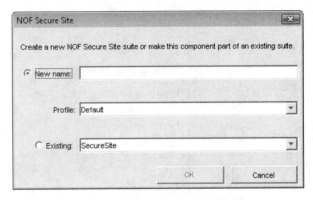

In addition, all of the components (including the Secure Page component) have a General tab, where you configure the database connection and e-mail properties. Don't forget to use the wizard to create the database, as discussed in Chapter 13.

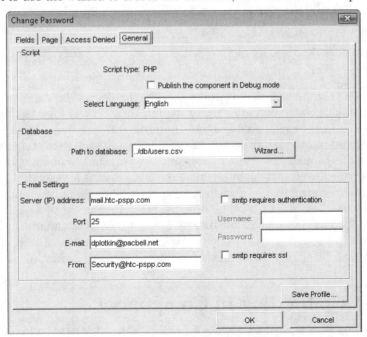

Allow Visitors to Sign Up for an Account

The Signup component is, not too surprisingly, the component where site visitors sign up for an account. Figure 14-10 shows a sample of what the Signup component might look like on your web site.

To establish the Signup component, select it from the NOF Secure Site section of the Custom Components panel. Click and drag on the page to establish the location and size. Once you've chosen the suite name from the NOF Secure Site dialog box, you can configure the component in the Signup dialog box.

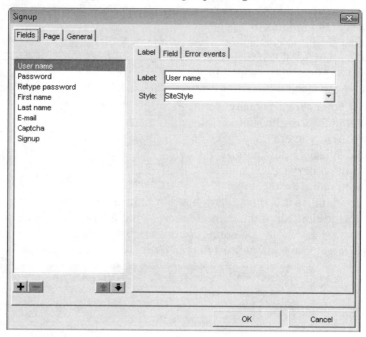

The Signup component works just like the Forms Handler component. The Fields tab enables you to define fields for the information you want to capture by clicking the + button to add fields and the – button to remove them. You can establish the label and style in the Label sub-tab. Use the Field sub-tab to configure the field type (Edit field, check box, radio button, etc.) and set the parameters for the field type. Use the Error Events sub-tab to establish the error events for each field. There are some specialized error events available, such as Non-Matching Passwords for the Retype Password field and User Name Already Taken for the User Name field.

The Page tab enables the display of error messages and the designation of a "Sign Up Success" page. This is the page that site visitors will see when they have successfully submitted a request for a user name and password.

Set Up the Log In Component

The Log In component provides a page with the user name and password, along with a button to complete the login process (see Figure 14-11 for a sample).

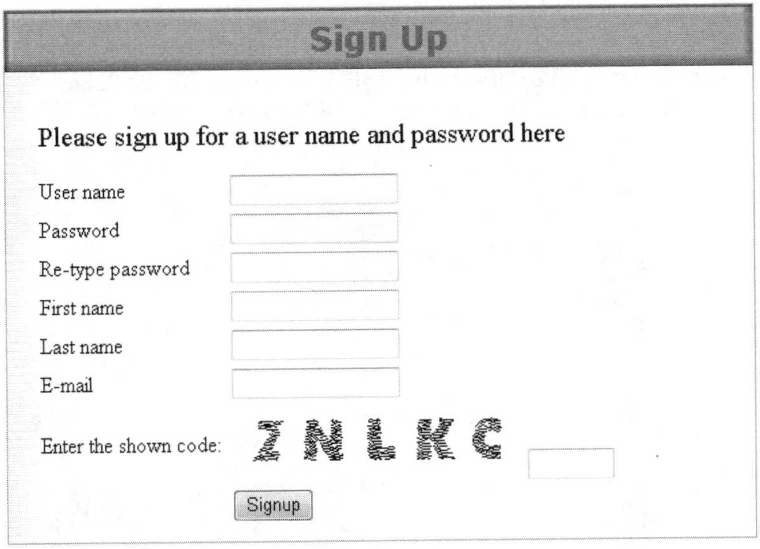

Sign Up

Please sign up for a user name and password here

User name

Password

Re-type password

First name

Last name

E-mail

Enter the shown code: Z N L K C

Signup

FIGURE 14-10   Site visitors sign up for a userid and password to access your site.

Note   The site administrator can disable an account using the Admin component—which would then display the "Account is disabled" error message when the visitor tries to log in.

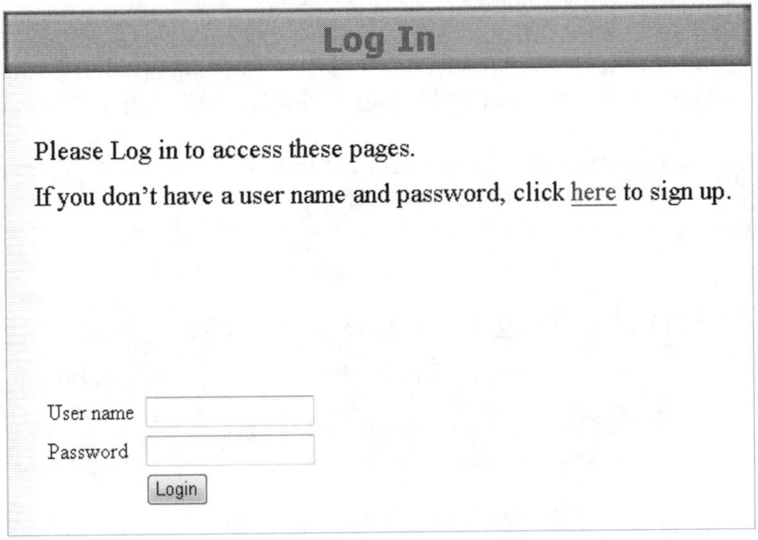

Log In

Please Log in to access these pages.

If you don't have a user name and password, click here to sign up.

User name

Password

Login

FIGURE 14-11   Log in to the site using the Log In component.

To establish the Log In component, select it from the NOF Secure Site section of the Custom Components panel. Click and drag on the page to establish the location and size. Once you've chosen the suite name from the NOF Secure Site dialog box, you can configure the component in the Login dialog box.

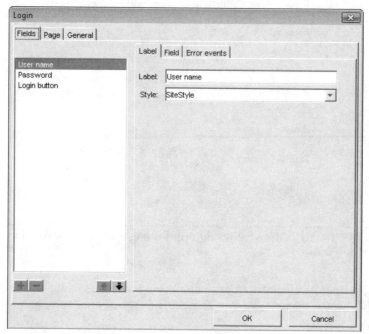

As with the Sign Up component, the Log In component has pretty much the same functionality as a standard Forms Handler. However, you can't add or remove fields, and the error events include specialized values such as "User name is invalid" and "Account is disabled" for the User name. The Page tab also has a Success Handling panel, where you can define the page to display if the site visitor successfully logs in.

Add links to this page to direct site visitors to the Get Password page, so that they can retrieve forgotten passwords.

Set Up the Log Out Component

The Log Out component provides a page with just a Log Out button, as shown here.

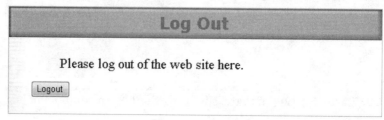

To establish the Log Out component, select it from the NOF Secure Site section of the Custom Components panel. Click and drag on the page to establish the location and size. Once you've chosen the suite name from the NOF Secure Site dialog box, you can configure the component in the Logout dialog box.

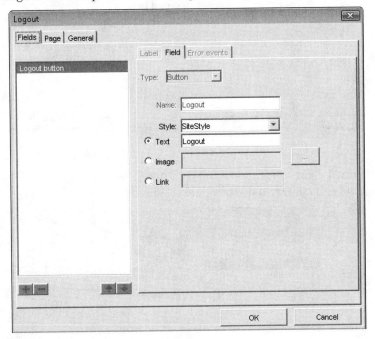

This dialog box is pretty simple—all you can configure in the Fields tab is the Log Out button, which can be text, image, or a link—but in all cases the action is to log out of the site. The Page tab provides the standard check boxes for error handling; though it escapes me under what circumstances the site visitor would encounter an error (even logging out without logging in doesn't produce an error)! You can also specify a Log Out Success page, which is displayed when the site visitor successfully logs out of the site.

Retrieve Lost Passwords

The Get Password component enables the site visitors to retrieve their password, as shown in Figure 14-12. You simply fill in your e-mail address and click Send to have your password e-mailed to you.

To establish the Get Password component, select it from the NOF Secure Site section of the Custom Components panel. Click and drag on the page to establish the

> ## Get Password
>
> Please retrieve your password here
>
> E-mail [   ]
>
> [Send]

FIGURE 14-12 Forgot your password? Retrieve it using this component.

location and size. Once you've chosen the suite name from the NOF Secure Site dialog box, you can configure the component in the Get Password dialog box.

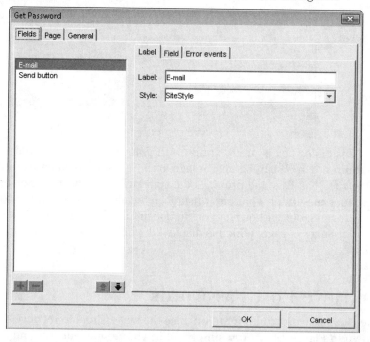

The Get Password component is also based on the Forms Handler dialog box, though here you get just the E-Mail field and Send button, and you can neither add nor delete fields. The E-Mail field has error events for "field value required," "E-mail not found," "E-mail address is invalid" (not a valid e-mail address), and "unable to retrieve password." The Fields tab provides a way to specify a "success" page for successfully completing the request to retrieve your password.

FIGURE 14-13   Change your own password with the Change Password page.

Allow Visitors to Change Their Own Passwords

The Change Password component creates a page that enables site visitors to change their own password by filling in the old password and the new password (twice), and then clicking the button (whose text you can specify) as shown in Figure 14-13.

To establish the Change Password component, select it from the NOF Secure Site section of the Custom Components panel. Click and drag on the page to establish the location and size. Once you've chosen the suite name from the NOF Secure Site dialog box, you can configure the component in the Change Password dialog box.

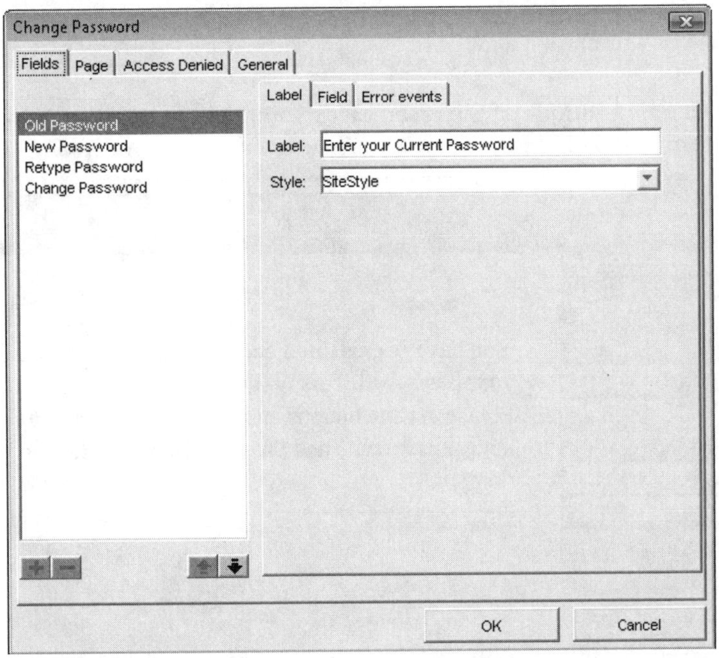

The Change Password dialog box (again, based on the Forms Handler) provides the necessary fields (which you cannot change). Error events handle issues for the Old Password (field value required, old password is invalid), New Password (field value required, field value too short, field value too long), and Retype Password (field value required, not match error). The Page tab enables you to specify a "success" page after successfully changing your password. The Access Denied tab provides a page to display if the site visitor tries to navigate directly to the Change Password page (perhaps by using a Navigation Bar) without logging in first.

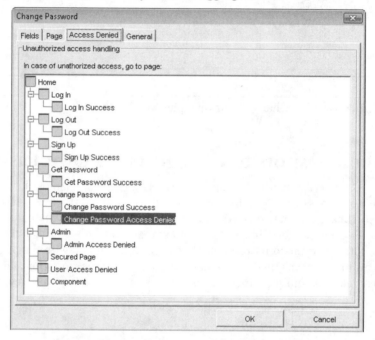

Here is a sample of the error pages you might encounter. Notice that the specifics of the error text help the site visitor figure out what went wrong!

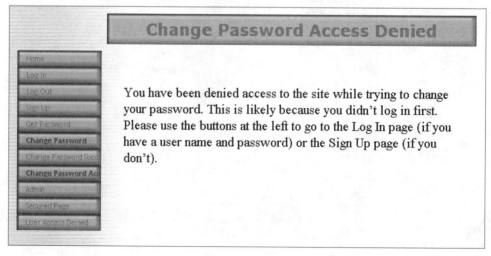

Add the Admin Component

The Admin component enables you to administer the list of users (see Figure 14-14). This includes adding new users, deleting users, validating a user (if you enable that functionality), and editing existing users. This is all done from a special page in the web site, which has its own username and password validation. To access this page, you must log in to the site (using the Log In page) with the administrator username and password. If you get it wrong, you'll end up on the page specified on the Access Denied tab of the Admin dialog box.

To establish the Admin component, select it from the NOF Secure Site section of the Custom Components panel. Click and drag on the page to establish the location and size. Once you've chosen the suite name from the NOF Secure Site dialog box, you can configure the component in the Admin dialog box.

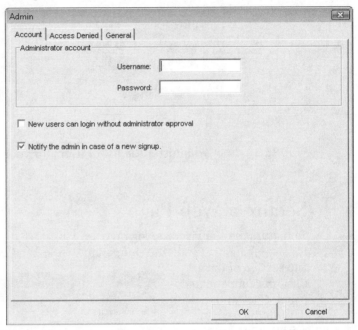

The Account tab is the only unique feature of this component's dialog box. This is where you fill in the user name and password for the administrator. If you want to be able to validate a signup request before allowing a user to have access to the site, leave the New Users Can Login Without Administrator Approval check box unselected. Otherwise, the new user can log in to the site immediately after requesting to sign up. In addition, you can receive an e-mail with the signup information when a new user signs up by selecting the Notify The Admin In Case Of A New Signup check box. A new user will also receive an e-mail once that user's user name and password are active.

Tip   If you don't allow immediate access to the web site (the administrator has to validate the signup information), you should have an e-mail sent to the administrator so that you know that you have a new signup you need to validate. The Signup Success page should warn the site visitor if immediate access isn't allowed.

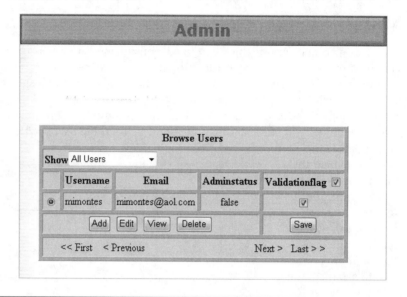

FIGURE 14-14 Administer the list of users for your web site.

Secure a Web Page

To require the site visitor to log in to see a page, that page must contain the Secure Page component. To add the component to the page, select it from the NOF Secure Site section of the Custom Components panel. Click and drag on the page to establish the location and size. Once you've established the Secure Page component, you can configure it in the Secure Page dialog box.

The Security tab enables you to show an image on the page to indicate that the page is secured, and pick the image by clicking the...button and choosing the image from the Picture File Open dialog box.

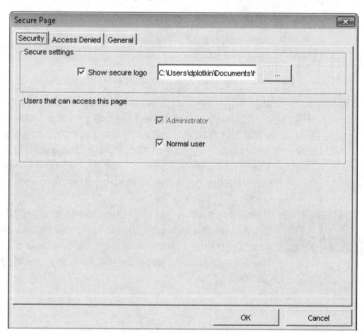

You can also decide whether the page should be accessible to a "Normal user" (one who has a user name and password) by selecting the Normal User check box. If the check box is left blank, only the site administrator can access the page. The Access Denied tab enables you to specify the page that site visitors will see if they attempt to access a page without logging in.

 Some pages—like the FAQ Admin page—should be accessible only to the site administrator, but are not secured by a password (unlike the Guestbook Admin page, which does require a password). You can add the Secure Page component to these pages, and leave the Normal User check box empty. In that case, only the site administrator can access that page.

Administer a Secured Web Site

The page containing the Admin component (seen previously in Figure 14-14) enables you to browse and administer the site users. The following functions are available:

- **Add**   Click Add to display the Add User panel, where you can fill in the information needed to establish a new user name and password. This information is e-mailed to the new user once the user is added (click Add User).

Admin	
Add User	
Firstname	
Lastname	
Email	
Username	
Password	
Adminstatus	false ▼
Validationflag	false ▼
	Add User Back

- **Edit**   Select an existing user by clicking the radio button to the left of the user and then click Edit. This displays the Edit User panel, which looks the same as the Add User panel, except that the existing information is filled in. Note that the user does *not* get an e-mail if you change the information here, so make sure to let the user know what has changed!

- **View**   Shows the selected user in a non-editable version of the Add User panel (called "View User").
- **Delete**   Deletes the selected user without any confirmation.
- **Save**   You can set the Validationflag (set the user name to "validated") right from the list of users. If you do select (or deselect) this check box, click Save to save the change. This is very handy if you have lots of new users, as you can validate them without viewing their details individually.
- **Change pages of users**   If you have many pages of users, you can move through the pages using the First, Previous, Next, and Last buttons at the bottom of the Browse Users list.

PART IV

Manage and Publish Your Web Site

15

Publish Static Data

HOW TO...

- Set up and publish a data source
- Define a new external data source
- Create a list of data records as a table of contents
- Configure the individual data records for viewing
- Publish the data with your web site

There are times when you need to publish large blocks of data, and you probably don't want to have to create a huge number of pages manually to hold that information. For example, I created a spreadsheet many years ago in which I cataloged articles in photo magazines that were of interest to me. If I wanted to share that spreadsheet on my web site, the task of creating a list of article titles, with each title linked to the details of the article (magazine name, issue, page number, and description) on a separate page would be overwhelming. There *must* be an easier way!

Understand Static Data Publishing

There is an easier way. Fusion enables you to link a "data list" to a data source (spreadsheet, flat file, or database). The data list displays a few of the fields in the data source (see Figure 15-1). Each line in the data list is then linked to a page containing the data fields from the data source you specify (see Figure 15-2). Each record in the data source is contained on one of the set of stacked pages, and you can navigate through the stacked pages using Smart links—which Fusion will build for you automatically if you wish. Further, you have considerable control over the position and format of the data fields and labels that appear on the stacked pages. And, each time you update the content and republish the site, the new content will appear on your web site.

Photo Articles List	

Article Title	Magazine Name
> 10 Best Minutes of the Day	Popular Photography
> 10 Recipes for Delicious Photos	PCPhoto
> 10 Tips for Better Panoramic Photos	PCPhoto
> 10 Tips for Better Printing	PCPhoto
> 10 Tips for Better Prints	PCPhoto
> 10 Tips for Positively Great Prints	PCPhoto
> 10 Tips for the Traveling Photographer	PCPhoto
> 16 Pro Tips For Traveling With Your Digital Camera	PCPhoto
> 4 Easy Backgrounds	Popular Photography
> 4 Filters Every Photographer Must Own	Popular Photography
> 50 Tips for Better Pictures	Popular Photography
> A Butterfly is Born	Popular Photography
> A Flash in the Night	PCPhoto
> A Personal Macro Studio	PCPhoto
> A Pleasant Change of Scenery	PCPhoto
> Accesorize Your Digital Camera	PCPhoto

Click here to jump to the full article description →

FIGURE 15-1 A list of articles—and the links to the full article page—is contained in this data list.

The data source is called an "external data source" because it is built externally to the web site. This source can be (in addition to a spreadsheet or text file) any database for which your machine contains an ODBC connection. With such a connection, the data can be extracted from the database and imported into the stacked pages containing the data fields. As will be discussed later in this chapter, you connect to a data source using a data source driver. Some of these drivers (such as the text file, Excel spreadsheet, and Access database drivers) are supplied with Windows. Others (such as ODBC drivers for databases) are installed when you install the database support files for the databases (such as Oracle, Sybase, DB2, and so on) that you use.

Note Installing and configuring ODBC drivers is beyond the scope of this book. If you regularly use ODBC drivers (located in the Administrative tools of the Control Panel), then you probably already know how to do that. If you have no idea what I'm talking about, you can still use the built-in drivers to create the data source.

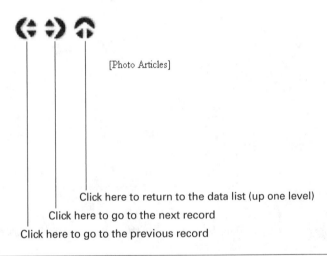

FIGURE 15-2   The full article description is shown on a stacked page.

How to...

Create a New Data Source Name

A "Data Source Name" (DSN) is a connection to a particular type of data source located in a specified directory—such as a spreadsheet in the Document directory, an Access database in the Documents directory, or a text file in My Documents. You must create a DSN to link and interpret a source of data before you can use the data in your web site. Once you *do* create the DSN on your computer, you can simply pick it any time you want to use that type of data source in a Fusion-built web site. For more information on picking a data source name to use, see "Set up the Data Publishing Parameters," later in this chapter.

  You can actually build a DSN from the Control Panel | Administrative Tools | Data Sources (ODBC). However, what we will cover here is how to do it within Fusion.

(continued)

To create a new DSN, use the following steps:

1. Choose the New External Data Source component from the Advanced Tools section of the Custom Components panel.
2. Click and drag on the web page to establish the size and position of the Data List component that will result when you're all done. This opens the Select Data Source dialog box. Click the Machine Data Source tab.

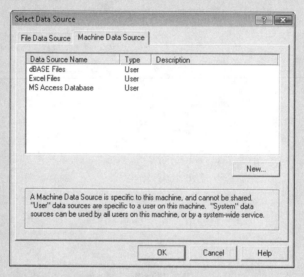

Note

If you have already defined a data source, you can just pick it from either the list in the File Data Source tab or the Machine Data Source tab, and then click OK to use that data source.

3. Click New to open the Create New Data Source dialog box. The first step is to decide whether you want a User Data Source or a System Data Source.

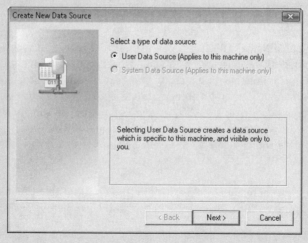

Note The only difference between a User Data Source and a System Data Source is that a User Data Source is visible only to the currently logged-in user. A System Data Source is visible to anyone who uses the machine. Due to a bug in Windows Vista, you may be unable to create a System Data Source through Fusion even if you are logged in with Administrative privileges.

4. Click Next to display the list of drivers available on your machine.

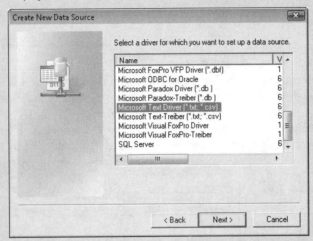

5. Select the driver you want to use and click Next. This displays the confirmation of the data source you have created (though you actually aren't done yet).

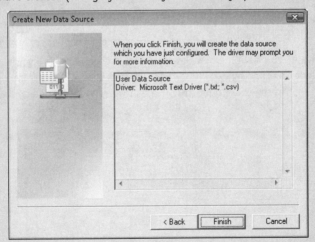

(continued)

6. Click Finish to display the ODBC Setup dialog box (a text setup, in this example).

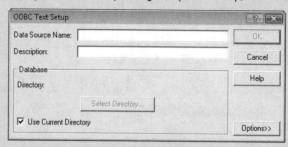

7. Finish setting up the ODBC data source by filling out the dialog box. The details are different for each driver. In the case of the text driver, you can follow the rest of the steps.
8. Give the Data Source a name by typing it into the Data Source Name field and add a description if you want.
9. Deselect the Use Current Directory check box and click Select Directory to pick the directory where the data source is located from the Select Directory dialog box.

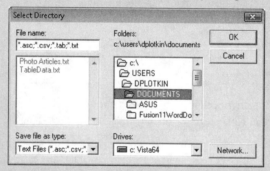

10. Click OK to create the new Data Source and choose the file you want to use from the Select dialog box that appears. Note that only files that match the type of the driver and that are present in the chosen directory will be displayed in the Select dialog box.

At this point the Data Publishing dialog box appears, and you can configure it as described in the next section "Set Up the Data Publishing Parameters."

Set Up the Data Publishing Parameters

Once you've defined a new external data source as a data source name (DSN), you can use it to display the contents of any of the type of files defined by the driver (such as a csv or txt file) located in the chosen directory.

Note The combination of the data source name (DSN) and a particular file of that type is called a "data object." Thus, once you have defined the DSN and picked the file using the Select dialog box noted earlier, you have created a "Data Object."

To pick the data object you want to use and configure the web pages to display the data, choose the Data List component from the Advanced Tools section of the Custom Components panel. Click and drag on the page to establish the size and location of data list. This list displays a subset of the fields in the data source (although you can show them all if you want to) along with a link to jump to the stacked page containing the entire record (or as much as you want to show). You can think of the data list as a "table of contents" for the data (see Figure 15-1, shown previously, for a sample of a completed data list).

Once you've clicked and dragged to define the region where you place the Data List component, Fusion opens the Data Publishing dialog box (see Figure 15-3). Pick the data object from the Data Object drop-down list, which includes any data objects you have built previously.

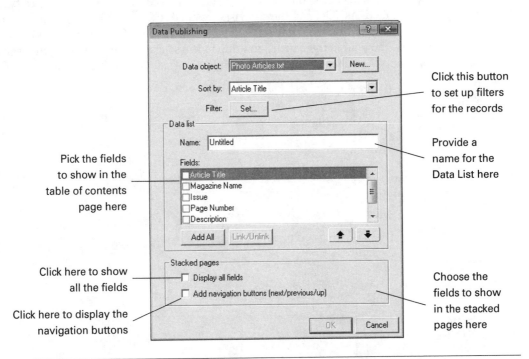

FIGURE 15-3   Set up data table of contents and detail fields you want to see.

Know? **The Data Publishing Dialog Box Appears When You Create a New DSN**

If you create a new DSN, the last step opens the Select dialog box with a list of the files that match the DSN. After you pick the file you want to use, the Data Publishing dialog box opens with the file shown in the Data Object drop-down list.

Note The stacked pages (each containing one record from the file or database) will be created automatically one level down from the table of contents page.

Configure the Data Object and Data List Parameters

The top section of the Data Publishing dialog box enables you to configure what will be displayed in the "data list" (table of contents) located on the main data page (called "Photo Articles List" in this example). The first step is to type a descriptive name into the Name field.

The next step is to choose the fields you want displayed by selecting the check box alongside each field. As a default, the site visitor can click the graphic link at the left end of each line to jump to the matching stacked page data record. If, in addition, you want to be able to click the field in the data list to jump to the stacked page containing the record, click Link/Unlink. This places an indicator (link) alongside each linked field.

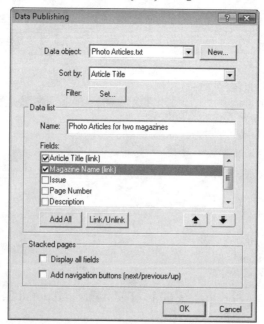

Click Link/Unlink again to remove the link if you change your mind.

You can rearrange the fields by selecting a field in the Fields list and using the up or down arrow to move the field in the list. If you wish, you can also click Add All to add all the fields to the table of contents. However, I don't advise that, since everything appears on one line (unlike the stacked pages) and some fields will have their contents truncated.

To sort the records in the order you want, pick the field to sort on from the Sort By drop-down list. You can also filter the contents of the data so that not all the records are shown. To do so, click Set to open the Filter dialog box.

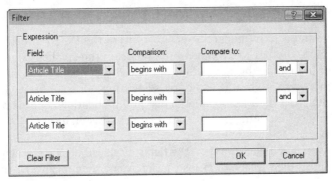

You can use the same data object on multiple pages, applying a different filter for each one. For example, you could create a list of the articles in one magazine on one page, and a list of the articles in another magazine on another page—even though both are stored in the same data file.

You can establish up to three filters. Each filter is based on a field (picked from the Field drop-down list), a comparison term (picked from the Comparison drop-down list), and a comparison criterion (which you fill in the Compare To field). You can choose any field you wish. For example, you could choose to display only a list of articles from one of the photo magazines included in this list (and it would probably be a good idea to include that information in a text box on the page). If you decide to use more than one filter line, you can combine the criteria with either an "and" (both lines must be true) or an "or" (either line must be true). For example, to display only the articles for 2006 for *PCPhoto,* you could use a filter such as Magazine Name begins with "PCPhoto" and Issue ends with 2006.

If you aren't going to use a filter line, choose "end" from the drop-down list at the left end of the last filter line you are using. This tells Fusion to ignore any other information in the filter lines below that one.

Did You Know?

Fusion Can Figure Out the Field Names

Even though the fields in the example are coming from a text file, Fusion is displaying the column names from the original spreadsheet. If the DSN was a spreadsheet, Fusion would still show the column names. This is because Fusion assumes that the first row in the text file or the spreadsheet contains the field names. Of course, if you are sourcing the data from a database table, Fusion uses the column names in the table as the field names.

Configure the Stacked Pages Parameters

The bottom portion (Stacked Pages section) of the Data Publishing dialog box enables you to pick whether to display all the fields on the stacked pages for each record, and whether to include the navigation buttons. Simply select the check boxes to make these choices. Note that if you don't select these check boxes, you'll have to add the data fields (and their associated labels) and navigation buttons by hand, using the Data Field components (as discussed later in this chapter).

Tip Even if you don't want *all* the fields displayed on the stacked pages, it's easiest to select the Display All Fields check box and then remove the fields you don't want.

Configure the Fields in the Data List

Once you've created the Data List on a page (see Figure 15-4), you can configure it in the following ways:

- **Adjust the displayed fields** If you want to add or remove fields from the Data List, double-click the list itself. This reopens the Data Publishing dialog box. While you can't change the Data Object, you can adjust the Filter (click Set), change the name, and add or remove fields by selecting or clearing the check boxes in the Fields list. You can also change the order and Link or Unlink the fields.
- **Adjust the size of the fields in the data list** If you display more than a single field in the Data list, you can adjust the split between the fields by moving the mouse over the border between the fields, and then clicking and dragging left or right to enlarge or shrink the field. You cannot change the field height manually.

You can also configure the Data List using the Data List Properties panel (also visible in Figure 15-4) in the following ways:

- **Display the column titles** The "column titles" are the field names that appear in the fields in the data list. To turn these off (they are on by default), deselect the Display Column Titles check box.

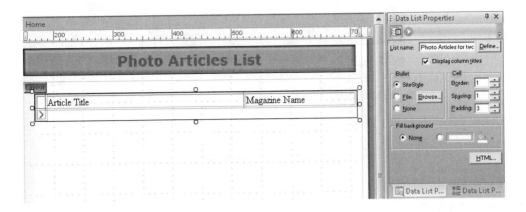

FIGURE 15-4   Adjust the Data List on the page to make your "TOC" look just right.

- **Choose the link bullet**   Pick the style of the link bullet you want to use from the Bullet section. To pick an image file of your own, choose the File radio button and click Browse. Pick the file you want from the Picture File Open dialog box.
- **Adjust the cell border, spacing, and padding**   The Data list is actually a table—so you can adjust the cell border, spacing, and padding, as described in Chapter 6.
- **Adjust the Fill background**   If you'd like to add a color fill to the Data list, select the radio button alongside the color rectangle and click the paint bucket icon to select a color from the ColorPicker.

Configure the Fields on the Stacked Pages

You can configure the fields in the stacked pages that contain the individual data records. And no, you don't have to configure each of the stacked pages. (Potentially there are a lot of them!) Fusion provides a single "parent" stacked page (see Figure 15-5). Changing the configuration of the single parent stacked page changes the formatting on all the pages (whew!).

The field labels you see in the figure are simply text boxes. As with any text boxes, you can click and drag them to relocate them on the page, or click and drag the sizing handles to resize them. You can also change the background color and image from the Text Properties panel, as well as attach actions to them.

You can also double-click in the text box, which makes the Format tab available—where you can change the font,

FIGURE 15-5 A sample stacked page—change the formatting to change the detailed record display.

size, color, background color, style, and paragraph alignment and formatting, as well as add a link or anchor to the text.

Tip Remember that you can also click Format to open the Object Format dialog box (from the Text Box tab) or the Span Setting dialog box (from the Format tab). Either way, you can change a wealth of settings for the text, as described previously in Chapter 4.

Add Your Own Fields to the Stacked Pages

If you decide you want to add another field to the stacked pages—or you have to add them all because you didn't use the Data Publishing dialog box—you certainly can do that. To do so, use the following steps:

1. Choose the Data Field component from the Advanced Tools section of the Custom Components panel.
2. Click and drag on the page to establish the initial size and location of the data field. This opens the Data Field dialog box.

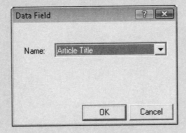

3. Pick the data field from the Name drop-down list.
4. Click OK to place the field on the page.

 Don't forget to add a text box for the label!

Clicking one of the data fields (containing sample data from the first record in the stacked pages) makes the Data Field Properties panel available. With the exception of being able to select the Text Box Is A Form check box (in the Text Box tab), this panel works identically to the Text Box panel. Double-clicking in the data field makes the Format tab available in the Data Field Properties panel, so you can adjust the text settings.

Preview the Data Publishing Results

You can preview the results for both the Data List (table of contents) and the stacked pages by either publishing your site locally or using the Preview tab. This can really help you visualize what your data will look like, and publishing locally even enables you to navigate through the records. Just be aware that if you have a lot of records in your database or file, it can take a *long* time to publish or preview the site. Fusion may even show as "Not Responding" in Windows, but be patient, it eventually comes back.

16

Publish Your Web Site

HOW TO...

- Connect to your web site for publishing
- Publish your web site
- Synchronize the local and remote copies of your web site
- Control the HTML output method

Before anyone can view, use, and enjoy all the hard work you've put into building your web site, you'll have to publish it to your site provider's server—called "publishing it remotely." In addition, you can't preview some of the components unless you publish it remotely.

To publish to your site provider, you have to supply the necessary parameters. Once the site is published, you can synchronize its contents with your local copy. You also have some choices to make about how to publish your web site.

Set Up the Connection to Publish Your Site

The first step in publishing your web site is to set up the connection. To do so, click the Publish Site tool in the Views bar to open the Publish Site dialog box.

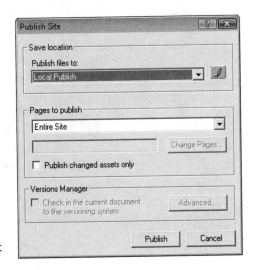

 If you accidentally click the Publish button (also in the Views bar), you'll find yourself looking at a different screen—the Publish View screen (discussed later in this chapter). Just click the Publish Site tool at that point to open the Publish Site dialog box.

Initially, the only option available in the Publish Files To drop-down list is Local Publish. To build the remote publish profile, click the Pencil icon to open the Publish Settings dialog box. This dialog box displays all your currently defined publish settings.

Note You can discard any publish settings you no longer need by selecting the Profile Name and clicking Remove.

To define your new Publish Settings profile, use the following steps:

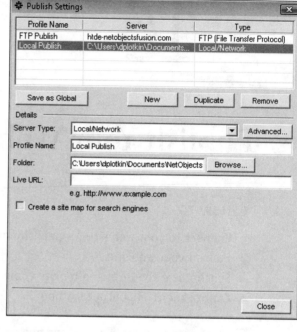

1. Click New to display the publishing parameters in the Details section of the dialog box.

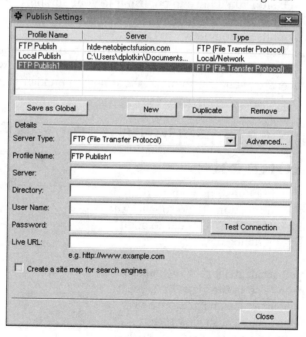

2. Choose the type of server you are publishing to from the Server Type drop-down list. The most common type is the default, FTP (File Transfer Protocol); however, other types are available in the list, and you'll have to find out what type your site provider uses.
3. Fill in the Server, Directory, User Name, Password, and Live URL (URL of the site). These parameters should all have been supplied to you by your site provider. The Live URL may not be necessary.
4. Click Test Connection. This uses the parameters you supplied to attempt to establish a connection to the web site. If you are successful, then you're done! Otherwise, check the parameters and try again.

If you wish, you can create a site map that enables search engines to more quickly "crawl" your site and add you to the search results. To do so, select the Create A Site Map For Search Engines check box. In addition, you can click Save As Global to create a Profile called Global FTP Publish. This profile is the default that will be used for publishing the site, and the name is not editable.

Publish Your Site

To publish your site for the first time, open the Publish Site dialog box and choose the following options:

- Choose the remote publishing settings (usually called FTP Publish) from the Publish Files To drop-down list.
- Select Entire Site from the Pages To Publish drop-down list.

When you're done, click Publish and wait while the site is published to the Internet.

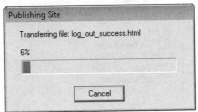

Publishing the entire site can be a lengthy process, especially if you are publishing data as described in Chapter 15. You can select the Publish Changed Assets Only check box to publish only those pages, images, files, and other assets that are different from what is on the web site. You can also choose to publish just the current page by picking Current Page Only from the Pages To Publish drop-down list. In addition, you can choose to publish only certain pages by picking Selected Page(s) from the Pages To Publish drop-down list. This opens the Site Structure – Select Pages(s) dialog box. Select the pages to publish by choosing the appropriate check boxes and clicking OK.

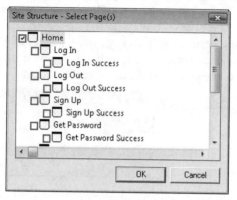

 To reopen the Site Structure – Select Page(s) dialog box and adjust your page choices, click the Change Pages button in the Publish Site dialog box.

Publish the Necessary Component Files

If you built a site using versions of Fusion previous to version 9 and are now migrating the site to the current version, you'll need to make sure to publish the supporting files to the web server for Email Page, FAQ, Forms Handler, and Secure Site. To do that, click Publish to switch to the Publish view, and choose Publish | Publish Components. Pick the components you used in order to publish them from the Publish Setup dialog box.

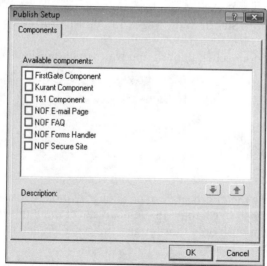

Synchronize Changes to Your Web Site

You can compare the contents of the web site on your machine with what you've published to the Internet. To do so, choose the Publish view from the Views bar (see Figure 16-1). This view shows the entire contents of your web site, including folders, scripts, assets, and pages (in the HTML folder). For each item, the current status of the item is displayed—that is, whether the item has ever been published either remotely or locally, and if so, when the last publish was done.

To connect to the remote web site and make the contents visible on the right side of the Publish view, select the publishing profile (such as FTP Publish) and click Connect. Once you are successfully connected, you can review the contents (see Figure 16-2) and drill into the various folders (double-click them). You can also check the last modification time to see if the web item has been modified since the last publish.

 To return to the parent folder, click the yellow folder icon with the arrow on it.

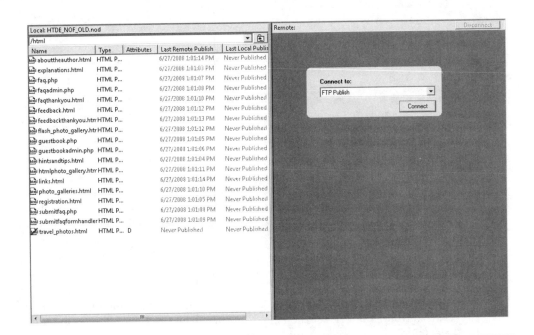

FIGURE 16-1   Check the status of all the items in your web site using the Publish view.

Click here to return to the parent folder

Click to disconnect from the remote web site

Click here to return to the parent folder

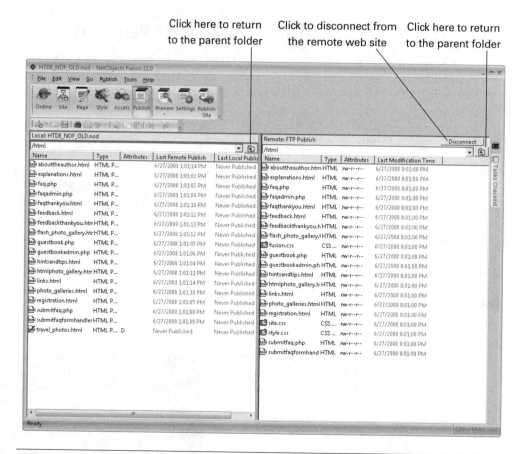

FIGURE 16-2 Compare the local and remote versions of the web site using the Publish view.

You can copy items from the local site to the remote site by clicking them in the local (left) side of the Publish view and dragging them to the remote (right) side panel.

Control the HTML Output

As you've been building your site, you may have noticed some options for configuring HTML output. You can set the default output from the Current Site Options dialog box (select Tools | Options | Current Site).

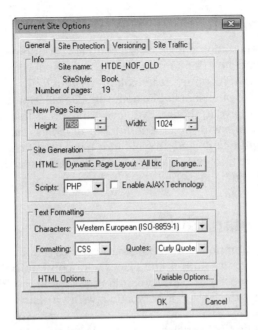

In the Site Generation section, click Change to open the Browser Compatibility dialog box. Then choose an option in the HTML generation section of the dialog box.

You can also override the HTML output at the page level by using the HTML output drop-down list in the Layout Properties panel.

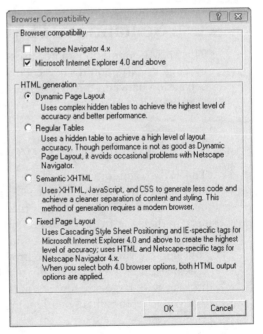

The choices on how to generate the HTML were much more important in the days of older (version 4 and older) browsers and a large preponderance of dial-up connections. In general, there isn't much reason to change from the default Dynamic Page Layout option. However, if you have overlapped objects on a page and you need them to appear as they are, you need to select Fixed Page Layout as the HTML output.

Use Dynamic Page Layout

This HTML generation choice uses a complex set of hidden tables to gain precise positioning with superior compatibly with browsers. The placement of your content is relative, so that it continues to look pretty much like you designed it in Page view. According to the publishers of Fusion, some JavaScript does not work properly with Dynamic Page Layout, though I've never run across this problem. Note that since everything is done with precise definitions of tables, the amount of HTML in the page can become quite large and unwieldy for hand modifications. On the other hand, HTML is just text, so even a lot of it loads quickly—and the whole point of using Fusion is to avoid hand-coding HTML!

Use Regular Tables

This HTML generation choice translates each Layout or Layout Region into a single table with rows and columns and places your content in the cells. The positioning is not quite as precise as with Dynamic Page Layout, but relative positioning is maintained and this option is compatible with virtually any browser.

 If you find that certain actions are not behaving the way you expect, try switching from Dynamic Page Layout to Regular Tables.

Use Semantic XHTML

This HTML generation choice uses XHTML, JavaScript, and CSS to generate the code, and it generally requires less code than other methods, as well as achieving a better separation between the page content and the style. However, only recent browsers will work with it, and you need to have set your security options to allow JavaScript to run.

Use Fixed Page Layout

This HTML generation choice uses Cascading Style Sheets (CSS) and layers to produce very accurate positioning. Since CSS is used, the HTML workarounds (such as empty table rows and transparent .gif files) are not needed—positioning is specified as a certain distance from the upper-left corner of the page. However, because CSS is used, some older browsers may not display everything correctly, or there may be considerable variation between browsers because older browsers didn't implement CSS the same way. Occasionally text boxes may expand and overlap other objects if a browser with large-size font settings is used. And again, if you have overlapping objects that you *want* to remain overlapping, you'll need to use this option to publish the page.

Index

References to figures are in italics.